하루 1 2 3분 영어 스피치

하루 1,2,3분 영어 스피치

초판 1쇄 인쇄 2025년 10월 29일
초판 1쇄 발행 2025년 11월 8일

지은이	박신규
발행인	임충배
홍보·마케팅	양경자
편집	김인숙
디자인	서해숙
펴낸 곳	도서출판 삼육오(PUB.365)
제작	(주)피앤엠123
출판신고	2014년 4월 3일
등록번호	제406-2014-000035호

(10882) 경기도 파주시 산남로 183-25
TEL 031-946-3196, FAX 031-946-3171
홈페이지 www.pub365.co.kr

ISBN 979-11-94543-40-4 03740
ⓒ 2025 박신규 & PUB.365

· 저자와 출판사의 허락 없이 내용 일부를 인용하거나 발췌하는 것을 금합니다.
· 저자와의 협의에 의하여 인지는 붙이지 않습니다.
· 가격은 뒤표지에 표시되어 있습니다.
· 잘못 만들어진 책은 구입처에서 교환해 드립니다.

하루 123분 영어 스피치

PUB 풉

머리말

영어 강의를 직업으로 삼은 지도 어느덧 30년이 흘렀습니다. 대학 시절 영어영문학을 전공하며 고등학교 3년 동안 영어 공부에 매진했던 열정은 제 삶의 중요한 기반이 되었습니다. 돌아보니, 영어를 공부한 시간만 거의 40년에 이릅니다. 그럼에도 불구하고 영어가 여전히 어렵게 느껴지는 이유는, 아마도 영어가 우리의 모국어가 아니기 때문일 것입니다. 그래서 오늘도 새로운 영어 표현을 배우고, 기회가 있을 때마다 이를 활용하려고 노력하고 있습니다.

영어 회화를 배우고자 하는 분들의 연령대와 배경은 정말 다양합니다. 30대 초반의 직장인부터 90대의 어르신까지, 남녀노소 많은 분들이 저와 함께 영어 공부를 하고 계십니다. 그런데 공통적으로 던지는 질문이 있습니다. 바로, **"어떻게 하면 영어 회화를 잘할 수 있을까요?"** 라는 질문입니다. 또한 **"배운 표현을 금방 까먹어서 힘들어요."** 라는 고민도 자주 듣습니다.

여러분의 고민에 깊이 공감합니다. 저 역시 같은 과정을 겪어봤기 때문입니다. 영어는 단순한 지식 습득을 넘어 익숙해지는 과정이며, 이 과정에는 반드시 반복이 필요합니다. 반복 없이 영어를 배우는 것은 마치 기초 없는 집을 짓는 것과 같습니다. 시간이 지나면 배운 것을 잊어버리는 것은 자연스러운 일이기에, 중요한 것은 지속적인 연습과 복습입니다.

제가 영어 회화를 가르치며 느낀 점은, 학습자들이 자신의 이야기나 경험에 대해서는 비교적 자연스럽게 말하지만, 자신과 관련이 없는 주제에 대해서는 어려움을 느낀다는 것입니다. 이는 익숙함과 연결된 문제로, 더 많은 연습과 자신감이 필요합니다.

이러한 고민을 해결하고, 영어 회화 실력을 향상시키고자 하는 분들에게 도움을 드리고자 『하루 1·2·3분 영어 스피치』를 집필하게 되었습니다. 목차에 나오는 다양한 주제를 제가 직접 영어로 표현하며 연습해 보았습니다.

먼저 각 주제를 기반으로 한 영어 대화를 들어본 후, 해당 주제와 관련된 내용을 영어로 1분, 2분 또는 3분 동안 말하는 연습을 하면 됩니다. 이렇게 하면 다양한 영어 표현을 익히는 데 도움이 됩니다. 또한, 각 주제에서 반드시 익혀야 할 유용한 표현들을 예문과 함께 정리했으니, 이러한 표현들이 자연스럽게 입에서 나올 때까지 반복해서 연습해야 합니다.

처음에는 귀에 잘 들리지도 않고 입으로 자연스럽게 나오지도 않습니다. 이는 당연한 일입니다. 하지만 시간을 두고 꾸준히 반복해서 연습하다 보면 어느 순간 자신도 모르게 익숙해진 표현들이 술술 나오게 될 것입니다. 저 역시 그렇게 해왔고 앞으로도 마찬가지입니다.

아무쪼록 이 교재가 영어 회화에 목마른 학습자들에게 조금이나마 도움이 되기를 진심으로 바랍니다. 단순한 영어 학습서를 넘어, 영어에 대한 자신감과 즐거움을 키울 수 있는 동반자가 되기를 바랍니다. 영어 학습 여정에 함께하게 되어 기쁩니다.

영원한 영어 강사 박신규

학습 방법

 STEP 1 　**스피치 가이드**

학습할 주제를 확인하고, 해당 주제에서 어떤 표현을 어떻게 말해야 할지 미리 안내합니다. 익숙한 주제라도 가이드를 읽고 시작하면, 어휘나 표현의 사용을 명확히 이해할 수 있습니다.

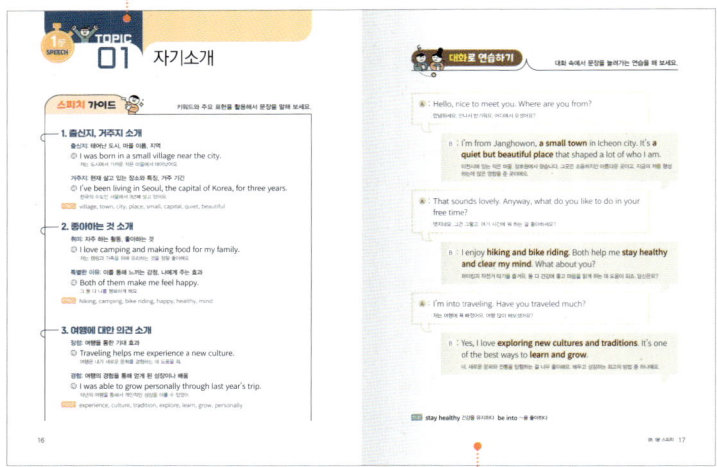

 **STEP 2** 　**대화로 연습하기**

짧은 롤플레이 형식으로 실제 대화를 연습하는 단계입니다.
"내가 이 상황에서라면 뭐라고 말할까?"를 떠올리며,
스피치 가이드를 참고하여 대사를 살짝 바꿔 말해 보세요.

 **내용 구성하기**

이제 본격적으로 스피치 내용을 구성해 봅니다.
제공된 문장을 활용해 나만의 내용으로 조리 있게 구성해보세요.

스피치 포인트는 말하기에서 내용을 풍부하게 하고,
시간도 늘려주는 말할거리의 뼈대입니다.
나만의 내용에 활용해 보세요.

 **1분 스피치**

말하기 준비가 끝났다면, 실제로 1분 동안 스스로 말해보는 시간입니다. 타이머를 1분으로 맞추고 중단 없이 말하기를 해보세요. 처음엔 버벅여도 괜찮습니다.
중요한 건 자신의 말하기 흐름을 만드는 것입니다.
말한 내용을 녹음해서 다시 들어보며 체크해 보세요.

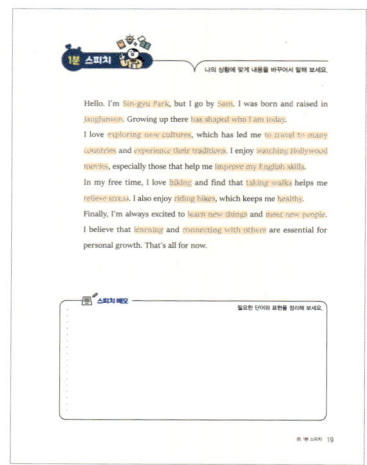

 **Review Quiz**

Part별로 학습한 표현과 문법을 복습하며 말하기에 필요한 핵심 요소들을 점검합니다. 문제를 풀면서 내가 빠뜨렸던 표현이나 문장을 체크해 보세요.

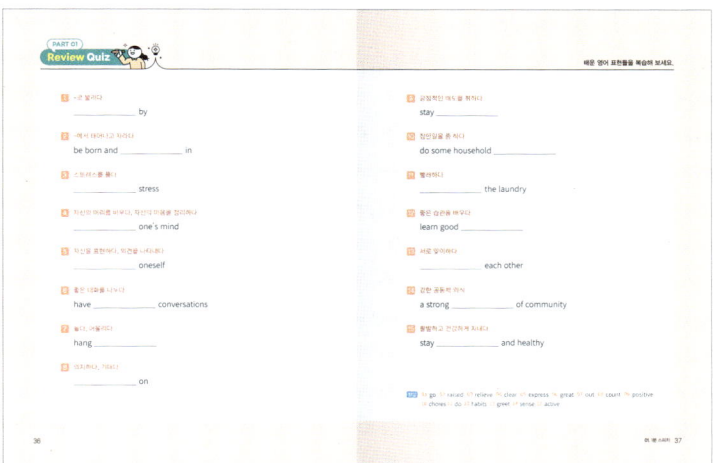

 **MP3 음원 활용**

MP3를 듣고, 한 문장씩 반복해서 소리 내어 말해보세요.
원어민 발음, 억양, 말하는 속도를 자연스럽게 익힐 수 있습니다.

목차

1분 스피치

PART 01 　 내 이야기　　　　　　　　　　　14
TOPIC 01　자기소개　　　　　　　　　　　16
TOPIC 02　여가생활　　　　　　　　　　　20
TOPIC 03　가족&친구　　　　　　　　　　24
TOPIC 04　집안일　　　　　　　　　　　　28
TOPIC 05　동네 이웃　　　　　　　　　　　32
Review Quiz　　　　　　　　　　　　　　36

PART 02 　 취미 생활　　　　　　　　　　38
TOPIC 06　영화　　　　　　　　　　　　　40
TOPIC 07　음악　　　　　　　　　　　　　44
TOPIC 08　게임　　　　　　　　　　　　　48
TOPIC 09　외식　　　　　　　　　　　　　52
TOPIC 10　여행　　　　　　　　　　　　　56
Review Quiz　　　　　　　　　　　　　　60

PART 03 　 일상생활　　　　　　　　　　62
TOPIC 11　반려동물　　　　　　　　　　　64
TOPIC 12　커피숍　　　　　　　　　　　　68
TOPIC 13　가족&친구　　　　　　　　　　72
TOPIC 14　음주　　　　　　　　　　　　　76
TOPIC 15　수면　　　　　　　　　　　　　80
Review Quiz　　　　　　　　　　　　　　84

2분 스피치

PART 04 인터넷 세상 — 86

TOPIC 16	온라인 쇼핑	88
TOPIC 17	스마트폰	92
TOPIC 18	유튜브	96
TOPIC 19	SNS	100
TOPIC 20	TV&라디오	104
Review Quiz		108

PART 05 사계절 — 110

TOPIC 21	날씨	112
TOPIC 22	계절	116
TOPIC 23	휴가	120
TOPIC 24	벚꽃놀이	124
TOPIC 25	단풍놀이	128
Review Quiz		132

PART 06 편의 시설 — 134

TOPIC 26	패스트푸드점	136
TOPIC 27	대중목욕탕	140
TOPIC 28	편의점	144
TOPIC 29	주유소	148
TOPIC 30	은행	152
Review Quiz		156

3분 스피치

PART 07 교통수단	158
TOPIC 31　버스&택시	160
TOPIC 32　지하철&기차	166
TOPIC 33　비행기&배	172
TOPIC 34　도보&자전거	178
TOPIC 35　GPS&구글 지도	184
Review Quiz	190

PART 08 공공시설	192
TOPIC 36　시청	194
TOPIC 37　우체국	200
TOPIC 38　동사무소	206
TOPIC 39　공영 주차장	212
TOPIC 40　공립도서관	218
Review Quiz	224

PART 09 건강과 질병	226
TOPIC 41　운동	228
TOPIC 42　건강	234
TOPIC 43　안과	240
TOPIC 44　치과	246
TOPIC 45　다이어트	252
Review Quiz	258

PART 10	K-콘텐츠	260
TOPIC 46	K-Pop	262
TOPIC 47	K-Food	268
TOPIC 48	K-Movie	274
TOPIC 49	K-Drama	280
TOPIC 50	K-Culture	286
Review Quiz		292

PART 01
내 이야기

TOPIC 01　자기소개
TOPIC 02　여가생활
TOPIC 03　가족&친구
TOPIC 04　집안일
TOPIC 05　동네 이웃

TOPIC 01 자기소개

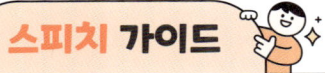

키워드와 주요 표현을 활용해서 문장을 말해 보세요.

1. 출신지, 거주지 소개

출신지: 태어난 도시, 마을 이름, 지역
- 예) I was born in a small village near the city.
  저는 도시에서 가까운 작은 마을에서 태어났어요.

거주지: 현재 살고 있는 장소와 특징, 거주 기간
- 예) I've been living in Seoul, the capital of Korea, for three years.
  한국의 수도인 서울에서 3년째 살고 있어요.

키워드 village, town, city, place, small, capital, quiet, beautiful

2. 좋아하는 것 소개

취미: 자주 하는 활동, 좋아하는 것
- 예) I love camping and making food for my family.
  저는 캠핑과 가족을 위해 요리하는 것을 정말 좋아해요.

특별한 이유: 이를 통해 느끼는 감정, 나에게 주는 효과
- 예) Both of them make me feel happy.
  그 둘 다 나를 행복하게 해요.

키워드 hiking, camping, bike riding, happy, healthy, mind

3. 여행에 대한 의견 소개

장점: 여행을 통한 기대 효과
- 예) Traveling helps me experience a new culture.
  여행은 내가 새로운 문화를 경험하는 데 도움을 줘.

경험: 여행의 경험을 통해 얻게 된 성장이나 배움
- 예) I was able to grow personally through last year's trip.
  작년의 여행을 통해서 개인적인 성장을 이룰 수 있었어.

키워드 experience, culture, tradition, explore, learn, grow, personally

A : Hello, nice to meet you. Where are you from?
안녕하세요. 만나서 반가워요. 어디에서 오셨어요?

B : I'm from Janghowon, **a small town** in Icheon city. It's **a quiet but beautiful place** that shaped a lot of who I am.
이천시에 있는 작은 마을, 장호원에서 왔습니다. 그곳은 조용하지만 아름다운 곳이고, 지금의 저를 형성하는데 많은 영향을 준 곳이에요.

A : That sounds lovely. Anyway, what do you like to do in your free time?
멋지네요. 그건 그렇고, 여가 시간에 뭐 하는 걸 좋아하세요?

B : I enjoy **hiking and bike riding**. Both help me **stay healthy and clear my mind**. What about you?
하이킹과 자전거 타기를 즐겨요. 둘 다 건강에 좋고 마음을 맑게 하는 데 도움이 되죠. 당신은요?

A : I'm into traveling. Have you traveled much?
저는 여행에 푹 빠졌어요. 여행 많이 해보셨어요?

B : Yes, I love **exploring new cultures and traditions**. It's one of the best ways to **learn and grow**.
네, 새로운 문화와 전통을 탐험하는 걸 너무 좋아해요. 배우고 성장하는 최고의 방법 중 하나예요.

어휘 stay healthy 건강을 유지하다 be into ~을 좋아하다

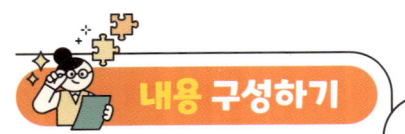

주제별로 구분하여 길게 말하는 연습을 해 보세요.

Hello. I'm Sin-gyu Park, but I ①**go by** Sam. I ②**was born and raised in** Janghowon. Growing up there has shaped who I am today.

안녕하세요. 저는 박신규라고 합니다만, 쌤이라는 이름으로 불리고 있어요. 저는 장호원에서 태어나고 자랐습니다. 그곳에서의 성장 경험이 오늘날의 저를 만들었습니다.

I love exploring new cultures, which has led me to travel to many countries and experience their traditions. I enjoy watching Hollywood movies, especially those that help me ③**improve my English skills**.

저는 새로운 문화를 탐험하는 것을 너무 좋아해서 여러 나라를 여행하며 각국의 전통을 경험해 왔습니다. 특히 영어 실력 향상에 도움이 되는 할리우드 영화를 즐겨 봅니다.

④**In my free time**, I love hiking and find that taking walks helps me ⑤**relieve stress**. I also enjoy riding bikes, which keeps me healthy.

자유 시간에는 하이킹을 즐기고 산책이 스트레스를 해소하는 데 도움이 된다고 생각합니다. 또한, 자전거 타기도 좋아해서 건강을 유지하는 데 큰 도움이 됩니다.

Finally, I'm always excited to learn new things and meet new people. I believe that learning and ⑥**connecting with** others are essential for personal growth. That's all for now.

마지막으로 저는 항상 새로운 것을 배우고 새로운 사람들을 만나는 것에 설렙니다. 배움과 사람들과의 소통이 개인적인 성장을 위해 꼭 필요하다고 믿습니다. 일단 여기까지입니다.

스피치 포인트

① **go by** ~로 불리다　② **be born and raised in** ~에서 태어나고 자라다　③ **improve one's English skills** 자신의 영어 실력을 향상시키다　④ **in one's free time** 자신의 자유 시간에　⑤ **relieve stress** 스트레스를 풀다　⑥ **connect with** ~와 가까워지다, ~와 소통하다

 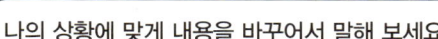

나의 상황에 맞게 내용을 바꾸어서 말해 보세요.

Hello. I'm Sin-gyu Park, but I go by Sam. I was born and raised in Janghowon. Growing up there has shaped who I am today.

I love exploring new cultures, which has led me to travel to many countries and experience their traditions. I enjoy watching Hollywood movies, especially those that help me improve my English skills.

In my free time, I love hiking and find that taking walks helps me relieve stress. I also enjoy riding bikes, which keeps me healthy.

Finally, I'm always excited to learn new things and meet new people. I believe that learning and connecting with others are essential for personal growth. That's all for now.

스피치 메모

필요한 단어와 표현을 정리해 보세요.

TOPIC 02 여가생활

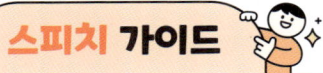

키워드와 주요 표현을 활용해서 문장을 말해 보세요.

1. 휴식 방법 소개

휴식 활동: 여러 가지 휴식 활동

> 예) When I need to relax, I just stay home and watch TV.
> 휴식이 필요할 때 난 그냥 집에 머물면서 TV를 시청해.

이유: 휴식이 필요한 배경 설명

> 예) I'm burned out, so I need to get some rest.
> 저는 지쳤어요. 그래서 휴식 좀 취해야겠어요.

키워드 hiking, ride bikes, watch TV, be burned out, recharge

2. 취미 활동 소개

영화 장르: 좋아하는 영화 장르

> 예) I enjoy Korean movies as well as Hollywood movies.
> 저는 한국 영화뿐만 아니라 할리우드 영화도 즐겨 봐요.

이유: 영화를 보는 목적과 이유

> 예) I enjoy comedy movies because they make me laugh and forget my worries.
> 저는 코미디 영화를 좋아해요. 웃게 해주고 걱정을 잊게 해주거든요.

키워드 Korean movies, Hollywood movies, improve, forget

3. 시간 보내는 방법 소개

영화 감상: 영화를 함께 감상하는 사람

> 예) I usually watch movies with my family. It's how we bond.
> 보통 가족과 영화를 봐. 그게 우리가 유대감을 형성하는 방법이야.

그 외 활동: 영화 감상 외에 하는 활동

> 예) I also enjoy playing board games or cooking with friends.
> 저는 보드게임을 하거나 친구들과 요리하는 것을 즐겨요.

키워드 family, friend, eat together, chat, watch movies, cook, bond

대화로 연습하기 — 대화 속에서 문장을 늘려가는 연습을 해 보세요.

A : Hey, how do you usually relax after a long day?
이봐요, 긴 하루 끝에 보통 어떻게 쉬세요?

B : I like spending time outdoors. **Hiking or riding my bike** really helps me **recharge**. How about you?
저는 밖에서 시간 보내는 걸 좋아해요. 하이킹이나 자전거 타기는 정말로 저를 재충전하게 해줘요. 당신은요?

A : I usually unwind by watching movies. Do you like movies too?
저는 보통 영화 보면서 긴장을 풀어요. 영화 좋아하세요?

B : Yes, especially **Hollywood movies**. They're fun, and I can **improve my English** while watching them.
네, 특히 할리우드 영화를 좋아해요. 재미있고, 보면서 영어 실력도 늘릴 수 있거든요.

A : That sounds great! Do you usually watch alone, or with friends and family?
정말 멋진 생각이에요! 혼자 보세요, 아니면 친구나 가족이랑 같이 보세요?

B : **Both**! I love spending time with them, whether we're **eating together or just chatting**. It's the best way to feel balanced.
둘 다요! 같이 밥을 먹든 수다를 떨든 그들과 함께 시간을 보내는 게 좋아요. 그게 균형 잡힌 느낌을 주는 가장 좋은 방법이죠.

어휘 recharge 재충전하다 unwind 긴장을 풀다, 편안하게 쉬다 feel balanced 균형 잡힌 기분이 들다, 마음이 안정되다

내용 구성하기

주제별로 구분하여 길게 말하는 연습을 해 보세요.

In my spare time, I enjoy exploring nature because it helps me stay healthy. When I need to relieve stress or recharge ①**after a long day**, hiking and traveling are my favorite activities.

여가 시간에 저는 자연을 탐험하는 걸 즐기는데, 건강을 유지하는 데 도움이 되기 때문입니다. 긴 하루 끝에 스트레스를 해소하거나 재충전이 필요할 때 하이킹과 여행은 제가 가장 좋아하는 활동입니다.

I also love riding my bike. It's not only a great way to stay fit but also helps me ②**clear my mind** and ③**feel refreshed**.

저는 또한 자전거 타는 것을 너무 좋아합니다. 건강을 유지할 수 있는 좋은 방법일 뿐만 아니라 머리를 비우거나 개운하게 해줍니다.

Plus, I like to relax by watching Hollywood movies. They're entertaining and a fun way to improve my English skills. I enjoy learning how native speakers ④**express themselves**.

게다가, 할리우드 영화를 보며 쉬는 것을 좋아합니다. 영화는 재미있고 영어 실력을 향상시킬 수 있는 즐거운 방법이기도 합니다. 저는 원어민들이 어떻게 말하는지 배우는 것을 즐깁니다.

Finally, spending time with my friends and family is very important to me. Whether we eat together, ⑤**have great conversations**, or simply ⑥**enjoy each other's company**, these moments make me happy.

마지막으로 친구들과 가족들과 시간을 보내는 것은 저에게 매우 중요합니다. 함께 식사를 하거나, 좋은 대화를 나누거나, 그냥 서로 함께 하는 것을 즐기거나, 이런 순간들이 저를 행복하게 만들어 줍니다.

스피치 포인트

① **after a long day** 긴 하루 끝에 ② **clear one's mind** 자신의 머리를 비우다, 자신의 마음을 정리하다 ③ **feel refreshed** 개운하다 ④ **express oneself** 자신을 표현하다, 의견을 나타내다 ⑤ **have great conversations** 좋은 대화를 나누다 ⑥ **enjoy each other's company** 서로 함께 하는 것을 즐기다

나의 상황에 맞게 내용을 바꾸어서 말해 보세요.

In my spare time, I enjoy exploring nature because it helps me stay healthy. When I need to relieve stress or recharge after a long day, hiking and traveling are my favorite activities.

I also love riding my bike. It's not only a great way to stay fit but also helps me clear my mind and feel refreshed.

Plus, I like to relax by watching Hollywood movies. They're entertaining and a fun way to improve my English skills. I enjoy learning how native speakers express themselves.

Finally, spending time with my friends and family is very important to me. Whether we eat together, have great conversations, or simply enjoy each other's company, these moments make me happy.

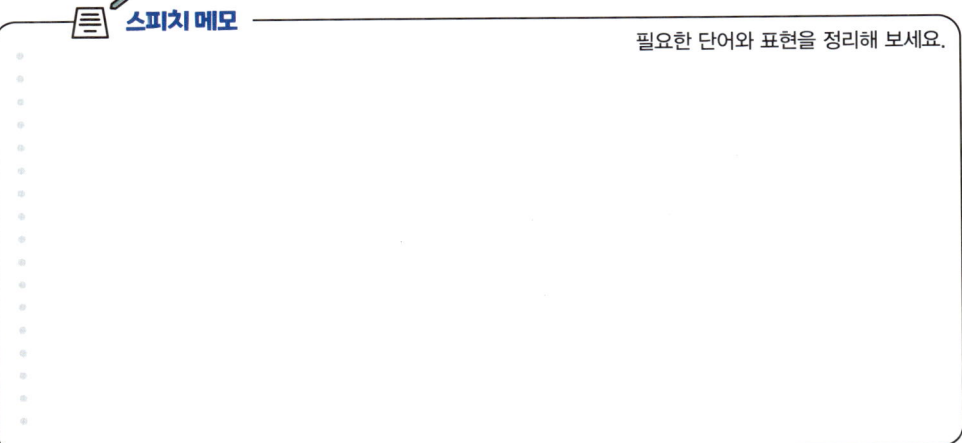

필요한 단어와 표현을 정리해 보세요.

TOPIC 03 가족&친구

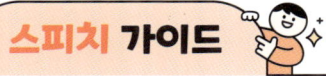

키워드와 주요 표현을 활용해서 문장을 말해 보세요.

1. 가족이나 친구 소개

소개: 지인에게 가족, 친구 소개

예) I'm really close to my family. We love spending time together every day.
저는 가족과 정말 친해요. 매일 함께 시간을 보내는 걸 좋아해요.

감정: 감정과 이유

예) When I'm with my family or friends, I always feel so happy.
가족이나 친구들과 함께 있으면 항상 행복해요.

키워드 family, friend, lucky, amazing, close, happy

2. 가족과 함께 하는 활동 소개

활동: 활동을 구체적으로 설명

예) We go hiking, play board games, or cook meals together.
우리는 하이킹을 하거나 보드게임을 하고, 같이 요리를 해.

빈도: 빈도수를 언급하기

예) My family and I usually watch TV together at home after dinner.
가족과 저는 보통 저녁 식사 후에 집에서 함께 TV를 시청해요.

키워드 go hiking, watch movies, chat about, always, usually

3. 가족과 친구의 의미 소개

존재감: 본인에게 어떤 의미인지 설명

예) My friends mean a lot to me.
제 친구들은 제게 정말 소중한 존재예요.

감정: 감사, 영감, 행운과 같은 긍정적인 감정

예) They always cheer me up and encourage me to do my best.
그들은 늘 제 기운을 북돋아 주고 최선을 다하도록 응원해 줘요.

키워드 a lot, cheer up, encourage, inspire, stay positive

 대화로 연습하기

대화 속에서 문장을 늘려가는 연습을 해 보세요.

A : I feel **so lucky to have amazing family and friends** in my life. **They're always there for me**.
내 인생에 멋진 가족과 친구들이 있다는 게 정말 행운이라고 느껴. 그들은 항상 내 곁에 있어주거든.

B : That's great to hear! What kinds of things do you enjoy doing with them?
그거 참 잘됐네! 그들과 주로 어떤 걸 즐겨 해?

A : We love **hiking, watching movies, or just chatting about our day**. It's **always** fun.
우리는 하이킹을 하거나, 영화를 보거나, 그냥 하루 일과를 이야기하는 걸 좋아해. 항상 즐거워.

B : That's wonderful! Having people who support you no matter what is truly a blessing.
정말 멋지다! 어떤 상황에서도 널 지지해주는 사람들이 있다는 건 정말 큰 축복이야.

A : Absolutely. They **inspire** me to **work hard, stay positive, and be kind to others**.
맞아. 그들은 내가 열심히 일하고, 긍정적으로 살며, 다른 사람들에게 친절하게 하도록 영감을 줘.

B : That's the best kind of support system. You're lucky to have them!
그건 정말 최고의 응원군이야. 그런 사람들이 있다는 게 참 행운이야!

어휘 inspire 영감을 주다 support system 응원군, 버팀목, 든든한 존재

주제별로 구분하여 길게 말하는 연습을 해 보세요.

Family and friends are super important to me. ①**No matter what happens**, they are always there for me. I truly enjoy spending time with them, whether we're sharing a meal or simply talking about our day.

가족과 친구는 저에게 너무 소중합니다. 어떤 일이 있어도 그들은 항상 제 곁에 있어 줍니다. 저는 그들과 함께 시간 보내는 것을 정말 좋아하는데, 함께 식사를 하거나 하루에 대해 그냥 이야기하는 것만으로도 즐겁습니다.

My friends are like a second family. We love ②**hanging out** or watching movies. I know I can always ③**count on** them for advice or support when I need it.

제 친구들은 마치 또 다른 가족 같아요. 우리는 함께 놀러 다니거나 영화를 보는 걸 정말 좋아합니다. 제가 조언이나 지원이 필요할 때 항상 그들을 의지할 수 있다는 것을 압니다.

④**I feel so lucky to** have such amazing people in my life. They make me happy and help me grow as a person.

제 삶에 이렇게 멋진 사람들이 있다는 것이 정말 운이 좋다고 느낍니다. 그들은 저를 행복하게 해주고 제가 더 나은 사람이 되도록 도와줍니다.

Both my family and friends inspire me to work hard, ⑤**stay positive**, and be kind to others. ⑥**I'm truly grateful for** their love and support every day.

제 가족과 친구들 다 같이 제가 열심히 일하고, 긍정적으로 살며, 다른 사람들에게 친절하도록 영감을 줍니다. 매일 그들의 사랑과 지원에 진심으로 감사드립니다.

스피치 포인트

① **no matter what happens** 어떤 일이 있어도 ② **hang out** 놀다, 어울리다 ③ **count on** 의지하다, 기대다 ④ **feel so lucky to** ~하게 되어 정말 운이 좋다고 느껴요 ⑤ **stay positive** 긍정적인 태도를 취하다 ⑥ **be truly grateful for** ~에 진심으로 감사하다

1분 스피치

나의 상황에 맞게 내용을 바꾸어서 말해 보세요.

Family and friends are super important to me. No matter what happens, they are always there for me. I truly enjoy spending time with them, whether we're sharing a meal or simply talking about our day.

My friends are like a second family. We love hanging out or watching movies. I know I can always count on them for advice or support when I need it.

I feel so lucky to have such amazing people in my life. They make me happy and help me grow as a person.

Both my family and friends inspire me to work hard, stay positive, and be kind to others. I'm truly grateful for their love and support every day.

스피치 메모

필요한 단어와 표현을 정리해 보세요.

TOPIC 04 집안일

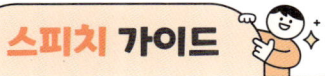

키워드와 주요 표현을 활용해서 문장을 말해 보세요.

1. 집안일 소개

집안일: 평소에 하는 집안일
- 예) I just finished doing the dishes.
  방금 설거지를 끝냈어요.

기분: 집안일 끝낸 후 기분
- 예) It's so satisfying to see the sink empty and clean.
  싱크대가 깨끗하게 비어 있는 걸 보면 정말 뿌듯해.

키워드 dish, laundry, floor, satisfying, great

2. 집안일 하는 이유 소개

세부사항: 집안일을 어떻게 했는지 설명
- 예) I used a scented floor cleaner to make the room smell nice and fresh.
  방이 향기롭고 상쾌하게 느껴지도록 향이 나는 바닥 세제를 사용했어.

이유: 집안일 하는 이유
- 예) I do housework to keep everything organized and easy to find.
  모든 걸 정돈하고 쉽게 찾을 수 있도록 집안일을 해요.

키워드 sweep, use, organized, fresh

3. 집안일과 관련된 습관 소개

횟수: 자주 하는지 여부 설명
- 예) I don't do it every day, but I try to help out whenever I can.
  매일은 아니지만, 할 수 있을 때는 돕는 편이야.

활동: 가족과 함께하는 활동 추가
- 예) On weekends, my family and I love baking cookies or trying new recipes together.
  주말에, 우리 가족과 저는 함께 쿠키를 굽거나 새로운 요리법을 시도하는 것을 좋아해요.

키워드 routine, every day, on weekends, cook, bake

대화로 연습하기

대화 속에서 문장을 늘려가는 연습을 해 보세요.

A : I just finished **folding the laundry**. It **feels great** to see everything neat and tidy.
방금 빨래 개는 걸 끝냈어. 모든 게 깔끔하게 정리된 걸 보면 정말 기분이 좋아.

B : That's awesome! Folding clothes can be oddly satisfying sometimes.
정말 멋지다! 옷 개는 게 묘하게도 만족감을 줄 때가 있지.

A : It really is. I also **swept the floor** earlier to **keep the house feeling fresh**.
진짜 그래. 그리고 아까 바닥도 쓸어서 집이 좀 더 상쾌해졌어.

B : You've been busy! Do you usually do a lot of chores every day?
정말 부지런하다! 평소에도 집안일을 많이 해?

A : Not every day, but I like helping out, especially **on weekends**. **We often cook together as a family**.
매일은 아니지만, 특히 주말엔 돕는 걸 좋아해. 우리 가족끼리 요리도 자주 같이 하거든.

B : That sounds nice. Doing chores together must make it more fun and less tiring!
정말 좋겠다. 같이 집안일 하면 훨씬 재미있고 덜 지루할 것 같아!

어휘 **awesome** 멋진, 대단한 **oddly** 묘하게도, 이상하게도 **especially** 특히

주제별로 구분하여 길게 말하는 연습을 해 보세요.

In my daily life, I ①**do some household chores** to keep things clean and organized. My main job is ②**doing the laundry**. I enjoy folding clean clothes because it feels satisfying to see everything neat.

일상 생활에서, 집안일을 해서 집을 깨끗하고 정돈되게 유지합니다. 제가 주로 맡는 일은 빨래입니다. 모든 것이 깔끔하게 보이는 게 만족스럽기 때문에 깨끗한 옷을 개는 걸 즐깁니다.

On weekends, I help in the kitchen. Sometimes I ③**prepare meals** or ④**do the dishes** after eating.

주말에는 부엌에서 일을 돕습니다. 가끔 음식을 준비하거나 식사 후 설거지를 합니다.

I believe doing chores together helps bring the family closer. For example, when we cook or clean as a team, we talk, laugh, and share stories.

저는 집안일을 함께 하면 가족이 더 가까워진다고 믿습니다. 예를 들어, 요리하거나 청소를 함께할 때 대화도 나누고 웃으며 이야기를 공유합니다.

Chores can be tiring, but I think they are important. They help us ⑤**learn good habits** and ⑥**make our home** more **comfortable** for everyone.

집안일은 피곤할 수 있지만, 그것들이 중요하다고 생각합니다. 집안일은 우리가 좋은 습관을 배우게 도와주고, 집을 모든 사람에게 더 편안한 곳으로 만들어 줍니다.

스피치 포인트

① **do some household chores** 집안일을 좀 하다 ② **do the laundry** 빨래하다 ③ **prepare meals** 음식을 준비하다 ④ **do the dishes** 설거지하다 ⑤ **learn good habits** 좋은 습관을 배우다 ⑥ **make one's home comfortable** 자신의 집을 편안하게 만들다

나의 상황에 맞게 내용을 바꾸어서 말해 보세요.

In my daily life, I do some household chores to keep things clean and organized. My main job is doing the laundry. I enjoy folding clean clothes because it feels satisfying to see everything neat.

On weekends, I help in the kitchen. Sometimes I prepare meals or do the dishes after eating.

I believe doing chores together helps bring the family closer. For example, when we cook or clean as a team, we talk, laugh, and share stores.

Chores can be tiring, but I think they are important. They help us learn good habits and make our home more comfortable for everyone.

스피치 메모

필요한 단어와 표현을 정리해 보세요.

TOPIC 05 동네 이웃

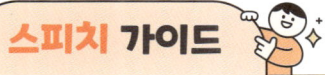

키워드와 주요 표현을 활용해서 문장을 말해 보세요.

1. 동네 소개

위치: 동네의 위치, 이름, 환경

예) I live in a peaceful neighborhood by the coast.
난 해안가에 있는 조용한 동네에 살아.

특징: 동네의 특징이나 장점 언급

예) It's a small community, so everyone knows each other and helps out.
작은 공동체라서 모두 서로 알고 도와주며 지내요.

키워드 coast, town, help, quiet, nature

2. 이웃 사람 소개

관계: 이웃들과의 관계나 활동

예) My neighbors are very kind. We often exchange tips about gardening.
이웃들은 매우 친절해요. 우리는 자주 원예에 관한 팁을 주고받죠.

도움: 서로를 돕는 행동

예) We help each other with tasks like picking up groceries.
우리는 장을 보는 일 같은 일들을 서로 도와줘요.

키워드 kind, friendly, gardening, vegetable, grocery, food

3. 동네 활동 소개

활동: 이웃들과 하는 야외 활동 얘기

예) We go for morning walks together, which helps us stay fit.
우리는 함께 아침 산책을 하는데, 건강을 챙기는데 도움이 돼요.

장소: 운동이나 취미 활동 하는 장소

예) My neighbors and I often exercise in the park in our area.
내 이웃들과 나는 자주 우리 동네 공원에서 운동을 해.

키워드 hiking, walk, trail, park, mountain

대화 속에서 문장을 늘려가는 연습을 해 보세요.

A : I live in a **small town** called Janghowon. It's **quiet and surrounded by beautiful nature**.

저는 장호원이라는 작은 마을에 살아요. 조용하고 아름다운 자연으로 둘러싸여 있죠.

B : That sounds so peaceful. Do you like living there?

정말 평화로울 것 같아요. 그곳에서 사는 게 마음에 들어요?

A : Yes, I love it! My neighbors are **so friendly**, and we even **share fresh vegetables or homemade food** sometimes.

네, 너무 좋아요! 이웃들이 정말 친절하고, 가끔 신선한 채소나 집에서 만든 음식을 나눠 먹기도 하죠.

B : I'm glad to hear that. It must make you feel close to everyone around you.

다행이네요. 그럼 주변 사람들과 가까워질 수 있겠네요.

A : Absolutely. We also enjoy **hiking together** since there are great **trails** nearby.

물론이죠. 그리고 근처에 멋진 산책로가 있어서 이웃들과 함께 하이킹도 즐깁니다.

B : Hiking with neighbors? That sounds like a great way to stay connected and healthy!

이웃들과 하이킹을 한다고요? 서로 친해지고 건강도 챙길 수 있는 좋은 방법 같아요!

어휘 **be surrounded by** ~에 둘러싸여 있다 **stay connected** 유대감을 유지하다

내용 구성하기

주제별로 구분하여 길게 말하는 연습을 해 보세요.

I'd like to ①**share a bit about** my neighborhood. I live in Jangho-won. It's a peaceful place surrounded by nature, and the people here are very ②**warm and welcoming**.
제 동네에 대해 잠시 소개해 드리고 싶습니다. 저는 장호원에 살고 있습니다. 자연으로 둘러싸여 있는 조용한 곳이며, 이곳 사람들은 매우 따뜻하고 우호적입니다.

My neighbors are kind and helpful. We often ③**greet each other** with smiles, and sometimes we exchange small gifts, like fresh vegetables. This creates ④**a strong sense of community**.
제 이웃사람들은 친절하고 도움을 잘 주시는 분들입니다. 우리는 종종 미소로 서로를 맞이하며, 때로는 신선한 채소 같은 작은 선물을 주고받기도 하죠. 덕분에 강한 공동체 의식이 생깁니다.

One thing I love about my neighborhood is that it's close to beautiful hiking trails. Many of us enjoy walking or cycling together to ⑤**stay active and healthy**.
제가 우리 동네에서 정말 좋아하는 점 중 하나는 아름다운 등산로가 가깝다는 점이에요. 우리 중 많은 사람들이 활발하고 건강하게 지내려고 함께 걷거나 자전거를 타는 걸 즐깁니다.

I'm truly grateful for my neighbors and the sense of harmony we share. We celebrate local festivals together, and it's always ⑥**a joyful time** to connect with one another.
저는 제 이웃들과 우리가 공유하는 조화로운 관계에 정말 감사하고 있습니다. 우리는 함께 지역 축제를 기념하며, 서로 교류할 수 있는 즐거운 시간을 항상 보냅니다.

스피치 포인트

① **share a bit about** ~에 대해 간단히 이야기해 보다　② **warm and welcoming** 따듯하고 호의적인　③ **greet each other** 서로 맞이하다　④ **a strong sense of community** 강한 공동체 의식　⑤ **stay active and healthy** 활발하고 건강하게 지내다　⑥ **a joyful time** 즐거운 시간

나의 상황에 맞게 내용을 바꾸어서 말해 보세요.

I'd like to share a bit about my neighborhood. I live in Janghowon. It's a peaceful place surrounded by nature, and the people here are very warm and welcome.

My neighbors are kind and helpful. We often greet each other with smiles, and sometimes we exchange small gifts, like fresh vegetables. This creates a strong sense of community.

One thing I love about my neighborhood is that it's close to beautiful hiking trails. Many of us enjoy walking or cycling together to stay active and healthy.

I'm truly grateful for my neighbors and the sense of harmony we share. We celebrate local festivals together, and it's always a joyful time to connect with one another.

스피치 메모

필요한 단어와 표현을 정리해 보세요.

PART 01 Review Quiz

1 ~로 불리다
_____ by

2 ~에서 태어나고 자라다
be born and _____ in

3 스트레스를 풀다
_____ stress

4 자신의 머리를 비우다, 자신의 마음을 정리하다
_____ one's mind

5 자신을 표현하다, 의견을 나타내다
_____ oneself

6 좋은 대화를 나누다
have _____ conversations

7 놀다, 어울리다
hang _____

8 의지하다, 기대다
_____ on

> 배운 영어 표현들을 복습해 보세요.

9 긍정적인 태도를 취하다

stay _____

10 집안일을 좀 하다

do some household _____

11 빨래하다

_____ the laundry

12 좋은 습관을 배우다

learn good _____

13 서로 맞이하다

_____ each other

14 강한 공동체 의식

a strong _____ of community

15 활발하고 건강하게 지내다

stay _____ and healthy

정답 01 go 02 raised 03 relieve 04 clear 05 express 06 great 07 out 08 count 09 positive
10 chores 11 do 12 habits 13 greet 14 sense 15 active

PART 02
취미 생활

TOPIC 06   영화
TOPIC 07   음악
TOPIC 08   게임
TOPIC 09   외식
TOPIC 10   여행

TOPIC 06 영화

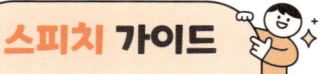

키워드와 주요 표현을 활용해서 문장을 말해 보세요.

1. 영화 소개

장르: 좋아하는 영화 장르
- 예) I really like watching action movies.
  나는 액션 영화를 정말 좋아해.

장점: 영화의 장점, 매력
- 예) Movies are a great way to escape from reality and relax.
  영화는 현실에서 벗어나 휴식을 취하는 좋은 방법이에요.

키워드 action, thriller, comedy, relax, power, differently

2. 영화의 영향 소개

교훈: 영화가 주는 교훈이나 감동
- 예) Some movies teach us important life lessons, like the value of friendship.
  어떤 영화들은 우정의 가치와 같은 중요한 인생의 교훈을 우리에게 가르칩니다.

관점: 영화가 새로운 관점을 열어주는 경험 공유
- 예) I watched a documentary on climate change, and it changed my perspective.
  기후 변화에 관한 다큐멘터리를 보고 내 시각이 바뀌었어.

키워드 lesson, change, perspective, connect, theme, universal

3. 영화와 영어 실력 향상 소개

학습: 영화가 언어 학습에 도움이 되는 방법
- 예) Watching movies helps me improve my listening skills.
  영화를 보면 듣기 실력 향상에 도움이 돼요.

경험: 영어 표현, 발음 향상 관련 경험 공유
- 예) I learned useful phrases from a comedy film I saw last week.
  지난주에 본 코미디 영화에서 유용한 표현들을 배웠어.

키워드 listening, speaking, improve, pick up, expression, pronunciation

대화로 연습하기

대화 속에서 문장을 늘려가는 연습을 해 보세요.

A : I think movies are amazing because they let me experience all kinds of emotions, stories, and cultures.
영화는 다양한 감정, 이야기, 문화를 경험할 수 있게 해줘서 정말 대단하다고 생각해요.

B : I agree! Movies really do **have the power** to take us to new places and make us **see things differently**.
저도 동감이에요! 영화는 정말 우리를 새로운 장소로 데려가서 세상을 다르게 볼 수 있게 만들어주는 힘이 있어요.

A : Exactly! They even inspire me to think about life in new ways.
맞아요! 영화는 새로운 방식으로 삶을 생각하도록 영감을 주기도 하죠.

B : That's true. Plus, movies **connect us with people** from around the world because **their themes are often universal**.
그건 사실이에요. 게다가, 영화는 그 주제들이 종종 보편적이기 때문에 전 세계 사람들과 연결해 주기도 합니다.

A : I also love how movies teach me valuable lessons, no matter the genre.
또한 장르에 관계없이 영화가 저에게 귀중한 교훈을 가르쳐주는 방식도 마음에 들어요.

B : And watching them helps **improve your English**, too! For example, you can **pick up natural expressions and improve your pronunciation**.
그리고 영화를 보는게 영어 실력 향상에도 도움이 됩니다! 예를 들어, 자연스러운 표현을 익히거나 발음을 향상시킬 수 있어요.

어휘 universal 보편적인, 일반적인 valuable 소중한, 귀중한 pick up 자연스럽게 배우다, 익히다

주제별로 구분하여 길게 말하는 연습을 해 보세요.

I think movies are amazing because they let me experience all kinds of emotions, stories, and cultures. They take me to new places, make me ①**see things differently**.

저는 영화가 정말 놀랍다고 생각해요. 왜냐하면 영화를 통해 여러 감정, 이야기, 그리고 문화를 경험할 수 있기 때문이에요. 영화는 저를 새로운 장소로 데려가고, 새로운 시각으로 세상을 보게 하죠.

I also love how movies can connect me with people ②**from around the world** since their themes and feelings ③**are** often **universal**.

영화가 전 세계 사람들과 연결될 수 있게 해주는 점도 좋아요. 왜냐하면 영화 속 주제나 감정이 보편적인 경우가 많거든요.

For me, movies are not just fun, but they also teach me valuable lessons. Whether it's drama, action, or comedy, I enjoy them all ④**in different ways**. Plus, watching movies helps me ⑤**improve my English** with new phrases and accents.

저에게 영화는 단순히 재미있는 것만이 아니라 가치 있는 교훈도 가르쳐줘요. 드라마든, 액션이든, 코미디든, 저는 각 영화마다 다른 매력을 느껴요. 게다가 영화를 보면 새로운 표현과 억양을 들을 수 있어서 영어 실력 향상에도 도움이 돼요.

Overall, I'm super thankful for movies because they're entertaining and give me a break ⑥**from my daily routine**. They really remind me of how connected we all are.

전체적으로 저는 영화에 정말 감사해요. 왜냐하면 영화는 재미있을 뿐만 아니라 일상에서 벗어나게 해주거든요. 영화는 우리 모두가 어떻게 연결되어 있는지 상기시켜줘요.

스피치 포인트

① **see things differently** 다른 시각(관점)으로 보다 ② **from around the world** 전 세계에서 ③ **be universal** 보편적이다, 모두에게 적용되다 ④ **in different ways** 다양한 방식으로 ⑤ **improve one's English** 자신의 영어 실력을 향상시키다 ⑥ **from one's daily routine** 자신의 일상으로부터

나의 상황에 맞게 내용을 바꾸어서 말해 보세요.

I think movies are amazing because they let me experience all kinds of emotions, stories, and cultures. They take me to new places, make me see things differently.

I also love how movies can connect me with people from around the world since their themes and feelings are often universal.

For me, movies are not just fun, but they also teach me valuable lessons. Whether it's drama, action, or comedy, I enjoy them all in different ways. Plus, watching movies helps me improve my English with new phrases and accents.

Overall, I'm super thankful for movies because they're entertaining and give me a break from my daily routine. They really remind me of how connected we all are.

스피치 메모

필요한 단어와 표현을 정리해 보세요.

TOPIC 07 음악

스피치 가이드

키워드와 주요 표현을 활용해서 문장을 말해 보세요.

1. 음악 소개

장르: 좋아하는 음악 장르
- 예) I really love listening to jazz music.
  저는 재즈 음악 듣는 걸 정말 좋아해요.

의미: 음악은 자신에게 어떤 의미
- 예) Music means a lot to me.
  음악은 내게 큰 의미가 있어.

키워드 music, jazz, soft rock, classical, big part, mean

2. 음악의 감정적 효과 소개

감정: 음악이 감정에 미치는 영향
- 예) Music can help me feel calm and relaxed when I'm anxious.
  음악은 내가 불안할 때 차분하고 편안한 느낌을 줄 수 있어요.

회복: 음악이 회복에 어떻게 도움 되는지 언급
- 예) Listening to my favorite song helps me unwind after a tough day.
  내가 좋아하는 노래를 듣는 것은 힘든 하루를 풀어주는 데 도움이 돼.

키워드 calm, relaxed, anxious, recover, unwind, escape, overwhelming

3. 음악과 사회적 연결 소개

연결: 음악이 관계를 형성하는 방식
- 예) Music can bring people together and create strong connections.
  음악은 사람들을 하나로 모으고 강한 관계를 형성할 수 있습니다.

공유: 음악을 통한 경험을 나누는 방법
- 예) I love sharing my favorite songs with friends.
  나는 좋아하는 노래들을 친구들과 공유하는 걸 너무 좋아해.

키워드 bring together, connection, share, background

대화로 연습하기

대화 속에서 문장을 늘려가는 연습을 해 보세요.

A : Music is **a big part** of my life. I love songs that evoke deep emotions, like **classical and soft rock**.

음악은 제 삶에서 큰 부분을 차지해요. 저는 클래식이나 소프트 록처럼 깊은 감정을 불러일으키는 노래를 좋아해요.

B : That's great! Do you listen to music when you're stressed to relax?

멋지네요! 스트레스를 받을 때 편안해지기 위해 음악을 듣나요?

A : Definitely. It feels like **a safe escape** when life **feels overwhelming**. What about you?

당연하죠. 삶이 벅찰 때 안식처럼 느껴지거든요. 당신은요?

B : Me too! I love discovering new artists and exploring different genres.

저도 그래요. 새로운 아티스트를 발굴하고 다른 장르를 탐구하는 걸 아주 좋아해요.

A : Music truly **brings people together**, no matter **their background**.

음악은 배경에 관계없이 진정으로 사람들을 하나로 묶어주죠.

B : I couldn't agree more with that. I think music really is a universal language.

그 점에는 전적으로 동의해요. 음악은 정말 보편적인 언어인 것 같아요.

어휘 evoke 불러일으키다, 자아내다 safe escape 안전한 피난처 overwhelming 압도적인

주제별로 구분하여 길게 말하는 연습을 해 보세요.

Music has always been a big part of my life. I listen to all kinds of music, but I especially love songs that ①**evoke deep emotions**.

음악은 항상 제 삶에서 큰 부분을 차지해왔습니다. 저는 모든 종류의 음악을 듣지만, 깊은 감정을 불러일으키는 노래를 특히 좋아합니다.

Sometimes, ②**when I'm feeling stressed** or overwhelmed, I ③**turn to music** to help me relax. It's like an escape. I also love discovering new artists and genres.

가끔 스트레스가 많거나 힘들 때 음악에 의지하며 편안함을 찾곤 해요. 음악은 마치 도피처 같은 느낌이에요. 또한 새로운 아티스트나 장르를 발견하는 것도 좋아해요.

Music has this unique power to bring people together, no matter where they're from or what language they speak. It's incredible how we can all ④**share the same feelings** just ⑤**through a song**.

음악은 사람들이 어디에서 왔든, 어떤 언어를 사용하든 관계없이 서로를 연결할 수 있는 특별한 힘을 가지고 있어요. 우리가 그냥 노래를 통해 같은 감정을 나눌 수 있다는 것이 믿기지 않아요.

To me, music is not just something I listen to, it's ⑥**a way to express** myself, connect with others, and even find peace in the chaos of life.

내 생각에 음악은 단지 듣는 것이 아니라, 나 자신을 표현하고, 다른 사람들과 교류하며, 심지어 삶의 혼잡 속에서 평화를 찾을 수 있는 방법이에요.

스피치 포인트

① **evoke deep emotions** 깊은 감정을 불러일으키다 ② **when I'm feeling stressed** 내가 스트레스 받을 때 ③ **turn to music** 음악에 의지하다, 음악을 찾다 ④ **share the same feelings** 같은 감정을 공유하다 ⑤ **through a song** 노래를 통해서 ⑥ **a way to express** 표현하는 방법

나의 상황에 맞게 내용을 바꾸어서 말해 보세요.

Music has always been a big part of my life. I listen to all kinds of music, but I especially love songs that evoke deep emotions.

Sometimes, when I'm feeling stressed or overwhelmed, I turn to music to help me relax. It's like an escape. I also love discovering new artists and genres.

Music has this unique power to bring people together, no matter where they're from or what language they speak. It's incredible how we can all share the same feelings just through a song.

To me, music is not just something I listen to, it's a way to express myself, connect with others, and even find peace in the chaos of life.

스피치 메모

필요한 단어와 표현을 정리해 보세요.

TOPIC 08 게임

스피치 가이드

키워드와 주요 표현을 활용해서 문장을 말해 보세요.

1. 게임 소개

장르: 좋아하는 게임 장르
- 예) I really enjoy playing strategy games.
  난 전략 게임하는 걸 정말 즐겨.

시간: 게임을 어느 때 하는지 언급
- 예) I usually play mobile games at home after work.
  저는 보통 퇴근 후에 집에서 모바일 게임을 해요.

키워드 strategy, mobile, game, after work, these days

2. 게임을 즐기는 방법 소개

도구: 게임을 하는 방법
- 예) When I feel like playing games, I play on my smartphone.
  게임이 하고 싶을 때, 스마트폰으로 해요.

영향: 게임이 몸에 미치는 영향
- 예) Spending too much time on games may result in poor posture.
  게임에 너무 많은 시간을 보내면 자세가 나빠질 수 있어요.

키워드 smartphone, computer, posture, poor, eyes, tired

3. 게임에 대한 개인 의견 소개

연결: 게임이 사람들과의 관계에 미치는 영향
- 예) Multiplayer games allow me to connect with friends online.
  멀티플레이어 게임을 하면 온라인에서 친구들과 교류할 수 있어.

의견: 게임하는 것에 대한 개인 의견, 생각
- 예) I believe gaming can be a great way to relax if done in moderation.
  적당히만 한다면 게임은 좋은 휴식 방법이 될 수 있다고 생각해요.

키워드 connect, catch up, time, waste, great, way

 **대화로 연습하기** — 대화 속에서 문장을 늘려가는 연습을 해 보세요.

A : Do you **play mobile games these days**?
요즘 모바일 게임 자주 해?

B : No, I used to, but I'm not into them anymore. What about you?
아니. 예전엔 했는데 이제는 흥미가 없어졌어. 너는?

A : Sometimes. I tried playing old arcade games **on my smartphone**, but the small screen **made my eyes tired quickly**.
가끔. 스마트폰으로 옛날 오락실 게임을 해봤는데, 화면이 작아서 금방 눈이 피로해지더라.

B : I know what you mean. On the subway, I see young people completely immersed in games on their smartphones.
무슨 말인지 알겠어. 지하철에서 난 스마트폰으로 게임에 완전히 몰입한 젊은 사람들을 자주 봐.

A : Yeah, but now playing games **feels like a waste of time**, so I only play when I want to **catch up with friends**.
응. 근데 이제 게임하는 게 시간 낭비처럼 느껴져서, 친구들과 연락하고 싶을 때만 해.

B : Same here. Anyway, I really miss the old arcades from my childhood.
나도 그래. 아무튼. 어렸을 때 다니던 동네 오락실이 정말 그리워.

어휘 be into ~을 좋아하다 arcade game 오락실 게임 immersed in ~에 몰입된 catch up with 연락을 주고받다

주제별로 구분하여 길게 말하는 연습을 해 보세요.

These days, many people ①**enjoy playing games** on smartphones or computers. I ②**used to play computer games** to relieve stress, but I no longer do. My interest has faded.

요즘 많은 사람들이 스마트폰이나 컴퓨터로 게임을 즐깁니다. 저도 한때는 스트레스를 풀려고 컴퓨터 게임을 했지만, 이제는 더 이상 하지 않습니다. 관심이 사라졌기 때문이죠.

When I played on my smartphone, I ③**downloaded old arcade games**, but the small screen made my eyes tired quickly, and I only played for about 10 minutes. I'm no longer interested in mobile games.

스마트폰으로 옛 오락실 게임을 다운받아 즐겼지만, 화면이 작아서 금방 눈이 피로해져 10분 정도만 했습니다. 이제는 모바일 게임에 흥미가 없습니다.

On the subway to Seoul, I often see young people ④**immersed in games**. It's interesting to see how focused they are, even while traveling.

서울로 가는 지하철에서 젊은 사람들이 게임에 몰입하는 모습을 자주 봅니다. 그들이 여행 중에도 게임에 집중하는 모습이 흥미롭습니다.

Honestly, as I get older, I often feel that playing mobile games on a computer or smartphone is a waste of time. When I was younger, I frequently ⑤**went to the arcade** in my neighborhood, but now ⑥**those days remain just a memory**.

솔직히 말해서 나이가 들어가니까 컴퓨터나 스마트폰으로 모바일 게임하는 게 왠지 시간이 아깝다는 생각이 자주 듭니다. 어렸을 때는 동네에 있는 오락실에 자주 갔었는데, 이제는 그런 시절이 추억 속에 남아있네요.

스피치 포인트

① enjoy playing games 게임을 즐기다 ② used to play computer games 컴퓨터 게임을 하곤 했다
③ download old arcade games 옛 오락실 게임을 다운받다 ④ immersed in games 게임에 완전 몰입된
⑤ go to the arcade 오락실에 가다 ⑥ those days remain just a memory 그 시절들은 단지 추억으로 남아 있다

나의 상황에 맞게 내용을 바꾸어서 말해 보세요.

These days, many people enjoy playing games on smartphones or computers. I used to play computer games to relieve stress, but I no longer do. My interest has faded.

When I played on my smartphone, I downloaded old arcade games, but the small screen made my eyes tired quickly, and I only played for about 10 minutes. I'm no longer interested in mobile games.

On the subway to Seoul, I often see young people immersed in games. It's interesting to see how focused they are, even while traveling.

Honestly, as I get older, I often feel that playing mobile games on a computer or smartphone is a waste of time. When I was younger, I frequently went to the arcade in my neighborhood, but now those days remain just a memory.

필요한 단어와 표현을 정리해 보세요.

TOPIC 09 외식

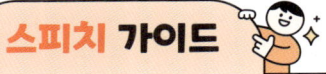

키워드와 주요 표현을 활용해서 문장을 말해 보세요.

1. 외식 소개

시간: 외식을 한 시간대
- I went out for lunch with my family on Friday.
  금요일에 가족이랑 점심 먹으로 외출했어.

이유: 외식을 하는 이유
- I usually eat out on weekends to relax and enjoy good food.
  저는 보통 주말에 외식하면서 휴식을 취하고 맛있는 음식을 즐깁니다.

키워드 lunch, dinner, on Friday, birthday, celebrate, relax

2. 외식 즐기는 방법 소개

장소: 좋아하는 외식 장소
- I often go to Italian restaurants because I love pasta.
  나는 파스타를 너무 좋아해서 이탈리안 레스토랑에 자주 가.

음식: 즐겨 먹는 음식
- When I go out for dinner, I usually order steak with some salad.
  저녁 외식을 할 때, 저는 보통 스테이크에 샐러드를 곁들여 주문해요.

키워드 Italian, Korean, Chinese, restaurant, steak, bulgogi, pasta

3. 외식에 대한 의견 소개

장점: 외식의 좋은 점
- Eating out is a great way to bond with family.
  외식은 가족과 유대감을 쌓는 좋은 방법이에요.

개인 경험: 외식을 통해 느낀 점이나 배운 점
- Having dinner together yesterday reminded me how important family time is.
  어제 함께 저녁을 먹으며 가족과의 시간이 얼마나 중요한지 깨달았어요.

키워드 bond, important, remind, realize, enjoy, more often

대화로 연습하기 대화 속에서 문장을 늘려가는 연습을 해 보세요.

A : Hey, how was your weekend?
이봐, 주말 어땠어?

B : It was great! We **went out for dinner** to **celebrate my mom's birthday**.
정말 좋았어! 어머니 생신을 기념해서 저녁 먹으러 외식했거든.

A : That sounds nice! Where did you go?
좋겠다! 어디 갔는데?

B : To **a Korean restaurant**. My mom loves **bulgogi**, so we went to one of her favorite places.
한식당에 갔어. 어머니께서 불고기를 좋아하셔서 좋아하는 식당 중 하나로 갔지.

A : Did she enjoy it?
어머니께서 만족하셨어?

B : Oh, absolutely! **Seeing her enjoy the meal so much** made me **realize we should eat out as a family more often**.
당연하지! 어머니께서 음식을 맛있게 드시는 모습을 보니, 우리 가족이 더 자주 외식해야겠다는 생각이 들더라.

어휘 absolutely 전적으로, 완전히 realize 깨닫다, 알게 되다

When ①**eating out**, my family ②**tends to go for Korean food** since everyone loves it. We usually look for well-known restaurants in the neighborhood.
외식을 할 때면 우리 가족은 모두 한식을 좋아하기 때문에 한식을 찾는 경향이 있습니다. 우리는 보통 동네에서 잘 알려진 식당을 찾습니다.

Last Friday was my mother's birthday, so our family went out for dinner ③**for the first time in a while**. Since my mother wanted to have bulgogi, we decided to visit a restaurant we ④**were familiar with**.
지난 금요일은 어머니의 생신이어서 오랜만에 가족들이 저녁 식사를 하러 나갔습니다. 어머니께서 불고기를 드시고 싶어 하셔서, 우리는 익숙한 식당을 방문하기로 결정했습니다.

When we arrived, the place was packed, so we had to wait for about 10 minutes before being seated. After sitting down, we ⑤**ordered our meals**. Watching my mom enjoy her bulgogi made me smile.
식당에 도착했을 때 이미 자리가 꽉 차 있어서 10분 정도 기다린 후 자리에 앉을 수 있었습니다. 자리에 앉은 후 우리는 식사를 주문했습니다. 어머니께서 불고기를 맛있게 드시는 모습을 보니 절로 미소가 나왔습니다.

On the way home, I thought we should ⑥**eat out together more often**. I suggested going out for dinner next weekend, and everyone seemed excited about it.
집에 오는 길에 우리는 더 자주 외식을 해야겠다고 생각했습니다. 다음 주말에 저녁 외식하자고 제안했더니 모두가 신나하는 것 같았습니다.

스피치 포인트

① **eat out** 외식하다 ② **tend to go for Korean food** 한식을 즐겨먹는 경향이 있다 ③ **for the first time in a while** 오랜만에 ④ **be familiar with** ~에 친숙하다, ~에 익숙하다 ⑤ **order one's meals** 자신의 음식을 주문하다 ⑥ **eat out together more often** 더 자주 외식하다

나의 상황에 맞게 내용을 바꾸어서 말해 보세요.

When eating out, my family tends to go for Korean food since everyone loves it. We usually look for well-known restaurants in the neighborhood.

Last Friday was my mother's birthday, so our family went out for dinner for the first time in a while. Since my mother wanted to have bulgogi, we decided to visit a restaurant we were familiar with.

When we arrived, the place was packed, so we had to wait for about 10 minutes before being seated. After sitting down, we ordered our meals. Watching my mom enjoy her bulgogi made me smile.

On the way home, I thought we should eat out together more often. I suggested going out for dinner next weekend, and everyone seemed excited about it.

필요한 단어와 표현을 정리해 보세요.

TOPIC 10 여행

스피치 가이드
키워드와 주요 표현을 활용해서 문장을 말해 보세요.

1. 여행 소개

유형: 선호하는 여행 종류
- 예) I enjoy solo trips because I can follow my own schedule.
  제 일정에 맞춰 다닐 수 있어서 혼자 여행하는 걸 즐겨요.

사람: 함께 여행하는 사람
- 예) I usually travel with my family because we love spending time together.
  함께 시간을 보내는 걸 좋아해서 보통 가족과 여행해.

키워드: travel alone, travel with, solo trip, backpacking trip, group tour

2. 여행 장소 소개

장소: 방문했던 장소, 국가
- 예) I visited New York last winter, and the city was breathtaking.
  작년 겨울에 뉴욕에 갔는데, 정말 멋진 도시였어요.

경험: 해외 여행한 빈도수
- 예) It was my second time traveling abroad, and I was so excited.
  해외여행은 두 번째였는데, 정말 설렜어.

키워드: New York, Dubai, Italy, Canada, first, second, time

3. 여행에 대한 생각 소개

배운 점: 여행을 통해 얻은 교훈
- 예) I realized that sharing moments with others is what makes traveling special.
  여행을 특별하게 만드는 건 다른 사람들과의 순간을 함께하는 거라는 걸 깨달았어요.

느낀 점: 여행에서 느낀 감정
- 예) Traveling with friends made the trip unforgettable.
  친구들과의 여행은 잊지 못할 추억이 되었어.

키워드: unforgettable, special, important, miss

대화로 연습하기 — 대화 속에서 문장을 늘려가는 연습을 해 보세요.

A : Do you prefer traveling alone or with others?
혼자 여행하는 걸 좋아해요, 아니면 다른 사람들과 가는 걸 더 좋아해요?

B : I used to love **solo trips**, but now I prefer **traveling with friends or family**.
예전에는 혼자 여행하는 걸 좋아했는데, 이제는 친구나 가족과 함께 여행하는 걸 더 좋아해요.

A : Did you travel with your family recently?
최근에 가족과 여행을 갔나요?

B : Yes, I **went to Dubai** with my little brother's family. It was **my first time traveling abroad** with them.
네, 남동생 가족과 두바이에 갔어요. 그들과 해외여행은 처음이었어요.

A : That must have been fun! Did you enjoy it more than traveling alone?
재밌었겠네요! 혼자 여행하는 것보다 더 즐거웠나요?

B : Definitely! I realized that who you travel with is **more important than** where you go, and I still **miss that time**.
당연하죠! 누구와 여행하느냐가 어디로 가느냐보다 더 중요하다는 걸 깨달았고, 그때가 아직도 그리워요.

어휘 solo trip 혼자 여행 definitely 틀림없이, 확실히

주제별로 구분하여 길게 말하는 연습을 해 보세요.

When I was younger, I enjoyed traveling alone, but as I get older, I've started to ①**get tired of solo trips**. Now, I try to travel with friends or family whenever possible.

어렸을 때는 혼자 여행하는 걸 좋아했는데, 나이가 점점 들어가면서 혼자 여행하는 게 싫증나기 시작했어요. 그래서 가능한 친구나 가족과 함께 여행을 하려고 하죠.

When traveling alone, I could ②**decide on any destination** I wanted, but when I travel with others, I often feel the pressure of having to ③**plan the trip** more **systematically**.

혼자 여행할 때는 가고 싶은 곳을 아무 곳이나 정해서 가면 되는데, 누구와 함께 가기로 마음먹으면 여행 일정을 체계적으로 잡아야 해서 부담을 느끼게 됩니다.

In 2022, I had the opportunity to travel to Dubai with my little brother's family. It was my first time ④**traveling abroad** with them, so I started ⑤**planning the itinerary** a week in advance by searching online.

2022년에 남동생 가족이랑 두바이 여행을 갈 기회가 생겼습니다. 동생 가족과 함께 해외여행은 처음이라 일주일 전부터 인터넷을 검색해서 여행 일정표를 짜기 시작했습니다.

During the trip, we had a great time, and I was happy to ⑥**make up for** the things I missed when traveling alone. I realized that who you travel with is more important than where you go.

여행 동안, 우리는 정말 좋은 시간을 보냈고, 혼자 여행할 때 놓쳤던 것들을 만회할 수 있어서 기뻤습니다. 저는 누구와 여행하느냐가 어디로 가느냐보다 더 중요하다는 것을 깨달았습니다.

스피치 포인트

① **get tired of solo trips** 혼자 여행하는 것에 지치다 ② **decide on any destination** 어디든지 목적지를 정하다 ③ **plan the trip systematically** 여행을 체계적으로 계획하다 ④ **travel abroad** 해외 여행하다 ⑤ **plan the itinerary** 여행 일정표를 짜다 ⑥ **make up for** 보상하다, 만회하다

나의 상황에 맞게 내용을 바꾸어서 말해 보세요.

When I was younger, I enjoyed traveling alone, but as I get older, I've started to get tired of solo trips. Now, I try to travel with friends or family whenever possible.

When traveling alone, I could decide on any destination I wanted, but when I travel with others, I often feel the pressure of having to plan the trip more systematically.

In 2022, I had the opportunity to travel to Dubai with my little brother's family. It was my first time traveling abroad with them, so I started planning the itinerary a week in advance by searching online.

During the trip, we had a great time, and I was happy to make up for the things I missed when traveling alone. I realized that who you travel with is more important than where you go.

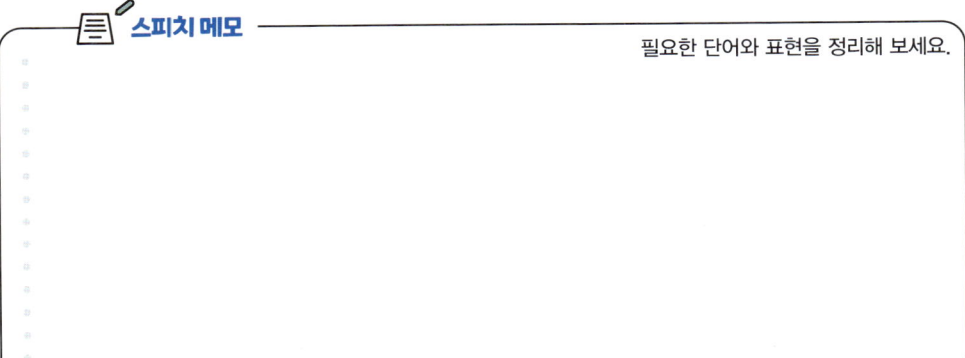

스피치 메모

필요한 단어와 표현을 정리해 보세요.

PART 02 Review Quiz

1 다른 시각(관점)으로 보다
see things _____

2 보편적이다, 모두에게 적용되다
be _____

3 자신의 영어 실력을 향상시키다
_____ one's English

4 깊은 감정을 불러일으키다
_____ deep emotions

5 음악에 의지하다, 음악을 찾다
turn to _____

6 같은 감정을 공유하다
share the _____ feelings

7 컴퓨터 게임을 하곤 했다
used to _____ computer games

8 게임에 완전 몰입된
_____ in games

배운 영어 표현들을 복습해 보세요.

9 오락실에 가다

go to the _____

10 한식을 즐겨먹는 경향이 있다

tend to go _____ Korean food

11 오랜만에

for the first _____ in a while

12 더 자주 외식하다

eat _____ together more often

13 혼자 여행하는 것에 지치다

get _____ of solo trips

14 여행을 체계적으로 계획하다

plan the trip _____

15 여행 일정표를 짜다

plan the _____

정답 01 differently 02 universal 03 improve 04 evoke 05 music 06 same 07 play 08 immersed
09 arcade 10 for 11 time 12 out 13 tired 14 systematically 15 itinerary

PART 03
일상생활

TOPIC 11	반려동물
TOPIC 12	커피숍
TOPIC 13	음주
TOPIC 14	수면
TOPIC 15	등산

TOPIC 11 반려동물

스피치 가이드

키워드와 주요 표현을 활용해서 문장을 말해 보세요.

1. 반려동물 소개

장소: 반려동물을 볼 수 있는 장소
- 예) I always run into puppies at the park.
  공원에서 강아지를 항상 마주쳐요.

반응: 반려동물을 발견할 때의 반응
- 예) I can't get over how cute that puppy is!
  저 강아지 너무 귀여워서 정신 못 차리겠어!

키워드 park, street, apartment, cute, get over, tiny

2. 반려동물 키운 경험 소개

유형: 과거에 키웠던 반려동물
- 예) When I was in my twenties, I had a golden retriever named Max.
  20대였을 때 맥스라는 골든 리트리버를 키웠어.

상황: 더 이상 키우지 않는 경우
- 예) I had a cat, but I left her with my parents when I moved out.
  고양이를 키웠는데, 이사하면서 부모님께 맡겼어요.

키워드 puppy, golden retriever, cat, move out, after moving

3. 반려동물과의 추억 소개

경험: 다른 집에 있는 반려동물과의 경험
- 예) Last year, I went to my cousin's place and spent hours playing with his cat.
  작년에 사촌 집에 가서 사촌 고양이랑 몇 시간 동안 놀았어요.

감정: 반려동물과의 추억이나 감정
- 예) Being around pets always brightens my day.
  반려동물과 함께 있으면 항상 기분이 좋아져.

키워드 cousin's, aunt's, place, visit, go, brighten, happy

대화로 연습하기 대화 속에서 문장을 늘려가는 연습을 해 보세요.

A : I can't help but say, "Your puppy is **so cute**!" whenever I see one **on the street**.
길에서 강아지를 볼 때마다 저절로 "너무 귀여운 강아지네요!"라고 말을 걸게 돼요.

B : That's nice! Have you ever had a puppy?
그거 좋네요! 강아지를 키워본 적 있나요?

A : Yes, I **had a puppy** for years, but I can't have one now **after moving**.
네, 몇 년 동안 강아지를 키웠지만 이사한 후에는 더 이상 키울 수 없어요.

B : That's too bad. Do you still get to spend time with puppies?
그거 아쉽네요. 아직도 강아지와 함께할 기회가 있나요?

A : Sometimes. Last month, I **visited my aunt's place** and played with her puppy, Choco. It made me **so happy** to spend time with Choco.
가끔요. 지난달에는 이모 집에 방문해서 이모의 강아지 초코와 놀았어요. 초코와 함께 시간을 보내서 정말 행복했어요.

B : That sounds like fun! Puppies always bring so much joy.
재미있겠네요! 강아지는 항상 많은 기쁨을 주죠.

어휘 can't help but 저절로 ~하게 되다 get to spend time with 함께 시간을 보낼 기회가 있다

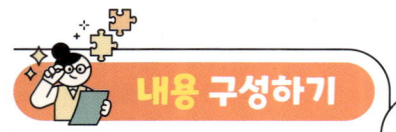

주제별로 구분하여 길게 말하는 연습을 해 보세요.

Whenever I see a small puppy, ①**I can't help but** find it adorable. Since my parents always loved dogs, we raised them at our rural home for a long time. But after moving, I haven't been able to keep one.

작은 강아지를 볼 때마다 저도 모르게 너무 귀엽다고 느끼게 됩니다. 부모님들이 항상 개를 좋아하셔서 저희는 시골집에서 오랫동안 개를 키웠습니다. 하지만 이사한 이후로는 개를 키우지 못하고 있었습니다.

②**That said**, my aunt in Yeongwol has a puppy named Choco. Last month, I visited her house to help make winter kimchi, and I had fun playing with Choco. I took pictures and videos and uploaded them to my blog to ③**relive the memories**.

그런데, 영월에 계신 이모님은 초코라는 이름의 강아지를 키우십니다. 지난달에는 겨울 김장을 도우러 이모님 댁에 갔었고, 초코와 놀며 즐거운 시간을 보냈습니다. 사진과 동영상을 찍고 난후 추억을 되새기려고 제 블로그에 올렸습니다.

When I travel abroad, I often see locals ④**walking their dogs**. I can't resist saying, "Your dog is so cute!". It usually ⑤**leads to a short conversation**.

해외여행을 갈 때면, 저는 종종 현지인들이 개와 함께 산책하는 모습을 봅니다. 저도 모르게 "개가 너무 귀여워요!"라고 말하게 됩니다. 보통 그로 인해 짧은 대화가 이어집니다.

I guess it's because of my past experience raising dogs. Even now, I find myself approaching owners when I see a cute dog and striking up a conversation ⑥**out of habit**.

아마도 개를 키운 제 과거 경험 때문인 것 같습니다. 지금도 귀여운 개를 보면 그 주인에게 다가가서 습관적으로 말을 걸게 됩니다.

스피치 포인트

① **I can't help but** ~하지 않을 수 없다 ② **that said** 그렇기는 하지만, 그런데 ③ **relive the memories** 추억을 되새기다 ④ **walk one's dogs** 자신의 개를 산책시키다 ⑤ **lead to a short conversation** 짧은 대화로 이어지다 ⑥ **out of habit** 습관적으로, 습관 때문에

1분 스피치

나의 상황에 맞게 내용을 바꾸어서 말해 보세요.

Whenever I see a small puppy, I can't help but find it adorable. Since my parents always loved dogs, we raised them at our rural home for a long time. But after moving, I haven't been able to keep one.

That said, my aunt in Yeongwol has a puppy named Choco. Last month, I visited her house to help make winter kimchi, and I had fun playing with Choco. I took pictures and videos and uploaded them to my blog to relive the memories.

When I travel abroad, I often see locals walking their dogs. I can't resist saying, "Your dog is so cute!". It usually leads to a short conversation.

I guess it's because of my past experience raising dogs. Even now, I find myself approaching owners when I see a cute dog and striking up a conversation out of habit.

스피치 메모

필요한 단어와 표현을 정리해 보세요.

TOPIC 12 커피숍

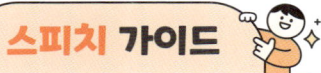

키워드와 주요 표현을 활용해서 문장을 말해 보세요.

1. 커피숍 소개

종류: 커피숍, 카페 종류
- 예) There are chain coffee shops and small local cafes.
  체인 커피숍과 작은 로컬 카페가 있어요.

분위기: 커피숍이나 카페 분위기 설명
- 예) Chain coffee shops are modern and tidy.
  체인 커피숍은 현대적이며 깔끔해요.

키워드 chain coffee shop, local cafe, atmosphere, tidy, modern, cozy

2. 커피 취향 소개

장소: 자주 가는 커피숍을 말할 때
- 예) I go to a local cafe for my morning coffee.
  나는 아침 커피를 마시려고 로컬 카페에 가.

때: 커피를 즐기는 시간
- 예) I drink coffee in the afternoon during my break.
  저는 오후에 쉬는 시간에 커피를 마셔요.

키워드 cafe, coffee shop, break, after class, morning, afternoon

3. 커피 부작용 소개

부작용: 커피의 부작용이나 피하는 이유.
- 예) I stay away from coffee late at night because it keeps me awake.
  늦은 밤에는 커피를 피해요. 커피가 잠을 못 자게 하거든요.

대체 방법: 커피 대신 마시는 음료
- 예) Instead of coffee, I tend to drink warm herbal tea.
  커피 대신에 따듯한 허브차를 마시는 편이야.

키워드 avoid, stay away from, at night, awake, herbal tea, water

대화로 연습하기

대화 속에서 문장을 늘려가는 연습을 해 보세요.

A : There are a lot of coffee shops these days. **Chain coffee shops are modern**, while **local cafes are cozy**.
요즘 커피숍이 많아요. 체인 커피숍은 현대적이고, 로컬 카페는 아늑해요.

B : I know! I usually grab a coffee after my English lessons or during a break.
맞아요! 저는 보통 영어 수업 후나 쉬는 시간에 커피 한 잔 마셔요.

A : I like **stopping by a cafe after class** to chat with others.
저는 수업 끝나고 카페에 들러서 사람들과 얘기하는 걸 좋아해요.

B : I'm not really into coffee, but I love a green tea latte when I want something sweet.
커피를 그렇게 좋아하진 않지만, 달달한 게 먹고 싶을 때는 녹차 라떼를 즐겨 마셔요.

A : **I avoid coffee at night since it keeps me awake**. **Warm water** works better for me.
저는 밤에 커피를 피해요. 커피가 잠을 못 자게 하거든요. 따뜻한 물이 저한테는 더 효과적이에요.

B : Same here! Warm water is perfect for the evening.
저도 그래요! 저녁에는 따뜻한 물이 딱 좋더라고요.

어휘 grab a coffee 커피 한 잔 마시다 stop by 잠시 들르다 be really into ~을 정말 좋아하다

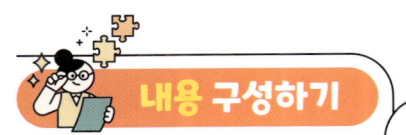

내용 구성하기

주제별로 구분하여 길게 말하는 연습을 해 보세요.

These days, when I walk around the city, I can see ①**countless coffee shops** around me. There are large chain stores, as well as small, locally operated coffee shops.

요즘 시내를 돌아다니다보면 주위에서 수많은 커피숍들을 볼 수가 있습니다. 대형 체인점도 있고, 소규모로 운영되는 커피숍도 있죠.

I ②**used to drink a lot of coffee**, but now I usually ③**have a cup of coffee** after my English lessons or during a short break between classes with the people taking the course.

예전에는 커피를 많이 마셨지만, 지금은 영어 강의 끝나고 커피 한 잔을 마시거나, 수업 중간 휴식 시간에 수업을 듣는 사람들과 잠깐 커피를 마십니다.

④**I'm** not really **a big fan of** drinking coffee. But since I don't drink alcohol, when I feel like something sweet, I ⑤**go for** my favorite, a green tea latte.

저는 커피를 마시는 걸 그다지 좋아하지 않습니다. 하지만 술을 마시지 않아서 뭔가 달콤한 게 당길 때는 제일 좋아하는 녹차 라떼를 찾게 됩니다.

However, I don't drink coffee or lattes at night. ⑥**Due to the caffeine**, it keeps me up at night, so instead of coffee, I prefer to drink warm water.

하지만 밤에는 커피나 라떼를 마시지 않습니다. 안에 들어 있는 카페인 때문에 잠을 거의 설쳐서, 커피 대신 따뜻한 물 마시는 걸 선호합니다.

스피치 포인트

① **countless coffee shops** 셀 수 없이 많은 커피숍들 ② **used to drink a lot of coffee** (예전에) 커피 많이 마시곤 했다 ③ **have a cup of coffee** 커피 한 잔 마시다 ④ **I'm a big fan of** 저는 ~을 정말 좋아해요, 저는 ~의 광팬이에요 ⑤ **go for** (무언가를) 선택하거나 결정하다 ⑥ **due to the caffeine** 카페인 때문에

나의 상황에 맞게 내용을 바꾸어서 말해 보세요.

These days, when I walk around the city, I can see countless coffee shops around me. There are large chain stores, as well as small, locally operated coffee shops.

I used to drink a lot of coffee, but now I usually have a cup of coffee after my English lessons or during a short break between classes with the people taking the course.

I'm not really a big fan of drinking coffee. But since I don't drink alcohol, when I feel like something sweet, I go for my favorite, a green tea latte.

However, I don't drink coffee or lattes at night. Due to the caffeine, it keeps me up at night, so instead of coffee, I prefer to drink warm water.

스피치 메모

필요한 단어와 표현을 정리해 보세요.

TOPIC 13 음주

스피치 가이드

키워드와 주요 표현을 활용해서 문장을 말해 보세요.

1. 음주 습관 소개

횟수: 술을 얼마나 자주 마시는지 묘사
- 예) I only drink on weekends, usually just one or two drinks.
  나는 주말에만 마셔, 보통 한두 잔 정도만.

권유: 누군가가 술 한 잔 하자고 할 때 반응
- 예) That sounds nice, but I'm not drinking tonight.
  좋은 제안이지만, 오늘밤에는 술 안 마실 거야.

키워드 drink, pass, weekend, hardly, tonight, these days

2. 술 못 하는 이유 소개

선호도: 술 마시는 걸 좋아하는지, 싫어하는지
- 예) I'm not a fan of alcohol.
  저는 술을 좋아하지 않아요.

영향: 가족의 영향이나 유전
- 예) I was raised in a family where no one drank, so I don't drink either.
  술을 마시지 않는 가족에서 자랐고, 그래서 저도 술을 마시지 않아요.

키워드 fan, enjoy, drinking, father, family, be raised

3. 음주를 피하는 이유 소개

건강: 건강이나 개인적 이유
- 예) I tend to avoid drinking because it affects my concentration.
  집중력에 영향을 주기에 술을 피하는 편이야.

직업: 직업 관련 이유
- 예) I don't drink much because I need to stay sharp for my job.
  내 일에 집중해야 하기에 술을 많이 마시지 않아.

키워드 concentration, sharp, job, avoid, alcohol, affect, class

대화로 연습하기

대화 속에서 문장을 늘려가는 연습을 해 보세요.

A : Hey, do you want to join us for drinks after work tonight?
이봐, 오늘 밤 퇴근 후에 우리랑 같이 술 한잔할래?

B : Thanks for the invite, but **I'll have to pass**. I **hardly drink these days**.
초대는 고마운데, 사양할게. 요즘 거의 술을 안 마셔.

A : Oh, really? Why's that?
아, 그래? 왜 그런데?

B : To be honest, I don't **enjoy drinking much**. **My father doesn't drink at all**, so I guess that influenced me.
솔직히 말하면, 술을 별로 좋아하지 않아. 우리 아버지도 전혀 술을 안 드시는데, 그게 나한테 영향을 준 것 같아.

A : That makes sense. But don't you ever feel like having just one beer?
그럴 수 있겠네. 그래도 가끔 맥주 한 잔 정도는 마시고 싶지 않아?

B : Sometimes I do have those thoughts, but as a freelance English teacher, I try to **avoid alcohol** so that it doesn't **affect my classes** the next day.
가끔 그런 생각이 들긴 하지만, 프리랜서 영어 강사로 일하다 보니 다음날 수업에 지장이 없도록 술은 피하려고 해.

어휘 to be honest 솔직히 influence 영향을 주다 make sense 일리가 있다

주제별로 구분하여 길게 말하는 연습을 해 보세요.

In social life, it's quite natural to have opportunities to drink with coworkers or friends. I was the same until my 30s. When meeting up with college friends or hometown friends, I would usually ①**have a drink**, like soju or beer.

사회생활을 하다 보면 직장 동료나 친구들과 음주를 할 기회가 생기는 일이 자연스럽기도 합니다. 저도 30대까지는 그런 경험이 많았죠. 대학 친구들이나 고향 친구들을 만날 때면 소주나 맥주를 간단히 마시곤 했습니다.

But as I get older, I have to ②**consider my health**, so nowadays I hardly drink. To be honest, I don't enjoy drinking. I think it's partly because my father doesn't drink at all.

그런데 나이가 들면서 건강을 생각해야 하기에 요즘은 거의 술을 마시지 않습니다. 솔직히 말하면 술을 즐겨하지 않습니다. 아버지께서 술을 전혀 하지 않으신 것도 영향을 미쳤다고 생각합니다.

If I ever have to drink, I usually just have a beer. I ③**'m particularly sensitive to alcohol**, and ④**my face turns red** immediately when I drink. Also, I don't like seeing myself drunk, so I don't enjoy drinking.

만약 어쩔 수 없이 술을 마셔야 하는 상황이 생긴다면 맥주 한잔 정도면 충분합니다. 저는 특히 술에 민감해서 술을 마시면 바로 얼굴이 빨갛게 변합니다. 또한 술에 취한 제 모습을 보고 싶지 않아서 음주를 즐기지 않습니다.

As a freelance English teacher, my schedule isn't fixed, and it's difficult to find time to meet others. I also try to ⑤**avoid drinking** because I don't want it to ⑥**affect my classes** the next day.

프리랜서 영어 강사로 일하다 보니 스케줄이 정해져 있지 않고 다른 사람들을 만날 시간을 내기가 어렵습니다. 또한 다음 날 수업에 영향을 미치지 않기를 바라기 때문에 술을 피하려고 노력합니다.

스피치 포인트

① **have a drink** 술 한 잔하다 ② **consider one's health** 자신의 건강을 고려하다(생각하다) ③ **be particularly sensitive to alcohol** 술(알코올)에 특히 민감하다 ④ **one's face turns red** 자신의 얼굴이 빨갛게 변하다 ⑤ **avoid drinking** 음주를 피하다 ⑥ **affect one's classes** 자신의 수업에 영향을 미치다

1분 스피치

나의 상황에 맞게 내용을 바꾸어서 말해 보세요.

In social life, it's quite natural to have opportunities to drink with coworkers or friends. I was the same until my 30s. When meeting up with college friends or hometown friends, I would usually have a drink, like soju or beer.

But as I get older, I have to consider my health, so nowadays I hardly drink. To be honest, I don't enjoy drinking. I think it's partly because my father doesn't drink at all.

If I ever have to drink, I usually just have a beer. I'm particularly sensitive to alcohol, and my face turns red immediately when I drink. Also, I don't like seeing myself drunk, so I don't enjoy drinking.

As a freelance English teacher, my schedule isn't fixed, and it's difficult to find time to meet others. I also try to avoid drinking because I don't want it to affect my classes the next day.

스피치 메모

필요한 단어와 표현을 정리해 보세요.

TOPIC 14 수면

스피치 가이드

키워드와 주요 표현을 활용해서 문장을 말해 보세요.

1. 불면증 소개

언제: 잠을 잘 못 잘 때 상황 설명
- 예) Sometimes I can't fall asleep no matter how tired I am.
  가끔은 아무리 피곤해도 잠이 안 올 때가 있어요.

원인: 불면증이나 수면 장애의 원인
- 예) I have trouble sleeping when I'm stressed about work.
  일에 대한 스트레스를 받을 때 잠을 잘 못 자요.

키워드 insomnia, fall asleep, stressed, sleep well, things, work

2. 바닥에서 자는 이유 소개

패턴: 자신의 수면 습관, 패턴
- 예) I tend to sleep on the floor rather than using my bed.
  나는 보통 침대에서 자는 것보다 바닥에서 자는 편이야.

이유: 바닥에서 잠을 청하는 이유 설명
- 예) I like sleeping on the floor because it feels warm and cozy.
  바닥에서 자면 따뜻하고 아늑한 느낌이 들어서 좋아.

키워드 sleep, bed, floor, warmth, warm, cozy, feel

3. 깊은 잠에 빠지는 상황 소개

상황: 피로한 상황 설명
- 예) When I've had a long day, I fall asleep the moment I hit the bed.
  긴 하루를 보낸 날에는 침대에 눕자마자 잠들어요.

묘사: 깊은 잠에 빠졌을 때 묘사
- 예) When I'm exhausted, I sleep so deeply that I don't even hear my alarm.
  정말 피곤할 때는 알람 소리도 못 들을 정도로 깊이 자요.

키워드 exhausted, hit the bed, deeply, deep sleep, fall into, alarm

대화로 연습하기

대화 속에서 문장을 늘려가는 연습을 해 보세요.

A : Good sleep is important, but it's not always easy.
좋은 잠은 중요하지만, 항상 쉬운 건 아니야.

B : I know! I try, but there are times **when I can't sleep well because of all the things** I have to do.
나도 알아! 노력하는데, 해야 할 일이 너무 많아서 잠을 잘 못 잘 때가 있어.

A : Same here. I usually get 7 hours of sleep, but if I'm really tired, I go to bed early.
나도 마찬가지야. 보통 7시간 자는데, 정말 피곤할 때는 일찍 잠자리에 들어.

B : Likewise. Sometimes I **sleep on the floor** just to **feel the warmth**.
나도 그래. 가끔은 바닥에서 자면서 온기를 느끼기도 해.

A : That's funny, I do the same. I'm not used to sleeping in a bed.
웃기네. 나도 그래. 난 침대에서 자는 게 익숙하지 않아.

B : **When I'm exhausted**, I **fall into such a deep sleep** that I wouldn't even notice if someone broke in.
정말 피곤할 때는 너무 깊은 잠에 빠져서 누가 들어와도 모를 정도야.

어휘 get 7 hours of sleep 7시간 자다 feel the warmth 온기를 느끼다 break in 침입하다, (대화에) 끼어들다

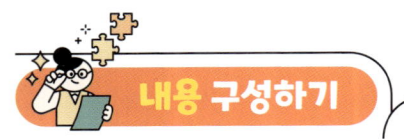

내용 구성하기

주제별로 구분하여 길게 말하는 연습을 해 보세요.

Everyone knows that good sleep is important. Of course, it's essential for [1]**both physical and mental health**. But as easy as it sounds, it's not always that simple.

숙면이 중요하다는 건 누구나 다 알고 있는 사실입니다. 물론 신체적이나 정신적으로 건강해지기 위해 숙면은 꼭 필요합니다. 하지만 말처럼 항상 쉽지만은 않습니다.

I try to [2]**get good sleep** whenever possible, but sometimes I can't sleep properly because of things I need to do. I usually sleep for about 7 hours, but when I'm very tired, I [3]**go to bed early**.

저는 되도록 숙면을 취하려 노력하지만 가끔은 해야 할 일 때문에 제대로 못 자는 경우가 있습니다. 보통 7시간 정도 자는데요, 몸이 너무 피곤할 때는 저녁 일찍 잠자리에 듭니다.

When I sleep, sometimes I sleep in bed, but other times I lay a blanket on the floor to feel its warmth and sleep on it. Since I'm not used to sleeping in a bed, I [4]**prefer sleeping on the floor**.

저는 잘 때 가끔 침대에서 자기도 하고, 다른 때는 바닥의 온기를 느끼기 위해 이불을 깔고 바닥에서 자기도 합니다. 침대에서 자는 게 익숙하지 않아서 바닥에서 자는 게 더 좋습니다.

I'm [5]**a light sleeper**, and it takes me a bit of time to fall asleep. But when I'm extremely tired, I [6]**fall into** such **a deep sleep** that I wouldn't even notice if a thief broke in.

저는 잠귀가 좀 밝은 편이고, 잠드는 데 시간이 좀 걸립니다. 하지만 몸이 너무 피곤할 때는 도둑이 들어와도 모를 정도로 깊은 잠에 빠집니다.

스피치 포인트

① **both physical and mental health** 신체적 건강과 정신적 건강 모두 ② **get good sleep** 잘 자다, 좋은 수면을 취하다 ③ **go to bed early** 일찍 잠자리에 들다 ④ **prefer sleeping on the floor** 바닥에서 자는 걸 선호하다 ⑤ **a light sleeper** 얕은 잠을 자는 사람 ⑥ **fall into a deep sleep** 깊은 잠에 빠지다

1분 스피치

나의 상황에 맞게 내용을 바꾸어서 말해 보세요.

Everyone knows that good sleep is important. Of course, it's essential for both physical and mental health. But as easy as it sounds, it's not always that simple.

I try to get some sleep whenever possible, but sometimes I can't sleep properly because of things I need to do. I usually sleep for about 7 hours, but when I'm very tired, I go to bed early.

When I sleep, sometimes I sleep in bed, but other times I lay a blanket on the floor to feel its warmth and sleep on it. Since I'm not used to sleeping in a bed, I prefer sleeping on the floor.

I'm a light sleeper, and it takes me a bit of time to fall asleep. But when I'm extremely tired, I fall into such a deep sleep that I wouldn't even notice if a thief broke in.

스피치 메모

필요한 단어와 표현을 정리해 보세요.

TOPIC 15 등산

스피치 가이드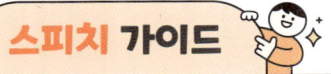

키워드와 주요 표현을 활용해서 문장을 말해 보세요.

1. 등산 포기한 이유 소개

핑계: 등산을 하지 못한 이유, 원인
예) I haven't been hiking lately because the weather's been awful.
요즘 날씨가 너무 안 좋아서 등산을 못 갔어요.

의지력: 등산에 대한 자신의 의지력
예) I know I should go hiking, but I just can't seem to find the energy.
등산을 가야 한다는 걸 알지만, 도통 기운이 나지 않아요.

키워드 lazy, busy, weather, awful, energy, willpower, lack

2. 등산 경험 소개

경험: 등산을 시작한 계기나 경험 설명
예) I started hiking because I wanted to challenge myself.
내 자신에게 도전하고 싶어서 등산을 시작했어.

성취감: 힘들었던 순간과 극복 방법
예) Even when I felt like giving up, I kept going step by step.
포기하고 싶을 때도 있었지만, 한 걸음씩 계속 걸었어.

키워드 challenge, give up, push through, step by step

3. 등산 스타일 소개

스타일: 자신만의 등산 방식이나 특징
예) I prefer hiking early in the morning to enjoy the crisp morning air.
저는 상쾌한 아침 공기를 즐기기 위해 아침 일찍 등산하는 걸 선호해요.

등산: 혼자 등산하는 이유, 함께 등산하는 이유
예) I like hiking alone because I can take breaks whenever I want.
원할 때 쉬어 갈 수 있어서 혼자 등산하는 걸 좋아해요.

키워드 enjoy, crisp, camera, view, break, speed, differ

대화로 연습하기 — 대화 속에서 문장을 늘려가는 연습을 해 보세요.

A : You haven't been hiking lately, right?
요즘 등산 안 가고 있지?

B : Yeah, I've been **too busy and lazy**. It's **a lack of willpower**.
응, 너무 바쁘고 게을러서. 의지가 부족해.

A : But you used to hike a big mountain every week!
그런데 너 예전에 매주 큰 산을 올라갔잖아!.

B : True, I'd **push through** even when I felt like **giving up**.
맞아. 포기하고 싶을 때도 있었지만, 끝까지 올라갔어.

A : Do you still hike alone?
여전히 혼자 등산해?

B : Yes, I prefer it because I don't like when **our speeds differ**. Plus, I always bring my **camera to capture the beautiful views** along the way.
응. 속도가 달라지면 불편해서 혼자 등산하는 걸 선호해. 그리고 등산 중에는 항상 카메라를 가지고 다니면서 멋진 풍경을 담으려고 해.

어휘 **willpower** 의지력 **push through** 끝까지 해내다 **feel like giving up** 포기하고 싶다 **along the way** 도중에

주제별로 구분하여 길게 말하는 연습을 해 보세요.

There are many people around me who ①**enjoy hiking**. I used to be one of them, but these days, I often use the excuse of being too busy to go hiking. Honestly, it's just ②**my lack of willpower**.

제 주변에는 등산을 즐기는 사람들이 많습니다. 저도 한때는 그랬지만 요즘은 너무 바쁘다는 핑계를 대며 등산을 자주 거르곤 합니다. 솔직히 의지가 부족한 탓입니다.

In the past, I made sure to ③**hike a big mountain** once a week. I would prepare by wearing hiking boots and comfortable clothes.

예전에는 일주일에 한 번씩 큰 산을 꼭 올라갔습니다. 등산화와 편안한 복장을 갖추고 가곤 했죠.

I usually ④**go hiking alone**. When I go with others, our hiking speeds tend to differ, which can be uncomfortable. That's why I prefer solo hikes.

등산은 대개 혼자 가는 경우가 많습니다. 일행과 함께 가면 각자의 속도가 달라 불편할 때가 있기 때문입니다. 그래서 저는 혼자만의 산행을 즐깁니다.

I believe spring and autumn are ⑤**the best seasons for hiking**, so I try to avoid hiking in winter. While I ⑥**understand the appeal of winter hikes**, I prioritize safety because I'm concerned about the risk of accidents.

등산하기 좋은 계절은 봄과 가을이라고 생각합니다. 그래서 겨울에는 등산을 피하려고 합니다. 겨울산의 매력을 알지만, 사고가 날까 걱정되어 안전을 우선시하는 편입니다.

스피치 포인트

① enjoy hiking 등산을 즐기다 ② one's lack of willpower 자신의 의지력 부족 ③ hike a big mountain 큰 산을 등산하다 ④ go hiking alone 혼자 등산하다 ⑤ the best seasons for hiking 등산하기에 가장 좋은 계절 ⑥ understand the appeal of winter hikes 겨울 등산의 매력을 이해하다

1분 스피치

나의 상황에 맞게 내용을 바꾸어서 말해 보세요.

There are many people around me who enjoy hiking. I used to be one of them, but these days, I often use the excuse of being too busy to go hiking. Honestly, it's just my lack of willpower.

In the past, I made sure to hike a big mountain once a week. I would prepare by wearing hiking boots and comfortable clothes.

I usually go hiking alone. When I go with others, our hiking speeds tend to differ, which can be uncomfortable. That's why I prefer solo hikes.

I believe spring and autumn are the best seasons for hiking, so I try to avoid hiking in winter. While I understand the appeal of winter hikes, I prioritize safety because I'm concerned about the risk of accidents.

스피치 메모

필요한 단어와 표현을 정리해 보세요.

PART 03 Review Quiz

1 추억을 되새기다
_____ the memories

2 자신의 개를 산책시키다
_____ one's dogs

3 습관적으로, 습관 때문에
out of _____

4 셀 수 없이 많은 커피숍들
_____ coffee shops

5 저는 ~을 정말 좋아해요, 저는 ~의 광팬이에요
I'm a big _____ of

6 카페인 때문에
due _____ the caffeine

7 술 한 잔하다
_____ a drink

8 자신의 얼굴이 빨갛게 변하다
one's face _____ red

배운 영어 표현들을 복습해 보세요.

9 음주를 피하다

_____ drinking

10 잘 자다, 좋은 수면을 취하다

_____ good sleep

11 얕은 잠을 자는 사람

a _____ sleeper

12 깊은 잠에 빠지다

fall _____ a deep sleep

13 자신의 의지력 부족

one's lack of _____

14 큰 산을 등산하다

_____ a big mountain

15 겨울 등산의 매력을 이해하다

understand the _____ of winter hikes

정답 01 relive 02 walk 03 habit 04 countless 05 fan 06 to 07 have 08 turns 09 avoid 10 get
11 light 12 into 13 willpower 14 hike 15 appeal

PART 04
인터넷 세상

TOPIC 16   온라인 쇼핑
TOPIC 17   스마트폰
TOPIC 18   유튜브
TOPIC 19   SNS
TOPIC 20   TV&라디오

TOPIC 16 온라인 쇼핑

키워드와 주요 표현을 활용해서 문장을 말해 보세요.

1. 온라인 쇼핑의 장점 소개

편리함: 온라인 쇼핑의 편리함 강조

예) I love online shopping because I can shop from home.
집에서 쇼핑할 수 있어서 온라인 쇼핑을 좋아해요.

시간: 온라인 쇼핑을 통한 시간 절약

예) Shopping online saves me a lot of time.
온라인 쇼핑이 시간을 많이 절약해줘요.

키워드 shop, home, convenient, save, time, online

2. 온라인 쇼핑의 특별한 이점 소개

직구: 온라인 쇼핑을 통해 해외 제품 직구

예) Online shopping is great for finding overseas products that you can't get nearby.
온라인 쇼핑은 근처에서 구할 수 없는 해외 제품을 찾기에 좋아요.

상품: 희귀한 물품 찾기

예) I once found a rare item online that I couldn't find anywhere else.
어디에서도 찾을 수 없던 희귀한 물건을 온라인에서 찾은 적이 있어요.

키워드 product, overseas, international, available, rare, find

3. 온라인 쇼핑의 발전 소개

배송: 빠른 배송 언급

예) These days, delivery is so fast that I often get my orders the next day.
요즘은 배송이 너무 빨라서 종종 다음 날에 주문한 물건을 받아.

발전: 기술의 발전 강조

예) Thanks to technology, shopping has become more convenient than ever before.
기술 덕분에 쇼핑이 그 어느 때보다 더 편리해졌어.

키워드 delivery, faster, order, thanks to, technology, smartphone

대화로 연습하기

대화 속에서 문장을 늘려가는 연습을 해 보세요.

A : I love online shopping because it's **so convenient** and **saves me time**.
온라인 쇼핑이 너무 편리하고 시간을 절약할 수 있기 때문에 온라인 쇼핑을 아주 좋아해요.

B : Same here! I always use discounts and compare prices to get the best deal.
저도 그래요! 저는 항상 할인도 이용하고 가격을 비교해서 가장 좋은 거래를 찾아요.

A : Me too. Plus, it's great for **finding international products** that **aren't available here**.
저도요. 게다가 현지에서 구할 수 없는 해외 제품을 찾는 데도 좋습니다.

B : Absolutely! I tend to buy Blu-rays from Amazon all the time.
물론이죠! 저는 항상 아마존에서 블루레이를 구매하는 편이에요.

A : **The delivery is so much faster now**, which is awesome. Plus, **thanks to smartphone apps**, I can shop anytime, anywhere.
이제 배송이 훨씬 더 빨라져서 정말 좋아요. 게다가 스마트폰 앱 덕분에 언제 어디서든 쇼핑할 수 있어요.

B : Yes, that's right. Technology has made shopping so much easier!
네, 맞아요. 기술 덕분에 쇼핑이 정말 더 쉬워졌죠!

어휘 **get the best deal** 가장 좋은 가격에 사다, 가장 좋은 거래를 얻다 **awesome** 엄청난, 굉장한

주제별로 구분하여 길게 말하는 연습을 해 보세요.

I ①**enjoy online shopping** because I can conveniently ②**shop from home** anytime. It's especially helpful in my busy daily life as it saves time. I also like being able to compare products and find cheaper options, with discounts and coupons making it even more affordable.

저는 온라인 쇼핑을 즐깁니다. 집에서 언제든 편리하게 쇼핑할 수 있다는 점이 좋습니다. 특히 바쁜 일상 속에서 시간을 절약할 수 있어 매우 유용합니다. 또한, 상품을 비교하며 더 저렴한 제품을 찾을 수 있고, 할인과 쿠폰을 활용하면 더 저렴하게 살 수 있어 매력적입니다.

Although some items don't always match their pictures, my overall experience has been positive. I usually ③**search online** first when I need something ④**before deciding to buy**.

비록 물건이 사진과 다를 때가 있지만, 전반적으로 만족스러운 경험을 하고 있습니다. 필요할 때는 항상 온라인에서 먼저 검색한 후 구매를 결정합니다.

Another great thing about online shopping is the access to international stores, which makes it easy to ⑤**find items unavailable locally**. As a movie fan, I often buy Blu-rays from Amazon for my collection. Delivery is also faster these days, so I can ⑥**receive my orders quickly**, which I love.

해외 쇼핑 사이트를 통해 국내에서 구하기 힘든 제품을 쉽게 구매할 수 있다는 점도 큰 장점입니다. 저는 영화를 좋아해서 종종 아마존에서 블루레이를 소장용으로 구매합니다. 요즘은 배송도 빨라져서 주문한 물건을 금방 받아볼 수 있어 정말 만족스럽습니다.

With smartphone apps, I can shop anytime, anywhere, making online shopping ⑦**an essential part** of my life. It's incredible how technology has made shopping so ⑧**effortless and accessible**.

스마트폰 앱을 통해 언제 어디서든 쇼핑할 수 있어 더 자주 이용하게 되었고, 온라인 쇼핑은 이제 제 삶에서 없어서는 안 될 중요한 부분이 되었습니다. 기술 덕분에 쇼핑이 이렇게 쉽고 접근 가능해졌다는 것이 정말 놀랍습니다.

스피치 포인트

① **enjoy online shopping** 온라인 쇼핑을 즐기다 ② **shop from home** 집에서 쇼핑하다 ③ **search online** 인터넷에서 검색하다 ④ **before deciding to buy** 구매 결정하기 전에 ⑤ **find items unavailable locally** 현지에서 구할 수 없는 물품을 찾다 ⑥ **receive one's orders quickly** 자신의 주문을 신속하게 받다 ⑦ **an essential part** 필수적인 부분 ⑧ **effortless and accessible** 수월하고 접근 가능한

2분 스피치

나의 상황에 맞게 내용을 바꾸어서 말해 보세요.

I enjoy online shopping because I can conveniently shop from home anytime. It's especially helpful in my busy daily life as it saves time. I also like being able to compare products and find cheaper options, with discounts and coupons making it even more affordable.

Although some items don't always match their pictures, my overall experience has been positive. I usually search online first when I need something before deciding to buy.

Another great thing about online shopping is the access to international stores, which makes it easy to find items unavailable locally. As a movie fan, I often buy Blu-rays from Amazon for my collection. Delivery is also faster these days, so I can receive my orders quickly, which I love.

With smartphone apps, I can shop anytime, anywhere, making online shopping an essential part of my life. It's incredible how technology has made shopping so effortless and accessible.

스피치 메모

필요한 단어와 표현을 정리해 보세요.

TOPIC 17

스피치 가이드

키워드와 주요 표현을 활용해서 문장을 말해 보세요.

1. 스마트폰 사용 목적 소개

용도: 스마트폰의 사용 용도
- 예) I use my smartphone to stay connected with friends.
  저는 스마트폰을 친구들과 소통하는 데 사용해요.

시간: 스마트폰을 사용하는 시간
- 예) On weekends, I tend to use my smartphone more than usual.
  주말에는 평소보다 스마트폰을 더 많이 사용하는 편이에요.

키워드 connect, call, search for, information, usual, overuse

2. 스마트폰의 장점과 단점 소개

장점: 스마트폰의 유용한 점
- 예) Smartphones make communication much easier and faster.
  스마트폰 덕분에 소통이 훨씬 더 쉽고 빨라졌어요.

단점: 스마트폰 사용의 부정적인 영향
- 예) Spending too much time on my smartphone makes me feel less productive.
  스마트폰을 너무 오래 사용하면 생산성이 떨어지는 기분이 들어요.

키워드 communication, productive, stare at, screen, tire, eyes

3. 스마트폰 사용 습관 소개

습관: 스마트폰 사용 습관
- 예) I set app timers to avoid spending too much time on social media.
  SNS에서 너무 많은 시간을 사용하지 않으려고 앱 타이머를 설정해.

그 외 활동: 스마트폰 사용을 줄이고 즐기는 야외활동
- 예) Instead of using my smartphone, I like to go for a walk in the park.
  스마트폰을 사용하는 대신에 공원에서 산책하는 걸 좋아해.

키워드 avoid, app timer, computer, tablet, walk, enjoy, outdoor activities

대화로 연습하기

대화 속에서 문장을 늘려가는 연습을 해 보세요.

A : I use my smartphone to check emails, read articles, and sometimes handle my banking.

저는 스마트폰으로 이메일 확인하고 기사를 읽거나 가끔 은행 업무도 봐요.

B : That sounds convenient! I mainly use mine **for calls and searching for information**, but I try **not to overuse** it.

편리하네요! 저는 전화나 정보 검색 정도로만 쓰고, 너무 많이 사용하지 않으려고 해요.

A : Yeah, I tend to keep my data plan cheap to avoid high bills.

맞아요. 저도 높은 요금을 피하려고 데이터 요금제를 저렴하게 유지하는 편이에요.

B : I get that. **Staring at a small screen** for too long **tires my eyes**.

이해해요. 작은 화면을 오래 보면 눈이 피로해져요.

A : That's why I often prefer using larger screens.

그래서 저는 자주 큰 화면을 사용하는 것을 선호하죠.

B : Me too. I prefer **using a computer or tablet**. And in my free time, I try to **enjoy outdoor activities** instead of using my smartphone.

저도 마찬가지에요. 컴퓨터나 태블릿 사용을 선호해요. 그리고 한가할 때는 스마트폰 사용 대신에 야외활동을 즐기려고 노력하죠..

어휘 **handle one's banking** 자신의 은행 업무를 처리하다 **overuse** 남용하다 **enjoy outdoor activities** 야외활동을 즐기다

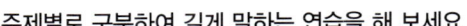

주제별로 구분하여 길게 말하는 연습을 해 보세요.

I use my smartphone for various tasks. First, I check my emails and read important articles of the day. Sometimes, I also ①**manage my banking**. When I'm feeling down, I search for my favorite music or videos to ②**lift my mood**.

저는 스마트폰으로 다양한 일을 합니다. 우선 이메일을 확인하고 오늘의 중요한 기사들을 읽습니다. 가끔은 은행 업무도 봅니다. 우울할 때는 제가 좋아하는 음악이나 동영상을 검색해서 기분을 좋게 만듭니다.

I mainly use my smartphone to make or receive calls and to ③**look up information** I need. I don't use it much beyond that. Sometimes, I'm concerned about the bills that will come if I ④**use my phone too much**, so I choose the cheapest data plan.

스마트폰은 전화를 걸거나 받을 때, 그리고 알고 싶은 내용을 검색할 때 주로 사용합니다. 그 외에는 그렇게 많이 사용하지는 않습니다. 가끔은 스마트폰을 많이 사용하면 다음에 청구될 요금이 걱정되기도 해서, 데이터 요금제를 제일 저렴한 것으로 선택합니다.

As I get older, I find it uncomfortable to look at the small screen ⑤**for extended periods**, so I try to ⑥**use my smartphone** only when necessary and prefer using larger screens, like on a computer or tablet.

나이가 들어감에 따라 작은 화면을 오랫동안 보는 것도 불편해져서, 웬만하면 스마트폰은 필요할 때만 사용하고, 큰 화면을 사용하는 컴퓨터나 태블릿을 이용하는 편입니다.

Also, staring at the small screen of a smartphone for a long time makes my eyes tired and ⑦**reduces my focus**, so I try to minimize the time I spend using it. When I do use my smartphone, I mainly use it ⑧**for practical purposes**, and in my free time, I enjoy other activities.

또한, 스마트폰의 작은 화면을 오래 들여다보면 눈이 피로하고, 집중력이 떨어지기 때문에 최대한 사용 시간을 줄이려고 노력합니다. 스마트폰을 사용할 때는 주로 실용적인 용도로만 쓰는 편이고, 여유 시간이 있을 때는 다른 활동을 즐깁니다.

스피치 포인트

① **manage one's banking** 자신의 은행 업무를 관리하다 ② **lift one's mood** 자신의 기분을 좋게 하다 ③ **look up information** 정보를 찾아보다, 정보를 검색하다 ④ **use one's phone too much** 자신의 휴대폰을 너무 많이 사용하다 ⑤ **for extended periods** 장기간, 오랫동안 ⑥ **use one's smartphone** 자신의 스마트폰을 사용하다 ⑦ **reduce one's focus** 자신의 집중력을 떨어뜨리다 ⑧ **for practical purposes** 실용적인 목적으로

나의 상황에 맞게 내용을 바꾸어서 말해 보세요.

I use my smartphone for various tasks. First, I check my emails and read important articles of the day. Sometimes, I also manage my banking. When I'm feeling down, I search for my favorite music or videos to lift my mood.

I mainly use my smartphone to make or receive calls and to look up information I need. I don't use it much beyond that. Sometimes, I'm concerned about the bills that will come if I use my phone too much, so I choose the cheapest data plan.

As I get older, I find it uncomfortable to look at the small screen for extended periods, so I try to use my smartphone only when necessary and prefer using larger screens, like on a computer or tablet.

Also, staring at the small screen of a smartphone for a long time makes my eyes tired and reduces my focus, so I try to minimize the time I spend using it. When I do use my smartphone, I mainly use it for practical purposes, and in my free time, I enjoy other activities.

스피치 메모

필요한 단어와 표현을 정리해 보세요.

TOPIC 18 유튜브

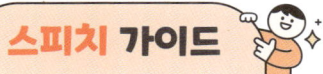

키워드와 주요 표현을 활용해서 문장을 말해 보세요.

1. 유튜브 콘텐츠 소개

콘텐츠: 즐겨보는 유형의 유튜브 콘텐츠
- 예) I enjoy watching cooking videos and travel vlogs in my free time.
  저는 여가 시간에 요리 영상과 여행 브이로그를 즐겨 봐요.

목적: 유튜브 동영상을 자주 보는 이유
- 예) Since I'm an English teacher, I watch a lot of English-related resources.
  저는 영어 선생님이라 영어 관련 자료를 많이 봐요.

키워드 teacher, English, resource, related, cooking, travel, watch

2. 영화나 음악 동영상 소개

영화: 영화 관련 동영상
- 예) It's fun to watch classic movie reviews and interviews with actors.
  고전 영화 리뷰와 배우 인터뷰 영상 보는 건 재밌어요.

음악: 음악 관련 동영상
- 예) I like watching live concert recordings and music video reactions.
  저는 라이브 콘서트 영상과 뮤직비디오 반응 영상을 보는 걸 좋아해요.

키워드 movie, song, material, listen to, classic, concert, reaction

3. 여행 동영상 소개

여행: 여행 관련 동영상
- 예) Travel documentaries allow me to learn about different cultures.
  여행 다큐멘터리를 통해 다른 문화를 배울 수 있어요.

장점: 여행관련 동영상의 좋은 점
- 예) Travel videos help me plan my trips.
  여행 영상은 여행을 준비하는 데 많은 도움이 돼요.

키워드 research, country, unfamiliar, learn, culture, help, trip

대화 속에서 문장을 늘려가는 연습을 해 보세요.

A : What do you usually watch on YouTube?
유튜브에서 주로 뭐 봐요?

B : Since I'm **an English teacher**, I mostly **watch English-related resources**.
영어 선생님이라 주로 영어 관련 자료를 많이 봐요.

A : Anything else?
다른 건 안 보세요?

B : I love movies, so I look up **movie materials** and sometimes **listen to old pop songs** from my college days.
영화도 좋아해서 영화 자료를 찾아보기도 하고, 가끔 대학 시절 듣던 옛날 팝송도 들어요.

A : How about Shorts?
쇼츠는요?

B : I watch those too! And I use YouTube to **research countries** before I travel. It makes new places **feel less unfamiliar.**
그것도 봐요! 그리고 여행 전에 유튜브로 가고 싶은 나라를 검색해요. 덕분에 새로운 곳도 덜 낯설게 느껴지죠.

어휘 **look up** (정보를) 찾아보다   **unfamiliar** 낯선, 익숙지 않은

주제별로 구분하여 길게 말하는 연습을 해 보세요.

YouTube has brought significant changes to my life. First of all, as an English teacher, ①**the ability to easily access** a vast amount of English-related resources is a huge advantage. I can comfortably ②**explore various types of** English from English-speaking countries at home, and listening to live English news has been a great pleasure for me.

유튜브는 제 인생에 큰 변화를 주었습니다. 우선, 영어 강사로서 방대한 영어 관련 자료를 손쉽게 접할 수 있다는 점이 큰 장점입니다. 집에서 편하게 영어권 국가들의 다양한 영어를 접할 수 있었고, 실시간으로 영어 뉴스를 청취할 수 있다는 점도 저에게 큰 즐거움이었습니다.

I③**'ve always been interested in** movies, so I also enjoy ④**searching for** movie-related materials on YouTube. Sometimes, I look up and listen to pop songs I used to enjoy as a college student, which makes me feel as if I've gone back to my twenties.

평소 영화에 관심이 많아 유튜브를 통해 영화 관련 자료를 찾아보는 것도 즐깁니다. 때로는 대학생 시절 즐겨 듣던 팝송을 검색해 들으며, 어느새 20대 시절로 돌아간 듯한 기분이 들기도 합니다.

Recently, one-minute videos like Shorts ⑤**have become a trend**, allowing me to enjoy a variety of content ⑥**without getting bored**. The content I encounter on YouTube is mostly related to my profession.

요즘은 쇼츠처럼 1분짜리 동영상이 대세라 지루하지 않게 다양한 콘텐츠를 즐기고 있습니다. 유튜브에서 접하는 내용은 대부분 제 직업과 관련된 자료들입니다.

⑦**As I mentioned earlier**, it's mostly limited to English-related resources, movies, or music. However, when I get the chance to travel abroad, I use YouTube to search for information about the countries I plan to visit and try to ⑧**gather as much material as possible**.

앞서 말했듯이 영어 관련 자료나 영화, 음악 정도로 한정적이죠. 하지만 해외여행 기회가 생기면, 유튜브를 통해 미리 여행할 나라의 정보를 검색하고 많은 자료를 얻으려고 합니다.

스피치 포인트

① the ability to easily access 쉽게 접근할 수 있는 능력 ② explore various types of 다양한 종류의 ~을 살펴보다 ③ have always been interested in 늘 ~에 관심이 있어 왔다 ④ search for 찾다, 검색하다 ⑤ have become a trend 유행이 되었다 ⑥ without getting bored 지루하지 않게, 지루함 없이 ⑦ as I mentioned earlier 앞서 말했듯이 ⑧ gather as much material as possible 가능한 많은 자료를 모으다

나의 상황에 맞게 내용을 바꾸어서 말해 보세요.

YouTube has brought significant changes to my life. First of all, as an English teacher, the ability to easily access a vast amount of English-related resources is a huge advantage. I can comfortably explore various types of English from English-speaking countries at home, and listening to live English news has been a great pleasure for me.

I've always been interested in movies, so I also enjoy searching for movie-related materials on YouTube. Sometimes, I look up and listen to pop songs I used to enjoy as a college student, which makes me feel as if I've gone back to my twenties.

Recently, one-minute videos like Shorts have become a trend, allowing me to enjoy a variety of content without getting bored. The content I encounter on YouTube is mostly related to my profession.

As I mentioned earlier, it's mostly limited to English-related resources, movies or music. However, when I get the chance to travel abroad, I use YouTube to search for information about the countries I plan to visit and try to gather as much material as possible.

필요한 단어와 표현을 정리해 보세요.

TOPIC 19 SNS

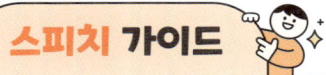

> 키워드와 주요 표현을 활용해서 문장을 말해 보세요.

1. SNS 활동 시작 소개

언제: SNS 활동을 처음 시작한 때
- 예) I've been sharing my travel experiences on my blog since 2016.
  2016년 이후로 내 블로그에 여행 경험을 공유해 왔어.

활동: 어떤 활동을 시작했는지 언급
- 예) I began posting about my hiking trips and outdoor adventures.
  하이킹 여행과 야외 모험에 대한 게시물을 올리기 시작했어.

키워드 2016, since, in, hiking, travel, photo, adventure, outdoor

2. SNS 활동 변화 소개

콘텐츠: SNS에서 주제로 추가한 콘텐츠
- 예) Over time, I started posting food recipes and workout tips.
  시간이 지나면서 음식 요리법과 운동 팁을 올리기 시작했어요.

진화: 콘텐츠를 어떻게 확장하거나 발전시켰는지 설명
- 예) My content has evolved, and now I focus on travel topics.
  내 콘텐츠가 점점 발전해서 지금은 여행 주제에 집중하고 있어요.

키워드 English, tip, recipe, material, food, content, evolve

3. SNS 활동의 의미 소개

의미: SNS 활동의 중요성, 의미
- 예) For me, my blog is like a digital scrapbook that I can look back on.
  저에게 블로그는 되돌아볼 수 있는 디지털 스크랩북 같은 존재입니다.

추억: 얼마나 자주 SNS을 살펴보며 추억을 되돌아보는지
- 예) Sometimes, I go through my past posts just to relive special moments.
  가끔은 특별한 순간들을 다시 느끼기 위해 예전 게시물을 훑어봐요.

키워드 digital, scrapbook, journal, memory, look back on, relive, sometimes

대화로 연습하기 — 대화 속에서 문장을 늘려가는 연습을 해 보세요.

A : I heard you've been blogging for a long time.
너 블로그 오래 했다고 들었어.

B : Yeah, I started in **2016** with **hiking and travel photos**.
응. 2016년에 등산하고 여행 사진으로 시작했어.

A : Do you still post the same things?
지금도 똑같은 것만 올려?

B : Not just that. I also share **English materials** and **food photos** now.
그것만은 아니야. 요즘은 영어 자료랑 음식 사진도 올려.

A : That's cool. Do you look back at old posts?
멋지다. 예전 글도 다시 봐?

B : **Sometimes**. It feels like **a journal full of memories**!
가끔 봐. 추억이 담긴 일기 같은 느낌이야!

어휘 **look back** 과거를 되돌아보다, 회상하다

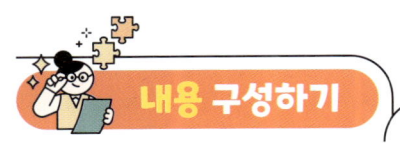
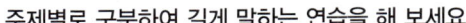

주제별로 구분하여 길게 말하는 연습을 해 보세요.

I've been ①**active on social media**, similar to blogging, since 2016. At first, I only posted hiking and travel photos, but after many years of teaching English, I started sharing a lot of educational materials I had collected ②**on my blog**.

저는 2016년부터 블로그와 같은 SNS 활동을 꾸준히 해왔습니다. 처음에는 주로 등산과 여행 관련 사진만 올렸지만, 오랜 시간 영어 강의를 하면서 수집한 다양한 학습 자료들도 함께 블로그에 공유하기 시작했습니다.

A few years ago, I developed an interest in good restaurants, so I began posting food photos from places I discovered during my travels. Over time, my blog has grown to include over 7,000 posts. Sometimes, I ③**look back** at my old posts and photos to ④**reminisce about** those times.

몇 년 전부터는 맛집에 관심이 생겨, 여행 중에 찾은 괜찮은 식당을 소개하려는 목적으로 음식 사진도 올리기 시작했죠. 그동안 제 블로그에는 7천 개가 넘는 글이 올라갔습니다. 가끔 예전에 올렸던 글이나 사진을 보면서 그때의 추억을 되새기곤 합니다.

Nowadays, almost everyone ⑤**has their own social media accounts**. It's great to be able to share things with others and ⑥**exchange opinions on** shared interests.

요즘은 거의 모든 사람이 자신의 소셜 미디어 계정을 가지고 있습니다. 다른 사람들과 공유하고 공유 관심사에 대해 의견을 교환할 수 있게 되어 기쁩니다.

It's hard to believe that 9 years have already passed since I ⑦**started my social media activity**. Even now, I continue to ⑧**post travel photos**, restaurant pictures, daily life moments, and English-related content whenever I have time. It has truly become a hobby, and my blog feels like a personal journal to me.

벌써 SNS 활동을 시작한 지 9년이 지났다는 게 믿기 힘듭니다. 여전히 시간이 날 때마다 여행 사진, 맛집 사진, 일상의 순간, 그리고 영어 관련 콘텐츠를 계속 올리고 있습니다. 이제는 그저 취미 생활이 되었고, 제 블로그는 마치 개인 일기처럼 느껴집니다.

스피치 포인트

① **active on social media** 소셜 미디어에서 활발히 활동하는 ② **on one's blog** 자신의 블로그에 ③ **look back** 되돌아보다 ④ **reminisce about** (과거를) 회상하다, 추억하다 ⑤ **have one's own social media accounts** 자신만의 소셜 미디어 계정을 가지다 ⑥ **exchange opinions on** ~에 대한 의견들을 교환하다 ⑦ **start one's social media activity** 자신의 소셜 미디어 활동을 시작하다 ⑧ **post travel photos** 여행 사진들을 올리다

나의 상황에 맞게 내용을 바꾸어서 말해 보세요.

I've been active on social media, similar to blogging, since 2016. At first, I only posted hiking and travel photos, but after many years of teaching English, I started sharing a lot of educational materials I had collected on my blog.

A few years ago, I developed an interest in good restaurants, so I began posting food photos from places I discovered during my travels. Over time, my blog has grown to include over 7,000 posts. Sometimes, I look back at my old posts and photos to reminisce about those times.

Nowadays, almost everyone has their own social media accounts. It's great to be able to share things with others and exchange opinions on shared interests.

It's hard to believe that 9 years have already passed since I started my social media activity. Even now, I continue to post travel photos, restaurant pictures, daily life moments, and English-related content whenever I have time. It has truly become a hobby, and my blog feels like a personal journal to me.

필요한 단어와 표현을 정리해 보세요.

TOPIC 20 TV&라디오

키워드와 주요 표현을 활용해서 문장을 말해 보세요.

1. TV&라디오 습관 소개

루틴: 자신의 일상 루틴 얘기하기

예) I usually spend my free time watching TV or listening to the radio.
보통 자유 시간이 있을 때 TV를 보거나 라디오를 들어.

방송: 특정 TV나 라디오 프로그램

예) In the mornings, I start my day with world news on a channel like CNN.
아침에는 CNN 같은 채널에서 세계 뉴스를 보면서 하루를 시작해.

키워드 TV, radio, watch, listen, catch up on, news, international, world

2. 뉴스 취향 소개

유형: 선호하는 뉴스 유형

예) Recently, I've been watching local news because I want to stay informed about my community.
최근에 우리 지역에서 어떤 일이 일어나는지 알고 싶어서 지역 뉴스를 보고 있어요.

비교: 국제 뉴스와 지역 뉴스 비교

예) I used to prefer international news, but now I think local news is more important.
예전에는 국제 뉴스를 더 선호했지만, 이제는 지역 뉴스가 더 중요하다고 생각해.

키워드 local, international, news, community, important, stay updated

3. TV 시청하기 소개

선택: TV 시청이나 라디오 청취에서 선택하기

예) After work, I prefer watching TV rather than listening to the radio.
퇴근 후에는 라디오를 듣기보다 TV를 보는 것을 선호해.

드라마: 한국 드라마에 대한 관심, 느낌

예) Lately, I've been really into Korean dramas.
최근 한국 드라마에 푹 빠졌어.

키워드 be into, emotional, drama, watch TV, skip, radio, drama

대화로 연습하기 — 대화 속에서 문장을 늘려가는 연습을 해 보세요.

A : What do you usually do in your spare time?
보통 여가 시간에 뭐 해?

B : **I watch TV**. In the mornings, I **catch up on international news** like CNN and BBC.
TV 봐. 아침에는 CNN이나 BBC와 같은 해외 뉴스를 시청해.

A : That sounds good! Do you always watch international news?
그거 괜찮네! 국제 뉴스를 항상 시청하는 거야?

B : Not really. Lately, **I've been watching more local news** to **stay updated** on what's happening around here.
그렇지 않아. 요즘은 주변에서 일어나고 있는 일들을 알기 위해 더 많이 국내 뉴스를 시청하고 있어.

A : That makes sense. What about after work?
이해가 돼. 퇴근 후에는?

B : **After work, I skip the radio and watch TV**. Lately, I've been really into Korean dramas. They're so **emotional** that I sometimes even tear up!
퇴근 후에는 라디오를 듣지 않고 TV를 봐. 요즘 한국 드라마에 푹 빠졌어. 드라마가 너무 감동적이라 가끔 눈물이 날 때도 있어!

어휘 catch up on (놓친 것을) 따라 잡다　stay updated 정보를 유지하다, 알고 있다　tear up 눈물이 나다

주제별로 구분하여 길게 말하는 연습을 해 보세요.

I watch TV in my free time. Before leaving for work, I usually ①**watch English news channels** like CNN, BBC, and ABC. However, lately, I tend to watch more domestic news to ②**stay informed** about what's happening in South Korea.

저는 한가할 때 TV를 시청합니다. 출근 전에는 보통 CNN, BBC, ABC와 같은 영어 뉴스 채널을 시청하지만, 최근에는 한국에서 일어나는 일들을 알기 위해 더 많이 국내 뉴스를 보는 편입니다.

③**On my way to work**, I ④**listen to EBS English radio** in the car. I usually listen for about 30 minutes, and when I hear useful English expressions, I often repeat them to myself.

출근길에는 차 안에서 EBS 영어 라디오를 듣습니다. 보통 30분 정도 듣는데, 유용한 영어 표현을 들으면 혼자서 반복하는 경우가 많습니다.

My work hours vary each day, so I try to listen to my favorite music stations on the drive home. It helps me ⑤**unwind from the stress** I've built up teaching English all day. When a song I love comes on, I sometimes ⑥**turn the volume up as loud as I can**.

퇴근 시간은 매일 다르기 때문에, 집으로 돌아올 때는 가급적 좋아하는 음악 방송을 듣습니다. 이렇게 하면 하루 종일 영어 강의를 하면서 쌓였던 스트레스가 풀립니다. 좋아하는 음악이 나오면 가끔은 볼륨을 최대로 올리기도 합니다.

After I get home, I skip the radio and ⑦**focus on watching TV**. I often watch the news, but I also enjoy movies. While I've always loved Hollywood films, I now prefer Korean movies and dramas. Lately, I⑧**'ve been hooked on** Korean dramas, sometimes tearing up without realizing it, probably because I'm a bit sentimental.

집에 도착한 후에는 라디오는 듣지 않고 TV를 보는 데 집중합니다. 뉴스를 자주 보지만 영화를 즐기기도 합니다. 할리우드 영화를 항상 좋아했지만, 이제는 한국 영화와 드라마를 더 선호하게 되었습니다. 최근에는 한국 드라마에 푹 빠져 있는데, 가끔 자신도 모르게 눈물이 나올 때가 있습니다. 아마도 제가 조금 감수성이 풍부해서 그런 것 같아요.

스피치 포인트

① watch English news channels 영어 뉴스 채널을 시청하다 ② stay informed 정보를 얻다, 최신 정보를 유지하다 ③ on one's way to work 자신의 출근길에 ④ listen to EBS English radio EBS 영어 라디오를 듣다 ⑤ unwind from the stress 스트레스를 풀다 ⑥ turn the volume up as loud as I can 내가 할 수 있을 만큼 볼륨을 크게 하다 ⑦ focus on watching TV TV 시청에 집중하다 ⑧ have been hooked on 푹 빠져있었다

2분 스피치

나의 상황에 맞게 내용을 바꾸어서 말해 보세요.

I watch TV in my free time. Before leaving for work, I usually watch English news channels, like CNN, BBC, and ABC. However, lately, I tend to watch more domestic news to stay informed about what's happening in South Korea.

On my way to work, I listen to EBS English radio in the car. I usually listen for about 30 minutes, and when I hear useful English expressions, I often repeat them to myself.

My work hours vary each day, so I try to listen to my favorite music stations on the drive home. It helps me unwind from the stress I've built up teaching English all day. When a song I love comes on, I sometimes turn the volume up as loud as I can.

After I get home, I skip the radio and focus on watching TV. I often watch the news, but I also enjoy movies. While I've always loved Hollywood films, I now prefer Korean movies and dramas. Lately, I've been hooked on Korean dramas, sometimes tearing up without realizing it, probably because I'm a bit sentimental.

필요한 단어와 표현을 정리해 보세요.

PART 04
Review Quiz

1 집에서 쇼핑하다

shop _____ home

2 인터넷에서 검색하다

_____ online

3 수월하고 접근 가능한

effortless and _____

4 자신의 기분을 좋게 하다

_____ one's mood

5 자신의 스마트폰을 사용하다

_____ one's smartphone

6 실용적인 목적으로

for _____ purposes

7 다양한 종류의 ~을 살펴보다

_____ various types of

8 유행이 되었다

have become a _____

배운 영어 표현들을 복습해 보세요.

9 앞서 말했듯이

as I _____ earlier

10 소셜 미디어에서 활발히 활동하는

active on _____ media

11 (과거를) 회상하다, 추억하다

_____ about

12 여행 사진들을 올리다

_____ travel photos

13 정보를 얻다, 최신 정보를 유지하다

stay _____

14 스트레스를 풀다

_____ from the stress

15 TV 시청에 집중하다

focus _____ watching TV

정답 01 from 02 search 03 accessible 04 lift 05 use 06 practical 07 explore 08 trend
09 mentioned 10 social 11 reminisce 12 post 13 informed 14 unwind 15 on

PART 05
사계절

TOPIC 21   날씨
TOPIC 22   계절
TOPIC 23   휴가
TOPIC 24   벚꽃놀이
TOPIC 25   단풍놀이

TOPIC 21 날씨

스피치 가이드

키워드와 주요 표현을 활용해서 문장을 말해 보세요.

1. 날씨가 좋을 때 하는 일 소개

날씨: 좋아하는 날씨를 언급하기
- 예) I like rainy days.
  저는 비 오는 날이 좋아요.

활동: 즐겨하는 야외 활동이나 취미 생활
- 예) When the weather is nice, I like going for a drive.
  날씨가 좋으면 드라이브하는 걸 좋아해요.

키워드 like, rainy, sunny, nice, go, drive

2. 자주 가는 장소 소개

장소: 자주 찾아가는 장소
- 예) On sunny days, I often go for a drive to Chuncheon.
  화창한 날엔 종종 춘천으로 드라이브 가.

이유: 방문하는 장소가 좋은 이유
- 예) I can take in the river view in Yeoju.
  여주에서 강 경치를 감상할 수 있어.

키워드 Chuncheon, Yeoju, Namhan River, visit, take in, walk, view

3. 비오는 날 하는 일 소개

일상: 비 오는 날 집에서 하는 활동
- 예) On rainy days, I like staying in and watching movies.
  비 오는 날엔 집에서 영화 보며 쉬는 걸 좋아해요

감정: 비 오는 날이 좋은 이유나 분위기
- 예) I love listening to the sound of rain. It's calming.
  빗소리 듣는 걸 좋아해요. 마음이 차분해져요.

키워드 stay, home, movie, watch, listen, calming, sound

 **대화로 연습하기** 대화 속에서 문장을 늘려가는 연습을 해 보세요.

A : When it's **sunny**, I love **going for a drive**. Staying home feels like such a waste.
날씨가 화창하면 드라이브하는 걸 정말 좋아해요. 집에 있는 게 너무 아깝게 느껴지거든요.

B : I agree! Where do you usually go?
저도 동감이어요! 주로 어디로 가세요?

A : Sometimes, I **visit the Namhan River in Yeoju** for **a walk**.
가끔 여주에 있는 남한강으로 가서 산책해요.

B : What about rainy days?
비 오는 날에는 어떻게 하세요?

A : I **stay home**, **watch movies**, and enjoy the sound of rain.
집에 있으면서 영화도 보고 빗소리를 즐겨요.

B : That sounds so relaxing! I love rainy days too.
정말 여유롭네요! 저도 비 오는 날을 좋아해요.

어휘 go for a drive 드라이브하러 가다 relaxing 편한

 **내용 구성하기**

주제별로 구분하여 길게 말하는 연습을 해 보세요.

When the weather is sunny, I can't help but take my car out for a drive. Staying home on such beautiful days feels like such a waste. Driving around ①**on sunny days** helps me unwind and naturally lifts my spirits. Sometimes, I also go hiking or head to the Namhan River in Yeoju to ②**enjoy a walk** along the riverside.

날씨가 화창한 날에는 차를 몰고 나가는 것을 멈출 수가 없습니다. 그렇게 좋은 날씨에 집에 머무르는 것은 정말 아깝게 느껴지기 때문입니다. 화창한 날에 드라이브를 하면 스트레스가 풀리고 자연스럽게 기분이 좋아지는 것을 느낍니다. 때로는 등산을 하기도 하고, 여주에 있는 남한강으로 가서 강변을 따라 산책을 즐기기도 합니다.

However, when it rains or snows, I ③**prefer staying home** and relaxing. Listening to my favorite music or lounging on the sofa to watch movies I haven't had the chance to see yet is ④**a delightful way** to spend my time.

하지만 비가 오거나 눈이 내리는 날에는 집에 머물며 휴식을 취하는 것을 선호합니다. 좋아하는 음악을 듣거나 소파에 편히 누워 아직 보지 못한 영화를 감상하는 것은 정말 즐거운 시간입니다.

I've always ⑤**loved rainy days**, even as a child, and that hasn't changed. Especially at night, ⑥**the sound of raindrops** as I fall asleep brings me a profound sense of peace and comfort.

저는 어렸을 때부터 비 오는 날을 좋아했는데, 지금도 변함이 없습니다. 특히 밤에 잠들 때 들리는 빗소리는 제게 깊은 평화와 편안함을 줍니다.

These days, winter mornings are ⑦**exceptionally cold**. I ⑧**take extra precautions** when driving and try to stay as safe as possible. On cold days, I believe the most important thing is to prioritize safety and avoid any injuries.

요즘은 겨울 아침이 유난히 춥습니다. 운전할 때는 더 조심하려고 하고 최대한 안전하게 다니려고 합니다. 추운 날에는 무엇보다 안전을 우선시하고 다치지 않는 것이 가장 중요하다고 생각합니다.

스피치 포인트

① on sunny days 화창한 날에 ② enjoy a walk 산책을 즐기다 ③ prefer staying home 집에 머무르는 걸 선호하다 ④ a delightful way 즐거운 방법 ⑤ love rainy days 비 오는 날을 너무 좋아하다 ⑥ the sound of raindrops 빗방울 소리 ⑦ exceptionally cold 유난히 추운 ⑧ take extra precautions 특별히 주의하다

2분 스피치

나의 상황에 맞게 내용을 바꾸어서 말해 보세요.

When the weather is sunny, I can't help but take my car out for a drive. Staying home on such beautiful days feels like such a waste. Driving around on sunny days helps me unwind and naturally lifts my spirits. Sometimes, I also go hiking or head to the Namhan River in Yeoju to enjoy a walk along the riverside.

However, when it rains or snows, I prefer staying home and relaxing. Listening to my favorite music or lounging on the sofa to watch movies I haven't had the chance to see yet is a delightful way to spend my time.

I've always loved rainy days, even as a child, and that hasn't changed. Especially at night, the sound of raindrops as I fall asleep brings me a profound sense of peace and comfort.

These days, winter mornings are exceptionally cold. I take extra precautions when driving and try to stay as safe as possible. On cold days, I believe the most important thing is to prioritize safety and avoid any injuries.

스피치 메모

필요한 단어와 표현을 정리해 보세요.

TOPIC 22 계절

2분 SPEECH

스피치 가이드
키워드와 주요 표현을 활용해서 문장을 말해 보세요.

1. 가장 좋아하는 계절 소개

계절: 좋아하는 계절 언급
- 예) I love autumn the most.
  저는 가을을 제일 좋아해요.

이유: 좋아하는 이유 설명
- 예) The cool breeze makes me feel calm.
  시원한 바람이 마음을 차분하게 해줘요.

키워드 spring, autumn, calming, feel, calm

2. 눈 오는 날 소개

활동: 눈 오는 날 즐기는 활동
- 예) On snowy days, I enjoy taking pictures of the snow-covered trees.
  눈 오는 날에는 눈 쌓인 나무들을 사진으로 담는 걸 즐겨.

기분: 눈 오는 날 어떤 기분인지 묘사
- 예) Everything looks so quiet and magical.
  모든 게 너무 조용하고 마법 같아 보여.

키워드 snowy, pictures, home, sip, watch, fall, quiet, peaceful

3. 가장 싫어하는 계절 소개

계절: 싫어하는 계절 언급
- 예) My least favorite season is Winter.
  제가 가장 싫어하는 계절은 겨울이에요.

이유: 싫어하는 이유 설명
- 예) It's too cold, and I don't like wearing heavy clothes all the time.
  너무 춥고, 항상 두꺼운 옷을 입는 게 싫어요.

키워드 winter, summer, least, favorite, season, cold, hot, tiring

# 대화로 연습하기

대화 속에서 문장을 늘려가는 연습을 해 보세요.

A : Korea has four distinct seasons, right? Which one do you like the most?
한국에는 사계절이 있죠? 그 중에서 어떤 계절을 제일 좋아하세요?

B : **I'd say spring and autumn**. They're **so calming**. What about you?
저는 봄과 가을을 좋아해요. 정말 차분한 느낌이 들어요. 당신은요?

A : I like winter. Snowy days feel exciting, don't they?
저는 겨울이 좋아요. 눈 오는 날은 정말 흥미롭죠. 그렇죠?

B : They do! I love **staying home, sipping tea, and watching the snow fall**. It **feels peaceful**.
맞아요! 저는 집에 있으면서 차를 마시고, 눈이 내리는 걸 보는 걸 좋아해요. 평화로운 기분이 들죠.

A : I can't stand summer, though. The heat just drains my energy.
그런데 여름은 정말 못 참겠어요. 더위가 제 에너지를 다 빼앗아 가요.

B : Same here. **Summer is my least favorite season**. It's **too hot and tiring**!
저도요. 여름은 제일 싫어하는 계절이에요. 너무 덥고 피곤해요!

어휘 drain one's energy 자신의 에너지를 빼앗아 가다

주제별로 구분하여 길게 말하는 연습을 해 보세요.

Korea has four distinct seasons, each with its own charm. I ①**particularly enjoy spring and autumn** for their calming atmosphere, while summer is ②**my least favorite** due to the heat and lack of motivation it brings. Winter, though cold, feels more bearable than summer.

한국은 사계절이 뚜렷하며, 각 계절마다 고유의 매력이 있습니다. 저는 특히 봄과 가을의 차분한 분위기를 좋아하는 반면, 여름은 더위와 의욕 상실로 인해 가장 싫어하는 계절입니다. 겨울은 비록 춥지만 여름보다는 더 견딜 만합니다.

In the past, I often went hiking during spring and autumn, but lately, I've been skipping it out of laziness. Even without hiking, these seasons still ③**bring a sense of peace**, and simply admiring the distant scenery ④**feels refreshing**.

예전에는 봄과 가을마다 자주 등산을 갔지만, 요즘은 귀찮아서 잘 가지 않게 되었습니다. 그래도 등산을 가지 않더라도, 이 계절들은 여전히 평온함을 주고, 멀리 풍경을 바라보는 것만으로도 상쾌함을 느낄 수 있습니다.

Summer ⑤**is unpleasant for** me. The heat often ⑥**leaves me irritable** and drained of energy. Winter, however, has a quiet charm. I enjoy staying home, writing, and watching snow fall outside.

여름은 저에게 불쾌한 계절입니다. 더위는 종종 저를 짜증나게 하고, 기운을 빠지게 합니다. 반면 겨울은 조용한 매력이 있습니다. 저는 집에 머물면서 글을 쓰고 밖에 눈이 내리는 것을 보는 것을 즐깁니다.

Since childhood, I've found snowy days exciting. While others ⑦**enjoy winter sports**, I prefer relaxing indoors with a warm cup of tea, ⑧**savoring the peacefulness** of the season.

어린 시절부터 눈 오는 날은 신나는 날이었습니다. 다른 사람들은 겨울 스포츠를 즐기는 반면, 저는 따뜻한 차 한 잔과 함께 실내에서 휴식을 취하며 계절의 평화로움을 만끽하는 것을 선호합니다.

스피치 포인트

① particularly enjoy spring and autumn 특히 봄과 가을을 즐기다 ② one's least favorite 자신이 가장 싫어하는 ③ bring a sense of peace 평화로운 느낌을 주다 ④ feel refreshing 상쾌함을 느끼다 ⑤ be unpleasant for ~에게 불쾌하다 ⑥ leave someone irritable 누군가를 짜증나게 만들다 ⑦ enjoy winter sports 겨울 스포츠를 즐기다 ⑧ savor the peacefulness 평화로움을 음미하다

나의 상황에 맞게 내용을 바꾸어서 말해 보세요.

Korea has four distinct seasons, each with its own charm. I particularly enjoy spring and autumn for their calming atmosphere, while summer is my least favorite due to the heat and lack of motivation it brings. Winter, though cold, feels more bearable than summer.

In the past, I often went hiking during spring and autumn, but lately, I've been skipping it out of laziness. Even without hiking, these seasons still bring a sense of peace, and simply admiring the distant scenery feels refreshing.

Summer is unpleasant for me. The heat often leaves me irritable and drained of energy. Winter, however, has a quiet charm. I enjoy staying home, writing, and watching snow fall outside.

Since childhood, I've found snowy days exciting. While others enjoy winter sports, I prefer relaxing indoors with a warm cup of tea, savoring the peacefulness of the season.

스피치 메모

필요한 단어와 표현을 정리해 보세요.

TOPIC 23 휴가

스피치 가이드

키워드와 주요 표현을 활용해서 문장을 말해 보세요.

1. 직업과 휴가 스타일 소개

직업: 자신의 직업 언급
- 예) I work at a travel agency.
  저는 여행사에서 근무해요.

일정: 자신의 직업에 따른 휴가 일정 말하기
- 예) I have fixed vacation days.
  저는 정해진 휴가일이 있어요.

키워드 travel, freelancer, vacation, fixed, take off, whenever

2. 과거나 현재 휴가 활동 소개

과거: 과거에 어떻게 휴가를 보냈는지 말하기
- 예) I used to travel abroad every summer.
  매년 여름마다 해외여행을 하곤 했어.

현재: 현재는 어떻게 휴가를 보내는지 말하기
- 예) These days, I usually stay home and relax during my vacation.
  요즘은 보통 집에서 쉬면서 휴가를 보내.

키워드 used to, travel, a lot, abroad, summer, 2022, home, relax

3. 올해 휴가 계획 소개

계획: 구체적인 계획 소개
- 예) I'm planning to go to Japan in July.
  7월에 일본에 갈 계획이에요.

미정: 휴가 미정일 경우 이유 설명
- 예) I'm not sure yet. The economy isn't great these days.
  아직 잘 모르겠어요. 요즘 경기가 좋지 않아서요.

키워드 Japan, July, decide, economy, great, bad

 **대화로 연습하기** 대화 속에서 문장을 늘려가는 연습을 해 보세요.

A : Do you have set vacation days for your job?
직장에서 정해진 휴가일이 있나요?

B : No, I work as a **freelancer**, so I can **take time off whenever I want**.
아니요, 저는 프리랜서라서 언제든지 휴식을 취할 수 있어요.

A : That's nice! Do you travel abroad often?
그거 좋네요! 자주 해외여행 가시나요?

B : I **used to travel a lot**, but **since 2022**, I've been staying home.
예전에는 여행 많이 갔었는데, 2022년 이후로는 집에만 있었어요.

A : Are you planning to travel abroad this year?
올해는 해외여행 갈 계획이 있나요?

B : **I'm still deciding. The economy is bad**, so I'm not sure if I should travel.
아직 결정하지 않았어요. 경기가 안 좋아서 여행을 갈지 고민 중이에요.

어휘 take time off 휴가를 내다, 쉬다, 일을 쉬다

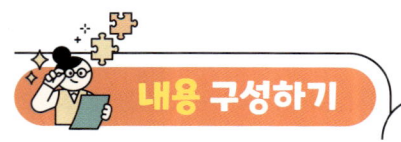 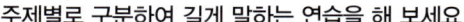

주제별로 구분하여 길게 말하는 연습을 해 보세요.

I've been working as a freelance English instructor for a long time, so I don't ①**have set vacation days**. I can take a break whenever I want. For me, a vacation is just a few days of rest at home, but at the end of December, when all my classes have finished, I can ②**take a longer vacation** of about a week. Around the fourth week of December, I can usually take a week off.

오랫동안 프리랜서 영어 강사로 일해 왔기에 저에게는 따로 휴가가 정해져 있지 않습니다. 언제든지 휴가를 갈 수 있죠. 제게 휴가는 그냥 집에서 며칠 쉬는 거지만, 모든 수업이 종강되는 12월 말쯤에는 일주일 정도 긴 휴가를 보낼 수 있습니다. 12월 넷째 주 정도면 일주일 정도 쉴 수 있어요.

Before COVID-19, I used to travel abroad every year during that time ③**for a winter vacation**. My last overseas trip was in 2022, and since then, I haven't been able to travel abroad and have just stayed home, doing nothing and resting. This year, I can also ④**take a week off** during the last week of December.

코로나가 발생하기 전에는 매년 그 시기에 겨울 휴가차 해외여행을 떠났습니다. 마지막 해외여행은 2022년에 갔었고, 그 이후로는 해외여행을 가지 못하고 그냥 집에서 아무것도 하지 않고 쉬었어요. 올해도 12월 마지막 주에 일주일 정도 쉴 수 있습니다.

I've been ⑤**repeating the same routine** every year, so this year, I'm only thinking about where to go, but with the current economy not doing well, I'm still just thinking about it. Honestly, I'm unsure whether to ⑥**take a winter vacation** or not.

매년 똑같은 생활을 반복하던 중이라 올해는 어디로 떠날까 고민만 하고 있는데, 요즘 경기가 좋지 않아서 아직 생각만 하고 있어요. 사실 겨울 휴가를 갈까 말까 고민 중입니다.

Whether I ⑦**spend my vacation at home** or go somewhere I've always wanted to visit, vacation gives me the time to ⑧**reflect on the past year**.

집에서 휴가를 보내든, 아니면 늘 방문하고 싶었던 곳을 찾아 떠나든, 휴가는 저에게 지난 한 해를 되돌아볼 수 있는 시간을 줍니다.

스피치 포인트

① have set vacation days 정해진 휴가일이 있다 ② take a longer vacation 좀 더 긴 휴가를 가지다 ③ for a winter vacation 겨울 휴가로 ④ take a week off 일주일 쉬다 ⑤ repeat the same routine 똑같은 일과를 반복하다 ⑥ take a winter vacation 겨울 휴가를 떠나다 ⑦ spend one's vacation at home 자신의 휴가를 집에서 보내다 ⑧ reflect on the past year 지난 한 해를 되돌아보다

나의 상황에 맞게 내용을 바꾸어서 말해 보세요.

I've been working as a freelancer English instructor for a long time, so I don't have set vacation days. I can take a break whenever I want. For me, a vacation is just a few days of rest at home, but at the end of December, when all my classes have finished, I can take a longer vacation of about a week. Around the fourth week of December, I can usually take a week off. Before COVID-19, I used to travel abroad every year during that time for a winter vacation. My last overseas trip was in 2022, and since then, I haven't been able to travel abroad and have just stayed home, doing nothing and resting. This year, I can also take a week off during the last week of December.

I've been repeating the same routine every year, so this year, I'm only thinking about where to go, but with the current economy not doing well, I'm still just thinking about it. Honestly, I'm unsure whether to take a winter vacation or not.

Whether I spend my vacation at home or go somewhere I've always wanted to visit, vacation gives me the time to reflect on the past year.

필요한 단어와 표현을 정리해 보세요.

벚꽃놀이

스피치 가이드

키워드와 주요 표현을 활용해서 문장을 말해 보세요.

1. 벚꽃놀이 장소와 활동 소개

장소: 어디로 가는지, 장소를 언급

예) One of my favorite places is Seokchon Lake in Seoul.
제가 가장 좋아하는 곳 중 하나는 서울의 석촌호수예요.

활동: 벚꽃놀이 중에 무엇을 하는지 말하기

예) I like taking photos and having a picnic under the trees.
저는 사진을 찍거나 나무 아래에서 소풍을 즐기는 걸 좋아해요.

키워드 Seokchon, lake, Chungju, Yangpyeong, take photos, blog, picnic

2. 벚꽃놀이 하는 이유와 시기 소개

이유: 벚꽃놀이를 하는 이유

예) I go cherry blossom viewing because it's relaxing and beautiful.
마음이 편안해지고 경치가 아름다워서 저는 벚꽃놀이를 즐겨요.

시기: 언제 벚꽃놀이를 가는지 말하기

예) I usually go cherry blossom viewing in early April.
저는 보통 4월 초에 벚꽃놀이를 가요.

키워드 April, at the beginning of, relaxing, beautiful

3. 특별한 기억이나 희망사항 소개

추억: 기억에 남는 벚꽃놀이 경험

예) Last year, I went with my family and we made a lot of great memories.
작년에 가족과 함께 가서 좋은 추억을 많이 만들었어요.

희망: 올해의 계획이나 희망사항

예) This year, I want to visit a new spot with my friends.
올해는 친구들과 새로운 장소에 가 보고 싶어요.

키워드 brother, photo, memory, visit, send, Japan, spot, new

대화로 연습하기

대화 속에서 문장을 늘려가는 연습을 해 보세요.

A : Every April, I drive to places like **Chungju and Yangpyeong** for cherry blossom viewing and **take photos for my blog**.
매년 4월에는 충주와 양평 같은 곳으로 벚꽃놀이를 가고, 블로그에 올릴 사진을 찍어요.

B : I heard the drive from Yangsuri to Cheongpyeong Dam is famous for its cherry blossom tunnel. Have you been there?
양수리에서 청평댐까지 가는 드라이브 코스가 벚꽃터널로 유명하다고 들었어요. 그곳에 가본 적 있나요?

A : Yes, it's my favorite spot. It's **beautiful**, so I always go there **at the beginning of April**.
네, 제가 제일 좋아하는 곳이에요. 아름다워서 저는 항상 4월 초에 그곳에 가죠.

B : Do you have any photos?
벚꽃 사진 있나요?

A : **My brother in Japan sends me cherry blossom photos** every February. When I see them, **I really want to visit Japan too**.
일본에 있는 제 동생이 매년 2월에 벚꽃 사진을 보내줘요. 그걸 보면 저도 일본에 가고 싶어져요.

B : Oh, really? I'm jealous!
오, 정말요? 부럽네요!

어휘 favorite spot 가장 좋아하는 곳 jealous 질투하는

 **내용 구성하기**

주제별로 구분하여 길게 말하는 연습을 해 보세요.

Every April, I drive to places like Chungju, Cheongpung Myeongwol, and Yangpyeong to ①**enjoy cherry blossom viewing**. It's already been 10 years since I started doing this. In April, I make sure to go cherry blossom viewing and ②**take as many photos as possible**, mainly to post them on my blog.

매년 4월이면 저는 벚꽃놀이를 즐기기 위해 충주, 청풍명월, 그리고 양평으로 드라이브를 갑니다. 이렇게 한 지도 벌써 10년이 지났네요. 4월에는 무조건 벚꽃놀이를 가고, 사진을 가능한 많이 찍습니다. 블로그에 올리기 위함이죠.

③**In my opinion**, the most famous cherry blossom tunnel is the drive course from Yangsuri to Cheongpyeong Dam. On both sides of the more than 20-kilometer stretch, old cherry trees ④**are planted like a tunnel**, so even if I can't find another place, I always make sure to visit this one.

제 생각에 벚꽃터널로 제일 유명한 곳은 양수리에서 청평댐으로 가는 드라이브 코스입니다. 20킬로미터 이상 길 양쪽으로 오래된 벚꽃나무들이 마치 터널처럼 잘 조성되어 있어서, 혹시 다른 곳을 못 찾아가도 이곳은 무조건 찾아갑니다.

Every February, my younger brother, who lives in Japan, sends me cherry blossom photos first. When I see these pictures, I ⑤**get eager to** see the cherry blossoms myself. Since the weather in Japan is warmer than in Korea, ⑥**the cherry blossoms bloom** earlier there, which is natural.

매년 2월이 되면 일본에 살고 있는 남동생이 먼저 벚꽃 사진을 저에게 보내줍니다. 이 사진들을 보면 빨리 벚꽃들을 보고 싶어집니다. 일본이 한국보다 날씨가 따뜻하기 때문에 벚꽃들이 빨리 피는 것이 당연하죠.

I ⑦**had a cherry blossom outing** this year, and I plan to do the same next year. I'm thinking about going to a different location for cherry blossom viewing next year, instead of the places I've been to so far. It's ⑧**a fun dilemma**.

올해도 벚꽃놀이를 했고, 내년에도 올해처럼 할 예정입니다. 내년에는 그동안 가본 곳 외에 다른 곳으로 벚꽃놀이를 하러 갈까 고민 중입니다. 즐거운 고민이에요.

스피치 포인트

① enjoy cherry blossom viewing 벚꽃 구경을 즐기다 ② take as many photos as possible 가능한 많은 사진들을 찍다 ③ in one's opinion 자신의 생각에는 ④ be planted like a tunnel 터널처럼 심어져 있다 ⑤ get eager to ~을 하고 싶어지다 ⑥ the cherry blossoms bloom 벚꽃이 피다 ⑦ have a cherry blossom outing 벚꽃 구경을 하다 ⑧ a fun dilemma 선택하기 어렵지만 즐거운 고민

나의 상황에 맞게 내용을 바꾸어서 말해 보세요.

Every April, I drive to places like Chungju, Cheongpung Myeongwol, and Yangpyeong to enjoy cherry blossom viewing. It's already been 10 years since I started doing this. In April, I make sure to go cherry blossom viewing and take as many photos as possible, mainly to post them on my blog.

In my opinion, the most famous cherry blossom tunnel is the drive course from Yangsuri to Cheongpyeong Dam. On both sides of the more than 20-kilometer stretch, old cherry trees are planted like a tunnel, so even if I can't find another place, I always make sure to visit this one.

Every February, my younger brother, who lives in Japan, sends me cherry blossom photos first. When I see these pictures, I get eager to see the cherry blossoms myself. Since the weather in Japan is warmer than in Korea, the cherry blossoms bloom earlier there, which is natural.

I had a cherry blossom outing this year, and I plan to do the same next year. I'm thinking about going to a different location for cherry blossom viewing next year, instead of the places I've been to so far. It's a fun dilemma.

필요한 단어와 표현을 정리해 보세요.

TOPIC 25 단풍놀이

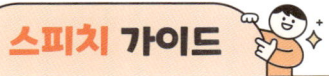

키워드와 주요 표현을 활용해서 문장을 말해 보세요.

1. 단풍놀이 명소 소개

장소: 매년 가는 곳이나 좋아하는 장소
- 예) I love going to Naejangsan National Park every fall.
  저는 매년 가을에 내장산 국립공원에 가는 걸 정말 좋아해요.

언제: 단풍이 아름다운 시기나 특징
- 예) The colors are amazing in late October.
  10월 말에는 단풍 색이 정말 아름다워요.

키워드 Woraksan, Naejangsan, October, by the end of, amazing, stunning

2. 단풍놀이 계획 소개

요일: 교통이나 요일 선택에 대한 언급
- 예) We chose a weekday to avoid heavy traffic.
  우리는 교통 체증을 피하려고 평일을 선택했어.

계획: 단풍놀이 계획을 세우는 상황
- 예) We're planning a day trip next weekend to see the leaves.
  우리는 다음 주말에 단풍을 보러 당일치기 여행을 계획하고 있어.

키워드 weekday, weekend, a day trip, traffic, avoid, worth, reach

3. 단풍놀이 좋은 점 소개

효과: 단풍놀이가 주는 감정적, 심리적인 효과
- 예) Being surrounded by fall colors always lifts my mood.
  가을 단풍 속에 있으면 기분이 항상 좋아져요.

의견: 단풍놀이에 대한 자신의 생각이나 의견
- 예) I think fall foliage trips are a perfect way to recharge.
  단풍놀이는 재충전하기에 완벽한 방법인 것 같아요.

키워드 lift, mood, agree, perfect, the best, enjoy, autumn

대화로 연습하기 대화 속에서 문장을 늘려가는 연습을 해 보세요.

A : Autumn is perfect for outdoor activities, especially in October when the fall foliage is at its peak.
가을은 야외 활동을 하기에 완벽한 계절로 특히 단풍이 절정에 이르는 10월에는 더더욱 그래.

B : I go hiking every year, and my favorite place is **Woraksan**, where the leaves are **absolutely stunning by the end of October**.
난 매년 하이킹 하고, 가장 좋아하는 곳은 월악산이야. 10월 말쯤에 단풍이 정말 아름답지.

A : I visit Seoraksan, although it gets crowded during peak season.
나는 설악산에 가는데, 성수기에는 사람이 많아.

B : I **prefer weekdays to avoid traffic. It's worth the effort to reach** Seoraksan.
차 막히는 걸 피하려 난 평일을 선호해. 설악산에 도착하는 것은 그만한 가치가 있어.

A : Being among the leaves clears my mind and reduces stress.
단풍 속에서 시간을 보내면 마음이 맑아지고 스트레스가 줄어들어.

B : **I totally agree**! It's **the best way to enjoy autumn**.
완전 동감해! 가을을 즐기는 가장 좋은 방법이야.

어휘 absolutely stunning 정말로 놀라운 만큼 아름다운 reduce stress 스트레스를 줄이다

 **내용 구성하기**

 주제별로 구분하여 길게 말하는 연습을 해 보세요.

Autumn is the perfect season for outdoor activities, especially from October when you can ①**enjoy fall foliage** across the country. Every year, I hike alone to nearby mountains to enjoy the leaves. My favorite place is Woraksan, where the entire mountain ②**becomes beautifully colored** by the end of October.

가을은 야외 활동을 하기에 가장 적합한 계절로, 특히 10월부터는 전국에서 단풍을 즐길 수 있어 더욱 좋습니다. 매년 저는 혼자서 단풍을 즐기기 위해 가까운 산을 찾습니다. 제가 가장 좋아하는 곳은 월악산으로, 10월 말쯤이면 온 산이 아름답게 단풍으로 물듭니다.

It takes about an hour by car from my house, and the old road to Woraksan is ③**great for a drive**. Another famous spot for fall foliage in Korea is Seoraksan in Gangwon Province, which ④**attracts many visitors** during peak season.

집에서 차로 1시간 정도 걸리며, 월악산으로 가는 옛 길은 드라이브하기에도 좋습니다. 한국의 단풍 명소 중 또 다른 곳은 강원도에 있는 설악산으로, 성수기에는 많은 방문객이 찾는 곳입니다.

The roads ⑤**are often congested**, so I prefer ⑥**visiting on weekdays** to enjoy the foliage. Though it's not easy to reach Seoraksan, the effort is always worth it.

도로가 혼잡한 경우가 많기 때문에 단풍을 즐기기 위해 평일에 방문하는 것을 선호합니다. 설악산에 도착하는 것은 쉽지 않지만 그 노력은 언제나 그만한 가치가 있습니다.

⑦**Spending time among the fall leaves** clears my mind and provides a chance to escape everyday stress. I believe that ⑧**enjoying the changing leaves** at autumn's end is the best way to truly appreciate the season.

단풍 속에서 보내는 시간은 마음을 정화시켜 주고, 일상의 스트레스로 부터 벗어날 수 있는 기회를 제공합니다. 저는 가을의 끝자락에서 단풍을 즐기는 것이 진정으로 계절을 만끽하는 최고의 방법이라고 생각합니다.

스피치 포인트

① **enjoy fall foliage** 단풍을 즐기다 ② **become beautifully colored** 아름답게 물들다 ③ **great for a drive** 드라이브하기에 좋은 ④ **attract many visitors** 많은 관광객들을 끌어들이다 ⑤ **be often congested** 종종 혼잡하다 ⑥ **visit on weekdays** 주중에 방문하다 ⑦ **spend time among the fall leaves** 단풍 속에서 시간을 보내다 ⑧ **enjoy the changing leaves** 변화하는 나뭇잎을 감상하다

나의 상황에 맞게 내용을 바꾸어서 말해 보세요.

Autumn is the perfect season for outdoor activities, especially from October when you can enjoy fall foliage across the country. Every year, I hike alone to nearby mountains to enjoy the leaves. My favorite place is Woraksan, where the entire mountain becomes beautifully colored by the end of October.

It takes about an hour by car from my house, and the old road to Woraksan is great for a drive. Another famous spot for fall foliage in Korea is Seoraksan in Gangwon Province, which attracts many visitors during peak season.

The roads are often congested, so I prefer visiting on weekdays to enjoy the foliage. Though it's not easy to reach Seoraksan, the effort is always worth it.

Spending time among the fall leaves clears my mind and provides a chance to escape everyday stress. I believe that enjoying the changing leaves at autumn's end is the best way to truly appreciate the season.

필요한 단어와 표현을 정리해 보세요.

PART 05
Review Quiz

1 집에 머무르는 걸 선호하다

prefer _____ home

2 유난히 추운

_____ cold

3 특별히 주의하다

take _____ precautions

4 자신이 가장 싫어하는

one's _____ favorite

5 상쾌함을 느끼다

feel _____

6 평화로움을 음미하다

_____ the peacefulness

7 좀 더 긴 휴가를 가지다

_____ a longer vacation

8 똑같은 일과를 반복하다

repeat the same _____

배운 영어 표현들을 복습해 보세요.

9 지난 한 해를 되돌아보다
_____ on the past year

10 자신의 생각에는
in one's _____

11 ~을 하고 싶어지다
get _____ to

12 벚꽃 구경을 하다
have a cherry blossom _____

13 단풍을 즐기다
enjoy fall _____

14 많은 관광객들을 끌어들이다
_____ many visitors

15 단풍 속에서 시간을 보내다
spend time _____ the fall leaves

정답 01 staying 02 exceptionally 03 extra 04 least 05 refreshing 06 savor 07 take 08 routine 09 reflect 10 opinion 11 eager 12 outing 13 foliage 14 attract 15 among

PART 06
편의 시설

TOPIC 26	패스트푸드점
TOPIC 27	대중목욕탕
TOPIC 28	편의점
TOPIC 29	주유소
TOPIC 30	은행

TOPIC 26 패스트푸드점

키워드와 주요 표현을 활용해서 문장을 말해 보세요.

1. 패스트푸드 메뉴 소개

메뉴: 평소에 자주 먹는 패스트푸드
- 예) I often eat a chicken burger with French fries.
  난 보통 치킨버거와 감자튀김을 먹어.

생각: 해당 메뉴에 대한 개인적인 생각, 의견
- 예) It's tasty and filling, but a bit greasy.
  맛있고 배도 부르지만 조금 기름지긴 해.

키워드 grab, chicken, burger, tasty, greasy, affordable, convenient

2. 패스트푸드의 장단점 소개

장점: 패스트푸드의 장점
- 예) Fast food is quick and cheap, perfect when you're short on time.
  패스트푸드는 빠르고 저렴해서 시간이 부족할 때 딱이에요.

단점: 패스트푸드의 단점
- 예) But it's usually high in calories and salt.
  하지만 보통 칼로리와 나트륨이 높아요.

키워드 quick, cheap, short, great, meal, health, good, salt

3. 건강에 좋은 패스트푸드 소개

선택: 건강에 좋은 메뉴
- 예) I usually choose a grilled chicken salad or a veggie wrap.
  저는 보통 구운 치킨 샐러드나 야채 랩을 선택해요.

이유: 그 메뉴를 선택한 이유
- 예) They're lighter and have more vegetables, so I feel better after eating them.
  그 메뉴들은 더 가볍고 채소가 더 많아서 먹고 나면 기분이 좋아요.

키워드 veggie, grilled, salad, low-calorie, better, popular

대화로 연습하기

대화 속에서 문장을 늘려가는 연습을 해 보세요.

A : I sometimes **grab a burger** for lunch. It's **affordable and convenient**.

가끔 점심으로 햄버거를 먹어요. 저렴하고 편리하거든요.

B : Me too! I used to get a shrimp burger and a Coke when I only had an hour for lunch.

저도요! 점심시간이 한 시간밖에 없을 때는 새우버거랑 콜라를 자주 먹곤 했어요.

A : Fast food is **great for a quick meal**, but we shouldn't eat it too often. Because **it's not good for our health**.

패스트푸드는 빠르게 한 끼를 해결하기엔 좋지만, 너무 자주 먹으면 안 됩니다. 건강에 좋지 않기 때문이죠.

B : I agree. These days, I try to pick healthier options.

동의해요. 요즘은 더 건강한 메뉴를 선택하려고 노력해요.

A : Right, **like salads or low-calorie meals**. They're **becoming popular** now.

맞아요, 샐러드나 저칼로리 음식처럼요. 요즘은 인기를 끌고 있어요.

B : Yes, and I try to choose them whenever I can!

네, 저도 가능하면 그런 메뉴를 고르려고 해요!

어휘 affordable and convenient 저렴하고 편리한

 **내용 구성하기**

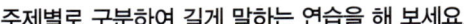

주제별로 구분하여 길게 말하는 연습을 해 보세요.

There are many ①**well-known fast-food restaurants** in my neighborhood. Occasionally, I ②**grab a burger for lunch** because it's affordable, time-saving, and convenient. However, since I know it's not good for my health, I rarely eat it these days.

우리 동네에는 잘 알려진 패스트푸드점들이 많이 있습니다. 가끔 점심으로 햄버거를 먹을 때도 있는데, 가격도 저렴하고 시간도 절약되며 편리하기 때문입니다. 하지만 건강에 좋지 않다는 것을 알기 때문에 요즘은 거의 먹지 않습니다.

In the past, I only had an hour between morning and afternoon classes, so I often ③**went to a nearby fast-food restaurant** to grab my favorite shrimp burger with a Coke. It was the perfect choice ④**for a quick and convenient lunch**.

예전에는 오전 수업과 오후 수업 사이에 점심시간이 한 시간밖에 없어서, 가까운 패스트푸드점에 가서 제가 좋아하는 새우버거와 콜라를 간단히 먹곤 했습니다. 빠르고 간편한 점심을 해결하기에는 완벽한 선택이었죠.

Not only children but also adults often ⑤**enjoy fast food**, such as pizza or burgers. As long as it's not consumed too often, it can be a convenient option for a quick meal. However, ⑥**for the sake of our health**, I believe it's important to limit how frequently we eat it.

아이들뿐만 아니라 어른들도 피자나 햄버거 같은 패스트푸드를 즐기는 경우가 많습니다. 너무 자주 먹지만 않는다면 빠른 식사로 괜찮은 선택이 될 수 있다고 생각합니다. 하지만 건강을 위해 우리가 얼마나 자주 먹는지 조절하는 것이 중요하다고 봅니다.

These days, fast-food restaurants are introducing more ⑦**health-conscious options**. Dishes like salads and low-calorie meals are ⑧**gaining popularity**, and I try to choose these whenever I can.

요즘에는 패스트푸드점에서도 건강을 고려한 메뉴들이 점점 더 나오고 있습니다. 샐러드나 저칼로리 식단 같은 요리들이 인기를 끌고 있으며, 저는 가능할 때마다 이런 메뉴를 선택하려고 노력합니다.

스피치 포인트

① **well-known fast-food restaurants** 잘 알려진 패스트푸드점 ② **grab a burger for lunch** 점심으로 햄버거를 먹다 ③ **go to a nearby fast-food restaurant** 근처 패스트푸드점에 가다 ④ **for a quick and convenient lunch** 빠르고 간편한 점심으로 ⑤ **enjoy fast food** 패스트푸드를 즐기다 ⑥ **for the sake of one's health** 자신의 건강을 위해서 ⑦ **health-conscious options** 건강을 고려한 선택지 ⑧ **gain popularity** 인기를 끌다

나의 상황에 맞게 내용을 바꾸어서 말해 보세요.

There are many well-known fast-food restaurants in my neighborhood. Occasionally, I grab a burger for lunch because it's affordable, time-saving, and convenient. However, since I know it's not good for my health, I rarely eat it these days.

In the past, I only had an hour between morning and afternoon classes, so I often went to a nearby fast-food restaurants to grab my favorite shrimp burger with a Coke. It was the perfect choice for a quick and convenient lunch.

Not only children but also adults often enjoy fast food, such as pizza or burgers. As long as it's not consumed too often, it can be a convenient option for a quick meal. However, for the sake of our health, I believe it's important to limit how frequently we eat it.

These days, fast-food restaurants are introducing more health-conscious options. Dishes like salads and low-calorie meals are gaining popularity, and I try to choose these whenever I can.

스피치 메모

필요한 단어와 표현을 정리해 보세요.

TOPIC 27 대중목욕탕

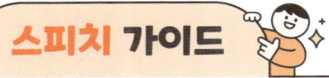

키워드와 주요 표현을 활용해서 문장을 말해 보세요.

1. 대중목욕탕에 가는 목적 소개

목적: 왜 대중목욕탕에 가는지 말해 보기

예) I tend to go to the public bathhouse to relax after a long day.
긴 하루를 보낸 후에 휴식을 취하려고 대중목욕탕에 가는 편이에요.

장소: 평소에 샤워하는 장소에 대해 말해 보기

예) I really love taking a shower at home.
집에서 샤워하는 걸 정말 좋아해요.

키워드 relax, feel, refreshed, at home, shower, take

2. 대중목욕탕에 가는 날 소개

요일: 보통 어느 요일에 가는지 말해 보기

예) I usually go on Sunday mornings when it's less crowded.
덜 붐비는 일요일 아침에 보통 가.

빈도: 얼마나 자주 가는지 말해 보기

예) I go to the public bathhouse twice a month.
한 달에 두 번 대중목욕탕에 가.

키워드 Sunday, weekday, usually, early, morning, twice, once, week, month

3. 대중목욕탕에 동행하는 사람 소개

동행: 누구와 함께 가는지 말해 보기

예) I go to the public bathhouse with my dad now and then.
저는 가끔 아버지와 함께 대중목욕탕에 가요.

활동: 목욕탕에서 주로 무엇을 하는지 말해 보기

예) After washing, I like to relax in the sauna for a while.
씻고 나서 사우나에서 잠깐 쉬는 걸 좋아해요.

키워드 dad, younger brother, relax, sauna, scrub, back

대화 속에서 문장을 늘려가는 연습을 해 보세요.

A : I enjoy **taking baths to feel refreshed**. I **usually shower at home**, but sometimes I go to the local bathhouse.
나는 상쾌함을 느끼기 위해 목욕하는 것을 즐겨. 보통은 집에서 샤워하지만, 가끔은 동네 목욕탕에 가.

B : There's a famous hot spring in Angseong, right?
앙성에 유명한 온천이 있지, 맞지?

A : Yeah, it's crowded on weekends, so I usually go **early in the morning on weekdays**. In fact, I go there **at least once a week**.
응. 주말엔 사람이 많아서 보통 평일 아침 일찍 가. 사실, 난 적어도 일주일에 한 번은 거기 가.

B : Since moving, I prefer showering at home.
이사한 후 집에서 샤워하는 걸 선호해.

A : When I go to a public bathhouse, I sometimes **go with my younger brother**, and **we scrub each other's backs**.
대중목욕탕에 갈 때 가끔 남동생과 함께 가는데, 우리는 서로 등을 밀어주기도 해.

B : That sounds great!
정말 좋겠네!

어휘 scrub each other's backs 서로의 등을 밀다

내용 구성하기

주제별로 구분하여 길게 말하는 연습을 해 보세요.

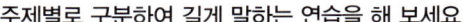

I ①**enjoy taking baths** because it makes me feel refreshed both physically and mentally. At home, I usually take showers, but sometimes I ②**visit the local public bathhouse** to relax and unwind while cleansing my body and relieving accumulated stress.

저는 목욕을 하면 몸과 마음이 상쾌해지기 때문에 목욕을 즐깁니다. 집에서는 주로 샤워를 하지만 가끔은 몸을 씻고 쌓인 스트레스를 해소하면서 휴식을 취하고 긴장을 풀기 위해 동네 목욕탕을 방문하기도 합니다.

About a 30-minute drive from my house, there's a village called Angseong, which is famous for its ③**carbonated hot springs**. It's so popular that the baths are often crowded with visitors early in the morning on weekends. That's why I usually ④**go on weekdays**, preferably early in the morning rather than in the afternoon, to enjoy a more peaceful experience.

집에서 차로 약 30분 거리에 탄산 온천으로 유명한 앙성이라는 마을이 있습니다. 주말에는 이른 아침부터 방문객들로 붐빌 정도로 인기가 많습니다. 그래서 저는 보통 평일에, 가급적 오후보다는 이른 아침에 가서 더 평온한 시간을 즐깁니다.

In the past, I didn't have a proper place to ⑤**take a bath at home**, so I often went to public bathhouses. However, after moving to a new house, I now ⑥**tend to shower comfortably** at home rather than visiting the local public bathhouse.

예전에는 집에서 목욕할 공간이 없어서 대중목욕탕을 자주 갔습니다. 하지만 새 집으로 이사한 후에는 이제 동네 대중목욕탕을 방문하기보다는 집에서 편하게 샤워하는 편입니다.

If I need to use a public bathhouse, I sometimes go alone, or other times, I go with my younger brother. When we go together, we often ⑦**scrub each other's backs**. I'm very satisfied that there's a carbonated hot spring ⑧**not far from my house**.

혹시 대중목욕탕을 이용해야 할 경우, 때로는 혼자 가기도 하고, 남동생과 함께 가기도 합니다. 같이 갈 때는 우리는 종종 서로의 등을 밀어주기도 합니다. 집에서 멀지 않은 곳에 탄산온천탕이 있어 정말 만족스럽습니다.

스피치 포인트

① **enjoy taking baths** 목욕하는 걸 즐기다 ② **visit the local public bathhouse** 지역 대중목욕탕을 방문하다 ③ **carbonated hot springs** 탄산 온천 ④ **go on weekdays** 주중에 가다 ⑤ **take a bath at home** 집에서 목욕하다 ⑥ **tend to shower comfortably** 편하게 샤워하는 경향이 있다 ⑦ **scrub each other's backs** 각자의 등을 밀어주다 ⑧ **not far from one's house** 자신의 집에서 멀지 않은

나의 상황에 맞게 내용을 바꾸어서 말해 보세요.

I enjoy taking baths because it makes me feel refreshed both physically and mentally. At home, I usually take showers, but sometimes I visit the local public bathhouse to relax and unwind while cleansing my body and relieving accumulated stress.

About a 30-minute drive from my house, there's a village called Angseong, which is famous for its carbonated hot springs. It's so popular that the baths are often crowded with visitors early in the morning on weekends. That's why I usually go on weekdays, preferably early in the morning rather than in the afternoon, to enjoy a more peaceful experience.

In the past, I didn't have a proper place to take a bath at home, so I often went to public bathhouses. However, after moving to a new house, I now tend to shower comfortably at home rather than visiting the local public bathhouse.

If I need to use a public bathhouse, I sometimes go alone, or other times, I go with my younger brother. When we go together, we often scrub each other's backs. I'm very satisfied that there's a carbonated hot spring not far from my house.

필요한 단어와 표현을 정리해 보세요.

TOPIC 28 편의점

스피치 가이드

키워드와 주요 표현을 활용해서 문장을 말해 보세요.

1. 주변 편의점 소개

근접성: 내 주변에 있는 편의점
- 예) There are two convenience stores near my house.
  우리 집 근처에 편의점이 두 개 있어요.

생필품: 편의점에서 자주 사는 물건
- 예) I often buy ready-to-eat meals or snacks.
  저는 보통 즉석식품이나 간식을 사요.

키워드 near, 2 minutes, house, snack, meal, ready-to-eat

2. 편의점의 편리성 소개

혜택: 할인이나 행사 같은 가격 혜택
- 예) Sometimes there are buy-one-get-one-free deals or small discounts.
  가끔은 하나 사면 하나 공짜인 행사나 작은 할인들이 있어요.

편리성: 편의점을 이용하는 이유
- 예) It's open 24/7, so I can go anytime I want.
  24시간 열려 있어서 언제든 갈 수 있어요.

키워드 two, item, price, deal, one, discount, 24/7, handy, cooking

3. 편의점의 다변화 소개

변화: 요즘 편의점에서 살 수 있는 다양한 물건
- 예) They sell daily necessities and even health products at convenience stores.
  편의점에서는 생필품은 물론 건강 제품까지도 판매해요.

식사: 간단한 식사도 가능한 점을 강조
- 예) You can have a quick meal like cup noodles or kimbap.
  컵라면이나 김밥 같은 간단한 식사도 할 수 있어요.

키워드 daily, everyday, health, item, diverse, quick, bite, meal, grab

대화로 연습하기

대화 속에서 문장을 늘려가는 연습을 해 보세요.

A : There are three convenience stores near me, and the closest is **just 2 minutes away**. I usually **buy meals or snacks**.

제 동네에는 편의점이 세 개 있는데, 가장 가까운 곳은 2분 거리에 있어요. 저는 보통 도시락이나 간식을 사요.

B : Sounds convenient! They're a bit expensive, but the proximity makes it worth it.

정말 편리하네요! 조금 비싸지만 가까워서 자주 가게 되죠.

A : Exactly. Sometimes you **get two items for the price of one**, and there are often small discounts. It's **really handy when I don't feel like cooking**.

맞아요. 때로는 하나 가격에 두 개를 살 수 있고, 가끔 작은 할인도 있어요. 요리하기 귀찮을 때 정말 편해요.

B : I've noticed they sell a lot of things now, even health products, and are open 24/7.

건강 제품을 포함한 많은 제품을 판매하고 24시간 연중무휴로 영업하고 있다는 것을 알게 되었어요.

A : Yeah, **they've become much more diverse lately**. You can even **buy everyday items or grab a quick bite** there.

네, 요즘 편의점이 훨씬 다양해졌어요. 생필품도 살 수 있고, 그곳에서 간단한 식사도 할 수 있어요.

B : That's why more people are going there now!

그래서 요즘 사람들이 더 자주 가는 것 같아요!

어휘 proximity 근접, 가까움 handy 편리한, 유용한 everyday item 생필품 grab a quick bite 간단하게 식사하다

 **내용 구성하기**

주제별로 구분하여 길게 말하는 연습을 해 보세요.

There are three convenience stores near my neighborhood. The closest one is just a 2-minute walk away, which is very convenient. When I ①**go to the convenience store**, I usually ②**buy ready-made meals or instant cup noodles**, but sometimes I also buy bread or milk as snacks.

저희 동네 근처에는 편의점이 세 곳 있습니다. 가장 가까운 곳은 도보로 2분 거리에 있어 매우 편리합니다. 편의점에 가면 주로 즉석식품이나 컵라면을 사지만 가끔은 간식으로 빵이나 우유를 사기도 합니다.

Of course, the items sold at convenience stores ③**tend to be more expensive than** those at regular discount stores, but I use them frequently because of their proximity. Sometimes, it's nice to be able to ④**buy two items for the price of one**.

물론 편의점에서 파는 물건들이 일반 할인 마트보다는 비싼 편이지만, 근접성 때문에 자주 이용합니다. 때로는 하나의 가격으로 두 개의 물건을 구입할 수 있어 좋습니다.

These days, convenience stores ⑤**sell a variety of items**, from fruits to emergency medicines. Additionally, since they ⑥**are open 24 hours**, I can visit them anytime, which is a big advantage.

요즘 편의점에서는 과일부터 비상약까지 다양한 품목을 판매하고 있습니다. 또한 24시간 영업하기 때문에 언제든지 방문할 수 있다는 점이 큰 장점입니다.

Recently, convenience stores have expanded their offerings to include not only simple drinks and snacks but also health foods and organic products, making them even more diverse. ⑦**Thanks to these changes**, more people seem to ⑧**visit convenience stores** more often than before.

최근 편의점은 간단한 음료와 간식뿐만 아니라 건강식품과 유기농 제품까지 다양하게 제공하고 있어 더욱 다양해지고 있습니다. 이러한 변화 덕분에 이전보다 더 많은 사람들이 편의점을 자주 찾는 것 같습니다.

스피치 포인트

① go to the convenience store 편의점에 가다 ② buy ready-made meals or instant cup noodles 즉석식품이나 컵라면 구매하다 ③ tend to be more expensive than ~보다 더 비싼 경향이 있다 ④ buy two items for the price of one 하나의 가격으로 두 개의 품목을 구매하다 ⑤ sell a variety of items 다양한 품목들을 판매하다 ⑥ be open 24 hours 24시간 영업하다 ⑦ thanks to these changes 이런 변화들 덕택으로 ⑧ visit convenience stores 편의점을 방문하다

나의 상황에 맞게 내용을 바꾸어서 말해 보세요.

There are three convenience stores near my neighborhood. The closest one is just a 2-minute walk away, which is very convenient. When I go to the convenience store, I usually buy ready-made meals or instant cup noodles, but sometimes I also buy bread or milk as snacks.

Of course, the items sold at convenience stores tend to be more expensive than those at regular discount stores, but I use them frequently because of their proximity. Sometimes, it's nice to be able to buy two items for the price of one.

These days, convenience stores sell a variety of items, from fruits to emergency medicines. Additionally, since they are open 24 hours, I can visit them anytime, which is a big advantage.

Recently, convenience stores have expanded their offerings to include not only simple drinks and snacks but also health foods and organic products, making them even more diverse. Thanks to these changes, more people seem to visit convenience stores more often than before.

스피치 메모

필요한 단어와 표현을 정리해 보세요.

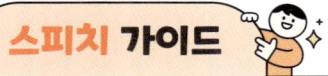 주유소

스피치 가이드

키워드와 주요 표현을 활용해서 문장을 말해 보세요.

1. 출근 방법과 주유 빈도 소개

수단: 차로 출근하거나 자주 운전하는지 언급
- 예) I usually take my car to work.
  난 보통 차로 출근해.

빈도: 주유소에 얼마나 자주 들르는지 말하기
- 예) I usually fill up once or twice a week, depending on how often I drive.
  보통 일주일에 한두 번 주유해. 얼마나 자주 운전하느냐에 따라 달라.

키워드 take, car, work, drive, every day, once, twice, week, fill up

2. 주유 비용 절약 방법 소개

절약 습관: 기름 값을 아끼는 방법
- 예) I try not to accelerate too quickly to save fuel.
  기름을 아끼기 위해 급가속은 하지 않으려고 해요.

주유소: 일반주유소 또는 셀프 주유소 선택 여부
- 예) I tend to use self-service gas stations.
  저는 셀프 주유소를 이용하는 편이에요.

키워드 save, gas, fuel, accelerate, self-service, cheaper, gas station

3. 주유 관련 지출 및 운전 습관 소개

비용: 한 달 주유 비용 구체적으로 언급
- 예) My monthly fuel expenses are around 250,000 won.
  한 달에 약 25만 원 정도 기름 값으로 써.

습관/느낌: 운전에 대한 습관이나 느낌
- 예) Driving helps me save time when commuting.
  운전은 출퇴근할 때 시간을 절약하는 데 도움이 돼.

키워드 monthly, a few, hundred thousand, save, time, happy, drive, work

대화 속에서 문장을 늘려가는 연습을 해 보세요.

A : I **drive to work every day**, so I stop by a gas station **about twice a week**.
저는 매일 차로 출근해요. 그래서 일주일에 두 번 정도는 주유소에 들립니다.

B : Are you trying to save money on gas?
기름 값을 아끼려고 하나요?

A : Yes, I always **try to save on gas**, so I **look for cheaper stations or self-service ones**.
네, 항상 기름 값을 아끼려고 하죠. 그래서 싼 주유소나 셀프 주유소를 찾아요.

B : That makes sense. Fuel costs can really add up.
그럴 만하네요. 기름 값이 많이 나올 수 있죠.

A : Exactly! I spend **a few hundred thousand won** on gas every month. But **I'm just happy that I can drive to work** every single day.
맞아요! 저는 한 달에 기름 값으로 몇 십만 원을 써요. 하지만 매일 차로 출근할 수 있다는 게 그저 행복해요.

B : Oh, really? That's good to hear.
아, 정말요? 그 말 들으니까 다행이네요.

어휘 save money on gas 기름 값을 아끼다 add up 누적되다, 쌓이다

내용 구성하기

주제별로 구분하여 길게 말하는 연습을 해 보세요.

I drive to work every day. Since I have to drive 70-80 kilometers round trip, I have to ①**stop at the gas station** about twice a week. These days, due to the economic situation, I try to ②**save on fuel costs** by looking for cheaper or self-service gas stations. If you drive, you can probably understand how I feel.

저는 매일 차로 출근합니다. 왕복으로 70~80킬로를 운전해야 하기에 일주일에 두 번 정도는 주유소에 들러야 합니다. 요즘 경기가 안 좋기에 조금이라도 기름 값을 아끼려고 싼 주유소를 찾아가거나 셀프 주유소를 찾습니다. 운전하는 사람이라면 제 마음을 이해할 수 있을 거예요.

I usually ③**spend** about 30,000 won **on fuel each time**, so it adds up to several hundred thousand won a month, making me ④**sensitive to fuel prices**.

보통 주유할 때마다 3만원 정도 넣는데, 한 달이면 몇 십 만원이 들어가니까 기름 값에 민감할 수밖에 없어요.

In the past, I didn't ⑤**have a driver's license**, so I had to use public transportation to commute, which was inconvenient. However, after getting my driver's license, it's great that I can ⑥**drive to work** whenever I want.

예전에는 운전면허가 없어서 출퇴근할 때 대중교통을 이용해야 해서 불편했습니다. 하지만 운전면허증을 취득한 후에는 원할 때 언제든지 운전해서 출근할 수 있어서 좋습니다.

These days, gas stations ⑦**offer car wash discount coupons** when you fill up a certain amount. It seems like they provide these benefits to customers ⑧**due to the competition** among gas stations.

요즘 주유소에서는 일정 금액을 주유하면 세차 할인권도 함께 줍니다. 주유소 간 경쟁으로 인해 고객에게 이러한 혜택을 제공하는 것 같습니다.

스피치 포인트

① stop at the gas station 주유소에 잠시 들르다 ② save on fuel costs 기름 값을 절약하다 ③ spend ~ on fuel each time 매번 기름에 ~을 쓰다 ④ sensitive to fuel prices 기름 가격에 민감하다 ⑤ have a driver's license 운전면허증을 가지다 ⑥ drive to work 차로 출근하다 ⑦ offer car wash discount coupons 세차 할인권을 제공하다 ⑧ due to the competition 경쟁 때문에

나의 상황에 맞게 내용을 바꾸어서 말해 보세요.

I drive to work every day. Since I have to drive 70-80 kilometers round trip, I have to stop at the gas station about twice a week. These days, due to the economic situation, I try to save on fuel costs by looking for cheaper or self-service gas stations. If you drive, you can probably understand how I feel.

I usually spend about 30,000 won on fuel each time, so it adds up to several hundred thousand won a month, making me sensitive to fuel prices.

In the past, I didn't have a driver's license, so I had to use public transportation to commute, which was inconvenient. However, after getting my driver's license, it's great that I can drive to work whenever I want.

These days, gas stations offer car wash discount coupons when you fill up a certain amount. It seems like they provide these benefits to customers due to the competition among gas stations.

필요한 단어와 표현을 정리해 보세요.

 은행

스피치 가이드

키워드와 주요 표현을 활용해서 문장을 말해 보세요.

1. 은행 방문 빈도 및 이유 소개

빈도: 평소에 은행에 얼마나 자주 가는지
- 예) I don't visit the bank often these days.
  요즘은 은행에 자주 가지 않아.

이유: 직접 방문해야 하는 이유
- 예) I only go when I need to renew a fixed deposit.
  정기 예금 갱신할 때만 가.

키워드 often, visit, not much, renew, fixed deposit

2. 은행 선택 기준 및 저축 습관 소개

선택: 주로 거래하는 은행
- 예) I use the same bank because I'm familiar with their services.
  그들의 서비스에 익숙해서 계속 같은 은행을 이용하고 있어.

저축: 저축 습관에 대한 말하기
- 예) I try to deposit 80% of my monthly salary into my bank account.
  매달 월급의 80%를 내 은행 계좌에 넣으려고 노력해.

키워드 same, bank, stick to, main, deposit, monthly, salary, most

3. 저축에 대한 의견, 목표 소개

의견: 저축에 대한 개인적인 생각이나 의견
- 예) To me, saving money is a good habit that brings peace of mind.
  저에게 저축은 마음의 안정을 주는 좋은 습관이에요.

목표: 저축을 하는 이유나 목표
- 예) I save regularly to prepare for unexpected expenses.
  예상치 못한 지출에 대비하기 위해 정기적으로 저축해요.

키워드 habit, peace, savings, grow, unexpected, prepare, retirement

대화로 연습하기

대화 속에서 문장을 늘려가는 연습을 해 보세요.

A : Do you visit the bank often?
은행 자주 가?

B : **Not much**. I handle most tasks on my phone but visit occasionally to **renew a fixed deposit**.
많이는 안 가. 대부분 스마트폰으로 처리하는데, 가끔 정기 예금 갱신하러 가.

A : Do you compare banks for better rates?
이율 높은 은행 비교도 해?

B : Sometimes, but I usually **stick to my main bank**. I **deposit most of my salary** there and place it into fixed deposits.
가끔 그렇긴 하지만, 보통은 주거래 은행을 이용해. 월급의 대부분을 거기에 저축하고 정기 예금에 넣어.

A : That's a good habit.
좋은 습관이네.

B : It **feels great to see my savings grow** as I **prepare for retirement**.
노후 준비하면서 저축이 늘어나는 걸 보면 기분이 좋아.

어휘 stick to 굳게 지키다 fixed deposit 정기 예금 retirement 노후, 퇴직, 은퇴

 **내용 구성하기**

주제별로 구분하여 길게 말하는 연습을 해 보세요.

In everyday life, I occasionally need to visit the bank. I go there to ①**open a fixed deposit account** or renew one when it matures. Since I ②**have multiple fixed deposit accounts**, I usually need to visit the bank every few months.

일상생활 속에서 가끔 은행에 갈 일이 생깁니다. 정기 예금 통장을 만들거나 만기가 되면 재 갱신을 위해 방문하기도 합니다. 저는 여러 개의 정기 예금 통장을 가지고 있어서 몇 달에 한 번은 꼭 은행에 가야 합니다.

Sometimes, I visit to ③**update my passbook**, but these days, I can ④**handle banking tasks easily** using my smartphone, so I don't go as often as I used to.

때로는 통장 정리를 위해 방문하는 경우도 있지만, 요즘은 스마트폰으로 간단히 은행 업무를 볼 수 있어서 예전처럼 자주 찾아가지는 않습니다.

When opening a new fixed deposit account, I compare various banks to find one ⑤**offering a higher interest rate**. However, since I already ⑥**have a primary bank**, I rarely switch to another.

새로운 정기 예금 통장을 만들 때는 여러 은행을 비교하며 이자가 더 높은 곳을 고려하기도 합니다. 하지만 주 거래 은행이 있어서 웬만하면 다른 은행으로 옮기지는 않습니다.

I'm not interested in stocks, so on payday, I ⑦**deposit about two-thirds of my salary** into my primary bank. Once I've saved up a decent amount, I immediately put it into a fixed deposit to secure the funds. Seeing the money in my bank account gradually grow gives me great satisfaction. As I grow older, I feel the need to prepare for my retirement, so I try to ⑧**save safely in the bank** whenever possible.

저는 주식에 관심이 없어서 월급날이면 월급의 약 3분의 2를 주 거래 은행에 입금합니다. 그리고 어느 정도 금액이 모이면 바로 정기 예금에 가입해 돈을 묶어둡니다. 은행 계좌에 돈이 조금씩 쌓이는 모습을 보면 기분이 좋아집니다. 나이가 들수록 노후를 준비해야 한다는 생각에 가능하면 은행에 안전하게 저축하려고 노력합니다.

스피치 포인트

① **open a fixed deposit account** 정기 예금 계좌를 개설하다 ② **have multiple fixed deposit accounts** 여러 개의 정기 예금 통장을 가지고 있다 ③ **update one's passbook** 통장 정리를 하다 ④ **handle banking tasks easily** 은행 업무를 쉽게 처리하다 ⑤ **offer a higher interest rate** 더 높은 이자율을 제공하다 ⑥ **have a primary bank** 주 거래 은행이 있다 ⑦ **deposit about two-thirds of one's salary** 자신 월급의 약 3분의 2를 입금하다 ⑧ **save safely in the bank** 은행에 안전하게 저축하다

나의 상황에 맞게 내용을 바꾸어서 말해 보세요.

In everyday life, I occasionally need to visit the bank. I go there to open a fixed deposit account or renew one when it matures. Since I have multiple fixed deposit accounts, I usually need to visit the bank every few months.

Sometimes, I visit to update my passbook, but these days, I can handle banking tasks easily using my smartphone, so I don't go as often as I used to.

When opening a new fixed deposit account, I compare various banks to find one offering a higher interest rate. However, since I already have a primary bank, I rarely switch to another.

I'm not interested in stocks, so on payday, I deposit about two-thirds of my salary into my primary bank. Once I've saved up a decent amount, I immediately put it into a fixed deposit to secure the funds. Seeing the money in my bank account gradually grow gives me great satisfaction. As I grow older, I feel the need to prepare for my retirement, so I try to save safely in the bank whenever possible.

필요한 단어와 표현을 정리해 보세요.

PART 06 Review Quiz

1 점심으로 햄버거를 먹다
_____ a burger for lunch

2 자신의 건강을 위해서
for the _____ of one's health

3 인기를 끌다
_____ popularity

4 목욕하는 걸 즐기다
enjoy _____ baths

5 집에서 목욕하다
take a bath at _____

6 각자의 등을 밀어주다
_____ each other's backs

7 즉석식품이나 컵라면 구매하다
buy ready-made meals or _____ cup noodles

8 다양한 품목들을 판매하다
sell a _____ of items

배운 영어 표현들을 복습해 보세요.

9 편의점을 방문하다

visit _____ stores

10 기름 값을 절약하다

save _____ fuel costs

11 기름 가격에 민감한

_____ to fuel prices

12 세차 할인권을 제공하다

offer car _____ discount coupons

13 통장 정리를 하다

_____ one's passbook

14 더 높은 이자율을 제공하다

offer a higher _____ rate

15 은행에 안전하게 저축하다

save _____ in the bank

정답 01 grab 02 sake 03 gain 04 taking 05 home 06 scrub 07 instant 08 variety
09 convenience 10 on 11 sensitive 12 wash 13 update 14 interest 15 safely

PART 07
교통수단

TOPIC 31   버스&택시
TOPIC 32   지하철&기차
TOPIC 33   비행기&배
TOPIC 34   도보&자전거
TOPIC 35   GPS&구글 지도

TOPIC 31 버스&택시

키워드와 주요 표현을 활용해서 문장을 말해 보세요.

1. 과거의 출퇴근 수단 소개

교통: 출퇴근 때 자주 이용했던 교통수단
- 예) I used to rely on buses and taxis before I had a license.
  면허 따기 전에는 버스랑 택시에 의존했어요.

불만: 대중교통을 이용하면서 불편했던 점
- 예) Most of the time, I took the subway. It was cheap but crowded.
  대부분 지하철을 탔어요. 저렴했지만 붐볐죠.

키워드 rely on, bus, taxi, subway, crowded, inconvenient

2. 운전면허 취득, 대중교통 이용 소개

운전면허: 운전면허 취득에 대한 아쉬웠던 점
- 예) Looking back, I should have gotten my driver's license earlier.
  돌아보면 더 일찍 운전면허를 땄어야 했어.

대중교통: 평소에 대중교통을 이용할 때
- 예) When I visit smaller cities, I usually take a local bus or grab a taxi.
  작은 도시에 가면 주로 시내버스를 타거나 택시를 타.

키워드 regret, driver's license, earlier, sooner, local, bus, taxi

3. 운전과 대중교통 비교 소개

운전: 운전을 할 때 주로 신경 쓰는 일
- 예) Driving in heavy traffic really makes me stressed because I need to stay alert.
  차가 많이 막힐 땐 항상 신경 써야 해서 스트레스를 정말 받아요.

활동: 대중교통을 이용할 때 주로 하는 일
- 예) I love taking the bus in spring because I can relax and enjoy the scenery.
  편하게 풍경을 감상할 수 있어 봄철엔 버스를 타는 걸 좋아해요.

키워드 alert, focus on, road, spring, enjoy, relax, take in, surrounding

대화로 연습하기

대화 속에서 문장을 늘려가는 연습을 해 보세요.

A : How did you usually get to work in the past?
예전엔 주로 어떻게 출퇴근했어요?

B : Before I got my driver's license, I mostly **took the bus or a taxi**. It was **pretty inconvenient**.
면허를 따기 전에는 주로 버스나 택시를 탔어요. 꽤 불편했죠.

A : What about after you got your license? 면허 따고 나니 어땠어요?

B : Everything became so much easier. I even **regret not getting it sooner**. 완전 편해졌어요. 왜 진작 안 땄나 후회될 정도였죠.

A : Do you still use public transportation these days?
요즘도 여전히 대중교통을 이용해요?

B : Hardly ever, but when I visit Gangneung, I take the KTX and **use local buses or taxis there**.
거의 이용 안 해요. 하지만 강릉 갈 땐 KTX 타고 그곳에서는 시내버스나 택시를 이용하죠.

A : What do you like about using public transportation?
대중교통을 이용하면 어떤 점이 좋아요?

B : When I drive, I have to **focus on the road**, but on a bus or train, I can just **relax and take in the surroundings**.
운전할 때는 도로에만 집중해야 하지만, 버스나 기차를 타면 주변을 편하게 감상할 수 있어요.

어휘 public transportation 대중교통 take in 감상하다, 섭취하다 surroundings 주변 환경

내용 구성하기

When I didn't have a driver's license a long time ago, I mostly ①**relied on buses or taxis** to get to work. When I had to give English lectures at university, I mainly took the bus, and when I had early morning classes at a foreign language academy, I either walked or took a taxi if I was in a hurry. ②**Back then,** I often felt inconvenienced.

오래전에 운전 면허증이 없었을 때, 저는 주로 버스나 택시를 이용해서 출근했습니다. 대학에서 영어 강의를 해야 할 때는 주로 버스를 탔고, 외국어 학원에서 새벽에 강의를 할 때는 걸어서 출근하거나 급할 경우 택시를 탔습니다. 그때는 종종 불편함을 느꼈습니다.

However, after I ③**got my driver's license**, all of those inconveniences disappeared ④**in an instant**. I regret not getting my driver's license sooner, as it would have made things much more convenient.

하지만 운전면허증을 취득한 후에는 그 모든 불편함이 순식간에 사라졌습니다. 운전 면허증을 더 빨리 취득하지 않은 것이 아쉽습니다. 그랬다면 훨씬 더 편리했을 텐데요.

These days, I ⑤**hardly ever use taxis or buses**. However, when I visit a city like Gangneung, located near the East Coast, I take the KTX instead of driving, and then ⑥**use local buses** within the city.

요즘은 택시나 버스를 이용하는 일이 거의 없습니다. 하지만 강릉처럼 동해 근처에 위치한 도시를 방문할 때는 자동차 대신 KTX를 타고, 그 후에는 시내에서 시내버스를 이용합니다.

It's a nice thing to ⑦**sit comfortably on the bus**, look around, and enjoy some personal time. If I felt like I was going to miss the returning train, I would ⑧**take a taxi** instead and hurry to Gangneung Station.

버스에 편안하게 앉아 주변을 둘러보며 개인적인 시간을 즐기는 것은 좋은 일입니다. 돌아오는 기차를 놓칠 것 같으면 대신 택시를 타고 서둘러 강릉역으로 갔어요.

주제별로 구분하여 길게 말하는 연습을 해 보세요.

Sometimes, [9]**using public transportation** allows me to experience the city in a different way. Watching people go about their daily lives, seeing local shops and streets pass by, and simply observing the atmosphere of a place make the journey more enjoyable. Unlike driving, taking a bus or train lets me relax and [10]**take in the surroundings** without any stress.

> 때때로 대중교통을 이용하면 도시를 색다르게 경험할 수 있어요. 사람들의 일상을 바라보고, 지역 상점과 거리가 지나가는 것을 보며, 그 장소의 분위기를 단순히 관찰하는 것만으로도 여행이 더 즐거워지죠. 운전할 때와 달리, 버스나 기차를 타면 스트레스 없이 편안하게 앉아 주변 환경을 감상할 수 있습니다.

Even though I now have the convenience of driving, I still appreciate [11] **the benefits of public transportation**. It's environmentally friendly, cost-effective, and sometimes even faster than driving, especially in cities with heavy traffic. While I don't use buses and taxis as often as before, I still find them to be a good alternative [12]**depending on the situation**.

> 비록 지금은 운전하는 것이 더 편리하지만, 여전히 대중교통의 장점을 높이 평가해요. 대중교통은 환경친화적이고, 경제적이며, 특히 교통이 혼잡한 도시에서는 운전보다 더 빠를 때도 있죠. 예전처럼 자주 버스나 택시를 이용하지는 않지만, 상황에 따라 여전히 좋은 대안이 될 수 있다고 생각해요.

스피치 포인트

① **rely on buses or taxis** 버스나 택시에 의존하다 ② **back then** 그때는, 그 당시에는 ③ **get one's driver's license** 자신의 운전 면허증을 취득하다 ④ **in an instant** 순식간에, 단번에, 곧바로 ⑤ **hardly ever use taxis or buses** 거의 택시나 버스를 사용하지 않는다 ⑥ **use local buses** 시내버스들을 이용하다 ⑦ **sit comfortably on the bus** 버스에 편안하게 앉다 ⑧ **take a taxi** 택시를 타다 ⑨ **use public transportation** 대중교통을 이용하다 ⑩ **take in the surroundings** 주변 환경을 감상하다 ⑪ **the benefits of public transportation** 대중교통의 장점(이점) ⑫ **depending on the situation** 상황에 따라

When I didn't have a driver's license a long time ago, I mostly relied on buses or taxis to get to work. When I had to give English lectures at university, I mainly took the bus, and when I had early morning classes at a foreign language academy, I either walked or took a taxi if I was in a hurry. Back then, I often felt inconvenienced.

However, after I got my driver's license, all of those inconveniences disappeared in an instant. I regret not getting my driver's license sooner, as it would have made things much more convenient.

These days, I hardly ever use taxis or buses. However, when I visit a city like Gangneung, located near the East Coast, I take the KTX instead of driving, and then use local buses within the city.

It's a nice thing to sit comfortably on the bus, look around, and enjoy some personal time. If I felt like I was going to miss the returning train, I would take a taxi instead and hurry to Gangneung Station.

Sometimes, using public transportation allows me to experience the city in a different way. Watching people go about their daily lives, seeing local shops and streets pass by, and simply observing the atmosphere of a place make the journey more enjoyable. Unlike driving, taking a bus or train lets me relax and take in the surroundings without any stress.

Even though I now have the convenience of driving, I still appreciate

나의 상황에 맞게 내용을 바꾸어서 말해 보세요.

the benefits of public transportation. It's environmentally friendly, cost-effective, and sometimes even faster than driving, especially in cities with heavy traffic. While I don't use buses and taxis as often as before, I still find them to be a good alternative depending on the situation.

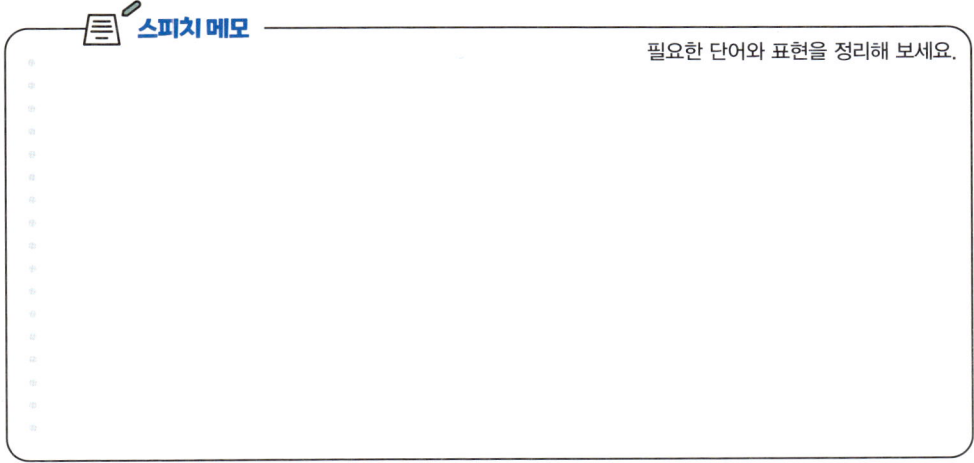

TOPIC 32 지하철&기차

스피치 가이드

키워드와 주요 표현을 활용해서 문장을 말해 보세요.

1. 기차역사 소개

기차역: 내 주변에 있는 기차역사 소개
- 예 There's a KTX station just 10 minutes from my house.
  우리 집에서 10분 거리에 KTX 역사가 있어요.

감정: 새로 생긴 기차역사에서 대한 느낌
- 예 A few months ago, a new train station opened, and it's been a game changer.
  몇 달 전에 새 기차역이 생겼는데, 삶의 질이 달라졌어요.

키워드 KTX, station, house, hometown, amazing, game changer

2. 지하철&기차 이용 방법 소개

지하철: 지하철을 이용하는 이유
- 예 I use the subway because it's fast and avoids traffic.
  난 빠르고 교통 체증을 피할 수 있어서 지하철을 이용해.

기차: 기차를 탈 때 걸리는 소요시간
- 예 It takes about 3 hours from Seoul to Busan by KTX.
  서울에서 부산까지 KTX로 3시간 정도 걸려.

키워드 easier, driving, fast, avoid, 3 hours, 50 minutes, by KTX

3. 지하철&기차 안에서의 활동 소개

활동: 지하철이나 기차 안에서 하는 활동
- 예 I usually listen to music while I'm on the subway or train.
  지하철이나 기차를 타고 있을 때 보통 음악을 들어요.

느낌: 그 활동에 대한 느낌
- 예 It's one of the few times I can truly relax.
  정말 여유롭게 쉴 수 있는 몇 안 되는 시간 중 하나예요.

키워드 listen, music, read, book, favorite, relax, relaxing, time

대화로 연습하기
대화 속에서 문장을 늘려가는 연습을 해 보세요.

A : A few years ago, **a KTX station opened in my hometown**. **It's amazing**! 몇 년 전에 제 고향에 KTX 역이 생겼어요. 정말 신기해요!

B : That's cool! How do you get to Seoul?
정말 멋지네요! 서울에는 어떻게 가세요?

A : I take the KTX to Pangyo and then the subway. **It's easier than driving**.
저는 KTX를 타고 판교까지 가고 그다음에는 지하철을 타요. 운전하는 것보다 그게 더 쉬워요.

B : Sounds convenient! Do you visit the East Sea by train?
정말 편리하네요! 동해에는 기차로 가시나요?

A : Yes, I take the KTX from Manjong to Gangneung. It's **about 50 minutes**.
네, 만종에서 강릉까지 KTX를 타요. 50분 정도 걸려요.

B : Really? That's nice. 정말요? 좋네요.

A : When I take the train, I **read a book or listen to my favorite music**. It's **such a relaxing time**
기차를 탈때 저는 책을 읽거나 좋아하는 음악을 들어요. 정말 여유로운 시간이죠.

B : That's true! I think you can feel more relaxed on a train than usual. 맞아요! 기차 안에서는 평소보다 여유를 더 느낄 수 있는 것 같아요.

어휘 relaxing 여유로운, 편안한

내용 구성하기

A few years ago, a KTX station called Gamgok-Janghowon Station was built ① **in my hometown**, Janghowon, and it has been operating since. When it first opened, I used it ②**at a discounted price** between Bubal and Chungju, and it was amazing to see something like this happening in my hometown.

몇 년 전에 제 고향 장호원에는 감곡장호원역이라는 KTX역사가 생겨 운영되고 있습니다. 처음 개통했을 때 부발에서 충주까지 할인 가격으로 이용했는데요. 이런 일이 고향에서 벌어지고 있다는 게 신기했죠.

Now, the KTX operates from Mungyeongseje to Pangyo, so whenever I go to Seoul, I ③**take the KTX** to Pangyo and then ④**switch to the subway**. It's more convenient to use the subway to get around in Seoul. Of course, I could drive, but the traffic is so heavy that the subway is much more comfortable.

지금은 문경세제부터 판교까지 KTX가 운영되고 있기에 서울에 갈 일이 있으면 판교까지 KTX를 이용하고 그 다음에는 지하철로 이동합니다. 서울에서 지하철을 타고 이동하는 게 편합니다. 물론 차를 이용해서 갈 수도 있지만 워낙 교통량이 많기에 지하철이 훨씬 편합니다.

Sometimes, when I want to visit the East Sea, I take the KTX from Manjong Station to Gangneung Station. It usually ⑤**takes about** 50 minutes, and on the train, I watch videos on my smartphone or ⑥**read the guidebook** provided on the train.

가끔 동해 바다에 가고 싶을 때는 만종역에서 강릉역까지 KTX를 이용해서 이동합니다. 보통 50분 정도 걸리는데요. 기차 안에서 스마트폰으로 동영상을 보거나 기차 내에 비치된 안내 책자를 읽습니다.

If I ⑦**have time**, I plan to visit Chuncheon from my hometown, ⑧**alternating between trains and subways**. Just thinking about it makes me excited.

시간이 되면 고향에서 춘천까지 기차와 지하철을 번갈아 타면서 가 볼 생각입니다. 생각만 해도 괜히 설렙니다.

주제별로 구분하여 길게 말하는 연습을 해 보세요.

⁹**One advantage of using the subway** or train is that I can leisurely ¹⁰**enjoy the surrounding scenery**. Watching fields, rivers, and mountains pass by through the window feels calming and gives me a sense of traveling. It's especially delightful to see the changing scenery as the seasons shift.

지하철이나 기차를 이용하면 주변 풍경을 여유롭게 감상할 수 있다는 장점이 있습니다. 창밖으로 지나가는 들판이나 강, 산을 바라보고 있으면 마음이 편안해지고 여행하는 기분이 듭니다. 특히 계절이 바뀔 때마다 풍경이 달라지는 것을 보는 재미가 쏠쏠합니다.

Also, ¹¹**taking the train or subway** is a great opportunity to read a book or listen to music while traveling. I usually enjoy my favorite playlist while admiring the scenery outside the window, and for that moment, I can ¹²**escape from my busy daily life** and find some peace.

또한 기차나 지하철을 타면 이동 중에 책을 읽거나 음악을 듣기에 좋습니다. 저는 주로 좋아하는 플레이리스트를 들으면서 창밖 풍경을 감상하는데, 그 순간만큼은 바쁜 일상에서 벗어나 여유를 찾을 수 있는 시간이 됩니다.

스피치 포인트

① **in one's hometown** 자신의 고향에서   ② **at a discounted price** 할인된 가격으로   ③ **take the KTX** KTX를 타다   ④ **switch to the subway** 지하철로 갈아타다   ⑤ **take about** 대략 걸리다   ⑥ **read the guidebook** 안내책자를 읽다   ⑦ **have time** 시간이 있다   ⑧ **alternate between trains and subways** 기차와 지하철을 번갈아 타다   ⑨ **one advantage of using the subway** 지하철 이용하는 것의 한 가지 장점   ⑩ **enjoy the surrounding scenery** 주변 풍경을 즐기다   ⑪ **take the train or subway** 기차나 지하철을 타다   ⑫ **escape from one's busy daily life** 자신의 바쁜 일상에서 벗어나다

A few years ago, a KTX station called Gamgok-Janghowon Station was built in my hometown, Janghowon, and it has been operating since. When it first opened, I used it at a discounted price between Bubal and Chungju, and it was amazing to see something like this happening in my hometown.

Now, the KTX operates from Mungyeongseje to Pangyo, so whenever I go to Seoul, I take the KTX to Pangyo and then switch to the subway. It's more convenient to use the subway to get around in Seoul. Of course, I could drive, but the traffic is so heavy that the subway is much more comfortable.

Sometimes, when I want to visit the East Sea, I take the KTX from Manjong Station to Gangneung Station. It usually takes about 50 minutes, and on the train, I watch videos on my smartphone or read the guidebook provided on the train.

If I have time, I plan to visit Chuncheon from my hometown, alternating between trains and subways. Just thinking about it makes me excited.

One advantage of using the subway or train is that I can leisurely enjoy the surrounding scenery. Watching fields, rivers and mountains pass by through the window feels calming and gives me a sense of traveling. It's especially delightful to see the changing scenery as the seasons shift.

나의 상황에 맞게 내용을 바꾸어서 말해 보세요.

Also, taking the train or subway is a great opportunity to read a book or listen to music while traveling. I usually enjoy my favorite playlist while admiring the scenery outside the window, and for that moment, I can escape from my busy daily life and find some peace.

스피치 메모

필요한 단어와 표현을 정리해 보세요.

TOPIC 33 비행기&배

스피치 가이드

키워드와 주요 표현을 활용해서 문장을 말해 보세요.

1. 이동 수단 선택이나 기준 소개

이동 수단: 여행할 때 자주 이용하는 이동 수단
- 예) I usually take a plane when I travel abroad.
  해외 여행할 때는 보통 비행기를 타요.

기준: 여행할 때 이동 수단 결정 기준 말하기
- 예) It depends on how far I'm traveling and how much time I have.
  여행 거리와 시간이 얼마나 있는지에 따라 달라요.

키워드 plane, ferry, choose, far, depending on, trip, time

2. 비행기&배의 장점 소개

비행기: 여행할 때 비행기의 장점
- 예) Flying saves time, especially when you have a tight schedule.
  일정이 빠듯할 때 비행기는 시간을 절약해줘요.

배: 여행할 때 배의 장점
- 예) The sea breeze and view make the journey itself enjoyable.
  바닷바람과 풍경 덕분에 여행 자체가 즐거워요.

키워드 save, time, faster, breeze, sea, enjoy, relaxed, pace

3. 배 여행의 특별한 경험 소개

경험: 배 여행에 대한 경험치 얘기
- 예) A ferry trip isn't just a means of transportation. It can be a special experience.
  배 여행은 단순한 이동 수단이 아니에요. 특별한 경험이 될 수 있죠.

추억: 배 여행에서 추억이 될 만한 순간
- 예) Watching the sunset on the ferry was a precious moment for me.
  배에서 일몰을 보는 것은 저에게 소중한 순간이었어요.

키워드 transportation, special, experience, precious, memorable, part

대화로 연습하기

대화 속에서 문장을 늘려가는 연습을 해 보세요.

A : I think it's important to **choose between a plane and a ferry depending on the trip**.
여행에 따라 비행기나 배를 선택하는 게 중요한 것 같아요.

B : What's the advantage of a plane? 비행기의 장점은 뭐죠?

A : **It's faster, saving a lot of time**, especially for long trips.
비행기는 더 빨라서 특히 긴 여행에서는 시간을 많이 절약할 수 있어요.

B : And what about ferries? 그렇다면 배는요?

A : They're slower, but you can **enjoy the sea at a relaxed pace**. 배는 느리지만, 여유로운 속도로 바다를 즐길 수가 있어요.

B : I couldn't agree more. 저도 전적으로 동의해요.

A : And a ferry trip **can be a special experience in itself**. The time spent on the sea can **become a memorable part** of your journey.
그리고 배 여행 자체가 특별한 경험이 될 수 있어요. 바다 위에서 보내는 시간이 여행의 소중한 추억이 될 수 있죠.

B : That's right. Planes are efficient, but ferries have a relaxed and unique charm.
맞아요. 비행기는 효율적이지만, 배는 여유롭고 색다른 매력이 있어요.

어휘 efficient 효율적인 charm 매력

I think it's important to choose between a plane and a ferry depending on the purpose and situation. When traveling abroad, ①**taking a plane** allows you to reach your destination in a short amount of time, while if you want to enjoy a more relaxed trip, ②**taking a ferry** is a better option.

저는 목적과 상황에 따라 비행기나 배 중 하나를 선택하는 게 중요한 것 같습니다. 해외여행을 할 때 비행기를 이용하면 빠른 시간 안에 목적지에 도착할 수 있고, 여유를 가지고 여행을 즐기고 싶다면 배를 선택하는 게 좋겠죠.

③**The biggest advantage** of a plane is its speed. It ④**saves a lot of time**, especially for long-distance or international travel, making it far more advantageous than a ferry.

비행기는 빠르다는 점이 가장 큰 장점입니다. 특히 장거리나 국제 여행에서는 시간을 많이 절약할 수 있어, 페리보다 훨씬 더 유리합니다.

On the other hand, a ferry is slower, but the journey itself can be an experience. It's perfect for those who want to ⑤**travel at a relaxed pace**, ⑥**enjoying the sea along the way**.

한편, 배는 느리지만 여행 자체가 하나의 경험이 될 수 있습니다. 여유로운 속도로 여행하며 바다를 즐기고 싶은 사람들에게 안성맞춤입니다.

When traveling by ferry, you can ⑦**enjoy beautiful views**, which can make the trip even more enjoyable. However, it takes a long time, and if the weather is bad, it can ⑧**become uncomfortable**.

배로 여행할 때 아름다운 경치를 감상할 수 있어 여행에 더욱 재미를 더할 수 있습니다. 하지만 시간이 많이 걸리고, 날씨가 나쁘면 불편할 수 있습니다.

주제별로 구분하여 길게 말하는 연습을 해 보세요.

⁽⁹⁾**Choosing the right mode of transportation** is crucial for a successful trip, and it's important to consider both the advantages of each option and your personal priorities. If you value speed and efficiency, a plane is the better choice. On the other hand, if you ⁽¹⁰⁾**prefer a relaxed atmosphere** and view the journey itself as part of the experience, taking a ferry can be more satisfying.

성공적인 여행을 위해 적절한 교통수단을 선택하는 것은 매우 중요하며, 각 교통수단의 장점과 개인의 우선순위를 함께 고려하는 것이 필요합니다. 빠른 이동과 효율성을 중시한다면 비행기가 더 좋은 선택입니다. 반면, 여유로운 분위기를 선호하며 여행 자체를 하나의 경험으로 여기고 싶다면 배를 이용하는 것이 더 만족스러울 수 있습니다.

Ultimately, what matters most are your trip's goals and priorities. If convenience and efficiency are your priorities, flying is ⁽¹¹⁾**the way to go**. If you value relaxation and unique experiences, a ferry trip may be more satisfying. Making a wise choice based on your situation will ⁽¹²⁾**lead to a more meaningful travel experience**.

결국 가장 중요한 것은 여행의 목표와 우선순위입니다. 편리함과 효율성을 우선순위로 생각한다면 비행이 가장 좋은 선택입니다. 만약 여유로움과 색다른 경험을 중시한다면 배 여행이 더 만족스러울 수 있습니다. 상황에 맞게 현명한 선택을 한다면 더욱 의미 있는 여행이 될 것입니다.

스피치 포인트

① **take a plane** 비행기를 타다 ② **take a ferry** 페리를 타다 ③ **the biggest advantage** 가장 큰 장점 ④ **save a lot of time** 많은 시간을 아끼다 ⑤ **travel at a relaxed pace** 여유로운 속도로 여행하다 ⑥ **enjoy the sea along the way** 가는 길에 바다를 감상하다 ⑦ **enjoy beautiful views** 아름다운 경치를 즐기다 ⑧ **become uncomfortable** 불편해지다 ⑨ **choose the right mode of transportation** 적절한 교통수단을 선택하다 ⑩ **prefer a relaxed atmosphere** 여유로운 분위기를 선호하다 ⑪ **the way to go** 가장 좋은 방법, 최선의 선택 ⑫ **lead to a meaningful travel experience** 의미 있는 여행 경험으로 이어지다

I think it's important to choose between a plane and a ferry depending on the purpose and situation. When traveling abroad, taking a plane allows you to reach your destination in a short amount of time, while if you want to enjoy a more relaxed trip, taking a ferry is a better option.

The biggest advantage of a plane is its speed. It saves a lot of time, especially for long-distance or international travel, making it far more advantageous than a ferry.

On the other hand, a ferry is slower, but the journey itself can be an experience. It's perfect for those who want to travel at a relaxed pace, enjoying the sea along the way.

When traveling by ferry, you can enjoy beautiful views, which can make the trip even more enjoyable. However, it takes a long time, and if the weather is bad, it can become uncomfortable.

Choosing the right mode of transportation is crucial for a successful trip, and it's important to consider both the advantages of each option and your personal priorities. If you value speed and efficiency, a plane is the better choice. On the other hand, if you prefer a relaxed atmosphere and view the journey itself as part of the experience, taking a ferry can be more satisfying.

Ultimately, what matters most are your trip's goals and priorities. If

나의 상황에 맞게 내용을 바꾸어서 말해 보세요.

convenience and efficiency are your priorities, flying is the way to go. If you value relaxation and unique experiences, a ferry trip may be more satisfying. Making a wise choice based on your situation will lead to a more meaningful travel experience.

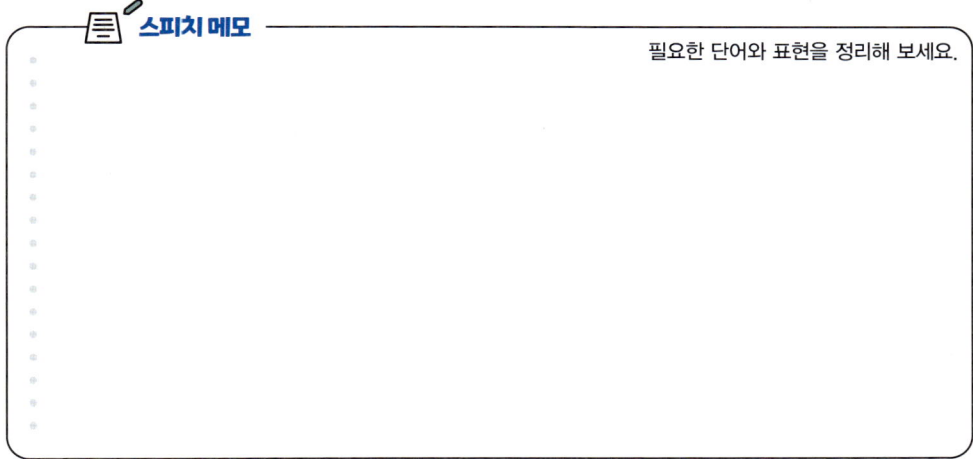

TOPIC 34 도보&자전거

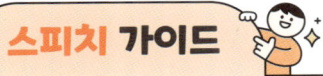
키워드와 주요 표현을 활용해서 문장을 말해 보세요.

1. 자전거 여행 소개

경험: 자전거 여행을 해 본 경험
예) I tried cycling around the island when I visited Jeju.
제주도에 갔을 때 섬을 자전거로 한 바퀴 도는 걸 시도했어요.

느낌: 자전거 여행에 대한 생각
예) It turned out to be more challenging than I had imagined.
상상했던 것보다 더 힘들었어요.

키워드 cycle, bike, around, island, harder, challenging, imagine

2. 도보&자전거 여행 선택 소개

도보: 도보 여행을 선택하는 이유
예) I prefer walking because it allows me to enjoy the scenery more.
저는 풍경을 더 즐길 수 있어서 걷는 걸 선호해요.

자전거: 자전거 여행을 선택하는 이유
예) Back then, I didn't have a car, so biking was the best option.
그때는 차가 없어서 자전거가 가장 좋은 방법이었어요.

키워드 prefer, walking, driver's license, back then, explore, unwind, option

3. 도보 여행 소개

기분: 도보 여행할 때 느끼는 기분
예) When I walk along the trail, I feel calm and peaceful.
산책로를 걸을 때 조용하고 편안한 느낌이 들어.

스타일: 자신만의 도보 여행 스타일
예) I like walking at a slow pace, so I often go on walking trips.
나는 여유롭게 걷는 걸 좋아해서 도보 여행을 자주 해.

키워드 calm, peaceful, at peace, prefer, walking, trip

대화로 연습하기

대화 속에서 문장을 늘려가는 연습을 해 보세요.

A : I often visit Jeju and Gangneung by myself. Last time in Jeju, I **biked around the island**, but it **was much harder than I expected**.

저는 제주도와 강릉을 혼자 자주 방문해요. 지난번 제주도에서는 섬을 자전거로 한 바퀴 돌았는데, 예상했던 것보다 훨씬 힘들었어요.

B : That sounds tough! What kept you going? 정말 힘들었겠네요! 뭐가 계속 가게 만들었어요?

A : **I didn't have a driver's license back then**, so I had no choice. Now, I rent a car whenever I go to Jeju.

그때는 운전 면허증이 없어서 어쩔 수 없었어요. 이제는 제주 갈 때마다 차를 렌트해요.

B : That's a good idea. How about Gangneung? 좋은 생각이에요. 강릉은 어때요?

A : I take the KTX and then walk around. **It's a great way to explore at a relaxed pace and unwind**.

KTX를 타고 나서 걸어 다녀요. 여유롭게 탐험하고 긴장을 풀 수 있는 좋은 방법이죠.

B : I bet walking by the East Sea is really calming! 동해 옆을 걷는 게 정말 평화로울 것 같아요!

A : That's right. Especially when I walk along the pine tree path, I **can't help but feel at peace**. That's why **I prefer walking when I'm in Gangneung**.

맞아요. 특히 소나무 길을 따라 걸을 때는 저도 모르게 마음이 평온해져요. 그래서 강릉에서는 걷는 것을 더 좋아해요.

B : That sounds amazing. We should go to Gangneung together sometime.

정말 멋지게 들리네요. 우리 언제 한 번 같이 강릉에 가요.

어휘 back then 그때는 explore 탐험하다 can't help but ~하지 않을 수 없다

I often visit Jeju Island or Gangneung. The charm of each place is different, so I tend to go there alone whenever I have time. When I went to Jeju Island, I ①**rented a bicycle** and traveled around the entire island by bike. Of course, it was much more difficult than I had expected, and there were times when I wanted to ②**give up halfway**. Every part of my body hurt, including my arms, legs, and even my buttocks.

저는 제주나 강릉을 자주 방문합니다. 두 장소의 매력이 서로 다르기 때문에 시간이 날 때마다 혼자 가는 편입니다. 제주도에 갔을 때는 저는 자전거를 빌려서 자전거를 타고 섬 전체를 여행했습니다. 물론 예상했던 것보다 훨씬 더 힘들었고, 중간에 포기하고 싶은 순간도 있었습니다. 제 몸의 모든 부위가 아팠습니다. 팔, 다리, 심지어 엉덩이까지요.

Even though it was raining, I ③**kept pedaling**. At that time, I didn't have a driver's license, so I had no choice. Now, I don't think I'd ④**have the courage** to do that again. Instead, these days, when I go to Jeju Island, I always rent a car.

비가 오는 중에도 계속 자전거 페달을 밟았습니다. 그때는 운전면허증이 없어서 어쩔 수 없는 상황이었죠. 지금은 그렇게 할 용기가 생기지 않네요. 대신 요즘은 제주도에 갈 때 차를 무조건 렌트합니다.

On the other hand, when I go to Gangneung, I take the KTX to Gangneung Station, and once I arrive, I try to ⑤**walk as much as possible**. It's great because it's good exercise and allows me to ⑥**explore leisurely**.

반면, 강릉에 갈 때는 강릉역까지는 KTX를 이용하고, 도착하면 그 이후에는 가능한 한 많이 걷습니다. 좋은 운동도 되고, 여유 있게 구경도 할 수 있어서 좋습니다.

Especially when I ⑦**walk along the pine tree path** with the East Sea right next to it, I can't help but ⑧**feel calm**. For this reason, I always walk when I'm in Gangneung.

특히 동해바다가 바로 옆에 보이는 소나무 길을 걷다 보면 저도 모르게 마음이 평온해집니다. 이런 이유로 강릉에서는 무조건 걷습니다.

주제별로 구분하여 길게 말하는 연습을 해 보세요.

Sometimes, I ⁹**think back to those tough moments** when I cycled around Jeju Island. Although it was exhausting and painful, I now ¹⁰**feel proud of myself** for not giving up. That experience gave me confidence, and I still cherish the memories of the beautiful scenery I witnessed along the way.

가끔 제주도를 자전거로 돌았던 그 힘든 순간들을 떠올립니다. 힘들고 아팠지만 포기하지 않았다는 점에서 지금은 스스로가 자랑스럽습니다. 그 경험 덕분에 자신감이 생겼고, 길을 따라 보았던 아름다운 풍경은 여전히 소중한 기억으로 남아 있습니다.

When I visit Gangneung, I often ⁱ¹**find myself thinking about** how peaceful life can be. Walking along the seaside paths and ¹²**listening to the sound of the waves** makes me realize how important it is to slow down sometimes. That's why I look forward to my trips to Gangneung whenever I need a break from my busy life.

강릉을 방문할 때면 종종 인생이 얼마나 평온할 수 있는지 생각하게 됩니다. 바닷가 길을 따라 걷고 파도 소리를 들으며 때로는 천천히 살아가는 것이 얼마나 중요한지 깨닫게 됩니다. 그래서 바쁜 일상에서 벗어나고 싶을 때 강릉 여행이 늘 기대됩니다.

스피치 포인트

① rent a bicycle 자전거를 빌리다 ② give up halfway 중도에 포기하다 ③ keep pedaling 페달을 계속 밟다 ④ have the courage 용기를 내다 ⑤ walk as much as possible 가능한 많이 걷다 ⑥ explore leisurely 여유롭게 탐험하다, 천천히 둘러보다 ⑦ walk along the pine tree path 소나무 길을 따라 걷다 ⑧ feel calm 차분해지다, 편안해지다 ⑨ think back to those tough moments 그 힘든 순간들을 떠올리다 ⑩ feel proud of oneself 스스로가 자랑스럽다 ⑪ find oneself thinking about 자신도 모르게 어떤 생각을 하게 되다 ⑫ listen to the sound of the waves 파도 소리를 듣다

I often visit Jeju Island or Gangneung. The charm of each place is different, so I tend to go there alone whenever I have time. When I went to Jeju Island, I rented a bicycle and traveled around the entire island by bike. Of course, it was much more difficult than I had expected, and there were times when I wanted to give up halfway. Every part of my body hurt, including my arms, legs, and even my buttocks.

Even though it was raining, I kept pedaling. At that time, I didn't have a driver's license, so I had no choice. Now, I don't think I'd have the courage to do that again. Instead, these days, when I go to Jeju Island, I always rent a car.

On the other hand, when I go to Gangneung, I take the KTX to Gangneung Station, and once I arrive, I try to walk as much as possible. It's great because it's good exercise and allows me to explore leisurely. Especially when I walk along the pine tree path with the East Sea right next to it, I can't help but feel calm. For this reason, I always walk when I'm in Gangneung.

Sometimes, I think back to those tough moments when I cycled around Jeju Isalnd. Although it was exhausting and painful, I now feel proud of myself for not giving up. That experience gave me confidence, and I still cherish the memories of the beautiful scenery I witnessed along the way.

나의 상황에 맞게 내용을 바꾸어서 말해 보세요.

When I visit Gangneung, I often find myself thinking about how peaceful life can be. Walking along the seaside paths and listening to the sound of the waves makes me realize how important it is to slow down sometimes. That's why I look forward to my trips to Gangneung whenever I need a break from my busy life.

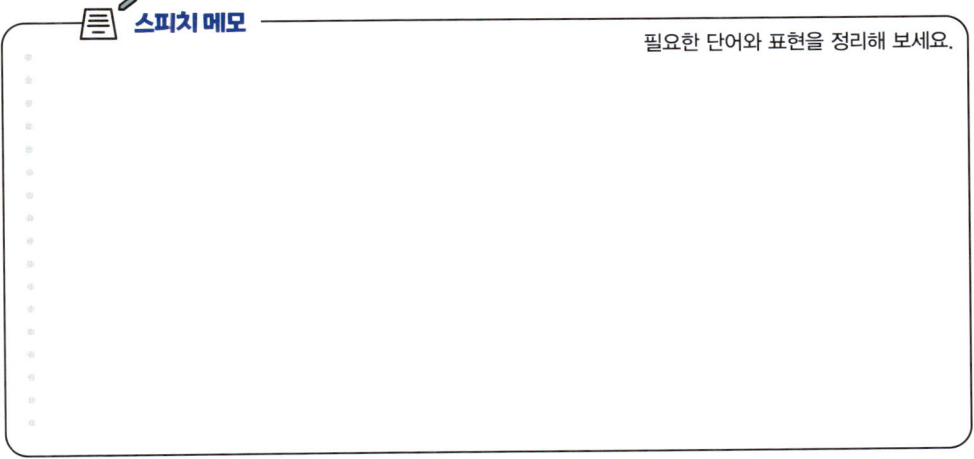

스피치 메모

필요한 단어와 표현을 정리해 보세요.

TOPIC 35 GPS&구글 지도

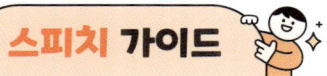

키워드와 주요 표현을 활용해서 문장을 말해 보세요.

1. GPS 소개

용도: 자신의 GPS 사용 습관

예) I tend to use my car's GPS whenever I go somewhere unfamiliar in Korea.
한국에서는 낯선 곳에 갈 때마다 차에 있는 GPS를 이용하는 편이야.

작동: GPS의 편리함 설명

예) The GPS is installed in the car and is very easy to use.
GPS가 차에 설치되어 있고 사용하기 정말 쉬워.

키워드 my car's, GPS, unfamiliar, new, place, simply, easy, use

2. 구글 지도 소개

언제: 구글 지도를 사용할 때

예) When traveling abroad, I always rely on Google Maps.
해외여행을 할 때는 항상 구글 지도를 의지해요.

이유: 구글 지도가 필요하지 않은 이유

예) If I already know the area well, I don't need Google Maps.
그 지역을 이미 잘 알고 있으면 구글 지도 필요하지 않아요.

키워드 abroad, rely on, Google Maps, taxi, driver, know, familiar

3. GPS 없이 길 찾기 소개

경험: GPS 없이 길을 찾은 경험

예) Sometimes I don't need GPS. I remember buildings or signs.
가끔은 GPS가 필요 없어요. 건물이나 표지판을 기억해요.

랜드마크: 랜드마크나 분위기를 따라간 경험

예) I just follow the atmosphere of the neighborhood, and somehow I find my way.
그 동네 분위기를 따라가다 보면 어떻게든 길을 찾게 돼요.

키워드 remember, signs, find, way, atmosphere, memorable, landmark, guide

대화로 연습하기

대화 속에서 문장을 늘려가는 연습을 해 보세요.

A : In Korea, I **use my car's GPS for new places. It's simple**.
한국에서는 처음 가는 곳은 차에 설치된 GPS를 사용해. 간단하지.

B : Abroad, I just rely on Google Maps. It's so convenient.
해외에서는 구글 지도를 의존해. 정말 편리하거든.

A : Same here. In Dubai, **even taxi drivers used Google Maps**, and I checked it too.
나도 그래. 두바이에서는 택시 기사들조차 구글 지도를 사용했고, 나도 같이 확인했어.

B : GPS or Google Maps is a must when traveling.
여행할 때 GPS나 구글 지도는 필수야.

A : True, but **I don't use it for familiar places**.
맞아. 하지만 익숙한 곳에선 거의 사용하지 않아.

B : Me neither! 나도 그래!

A : Sometimes **I can find my way without GPS. Landmarks or memorable buildings just guide me naturally**.
가끔은 GPS 없이도 길을 찾을 때가 있어. 랜드마크나 기억에 남는 건물이 있으면 자연스럽게 알게 되더라구.

B : That's right! And discovering a cool spot by accident makes it even better. 맞아! 그러다 멋진 장소를 우연히 발견하면 더 좋지.

어휘 **memorable** 기억에 남는 **cool spot** 멋진 장소 **by accident** 우연히

내용 구성하기

When visiting a place for the first time in Korea, I [1]**use the GPS** installed in my car to [2]**find my destination**. I just follow the directions it provides, so there's no need to worry.

국내에서 처음 가는 곳이라면 차에 설치된 GPS를 사용해 목적지를 찾습니다. 안내하는 대로 따라가기만 하면 되니 걱정할 필요가 없죠.

[3]**On the other hand**, when traveling abroad, I used to [4]**ask locals for help** to find the places I wanted to go. Nowadays, using Google Maps downloaded on my smartphone makes it easy to get anywhere, which is incredibly convenient.

반면, 해외여행을 할 때는 예전에는 현지 사람들에게 도움을 요청해서 목적지를 찾곤 했지만, 이제는 스마트폰에 다운로드된 구글 지도를 사용하면 어디든지 쉽게 찾아갈 수 있어서 정말 편리합니다.

Two years ago, when I visited Dubai with my younger brother's family, we often had to use local taxis instead of the subway. When taking a taxi, the driver would [5]**use Google Maps**, and I, sitting in the front seat, also used Google Maps to check our current location and make sure we weren't [6]**taking a longer route**. Being able to monitor it in real time was really helpful.

2년 전 남동생 가족과 두바이를 방문했을 때, 지하철 대신 현지 택시를 이용해야 하는 경우가 많았습니다. 택시를 탈 때 기사님도 구글 지도를 사용했는데, 조수석에 앉아 있던 저도 구글 지도를 보며 현재 위치가 어디인지, 혹시 먼 길로 돌아가고 있지는 않은지 실시간으로 확인할 수 있어 좋았습니다.

When traveling, [7]**GPS or Google Maps is a must**. However, since I[8]**'m not bad at** finding my way, I rarely use GPS if it's a place I've visited multiple times.

여행을 할 때 GPS나 구글 지도는 필수입니다. 하지만 저는 길치가 아니어서, 이미 여러 번 가 본 곳이라면 GPS를 거의 사용하지 않습니다.

주제별로 구분하여 길게 말하는 연습을 해 보세요.

Sometimes I can find my destination ⁹**without using GPS or Google Maps**. This is especially true when there are prominent landmarks or memorable buildings, which naturally guide me. Of course, GPS is still very helpful when visiting a new place or ⁱ⁰**navigating a busy city**.

가끔은 GPS나 구글 지도를 사용하지 않고도 목적지를 찾을 때가 있습니다. 특히 주요 랜드마크나 기억에 남는 건물이 있는 경우, 자연스럽게 길을 찾게 되더군요. 물론 처음 가는 장소나 복잡한 도심에서는 여전히 GPS가 큰 도움이 됩니다.

Finding your way during a trip is part of the fun. Walking down unfamiliar streets, discovering unexpected attractions, or ⁱⁱ**having casual conversations with locals** can make the journey even richer. That's why, even when using GPS or Google Maps, I try not to ⁱ²**miss out on the scenery** around me.

여행 중 길을 찾는 것도 즐거움 중 하나입니다. 새로운 거리를 걸으며 예상치 못한 명소를 발견하거나, 현지인들과 소소한 대화를 나누는 경험은 여행을 더욱 풍성하게 만들어 줍니다. 그렇기 때문에 저는 GPS와 구글 지도를 사용하더라도 주변 풍경을 놓치지 않으려 노력합니다.

스피치 포인트

① **use the GPS** GPS를 사용하다 ② **find one's destination** 자신의 목적지를 찾다 ③ **on the other hand** 다른 한편으로는 ④ **ask locals for help** 현지 사람들에게 도움을 요청하다 ⑤ **use Google Maps** 구글 지도를 사용하다 ⑥ **take a longer route** 더 돌아가는 길로 가다 ⑦ **GPS or Google Maps is a must** GPS나 구글 지도는 필수이다 ⑧ **be not bad at** ~을 못하지는 않다 ⑨ **without using GPS or Google Maps** GPS나 구글 지도를 사용하지 않고 ⑩ **navigate a busy city** 복잡한 도시에서 길을 찾다 ⑪ **have casual conversations with locals** 현지인들과 소소한 대화를 나누다 ⑫ **miss out on the scenery** 풍경을 놓치다

When visiting a place for the first time in Korea, I use the GPS installed in my car to find my destination. I just follow the directions it provides, so there's no need to worry.

On the other hand, when traveling abroad, I used to ask locals for help to find the places I wanted to go. Nowadays, using Google Maps downloaded on my smartphone makes it easy to get anywhere, which is incredibly convenient.

Two years ago, when I visited Dubai with my younger brother's family, we often had to use local taxis instead of the subway. When taking a taxi, the driver would use Google Maps, and I, sitting in the front seat, also used Google Maps to check our current location and make sure we weren't taking a longer route. Being able to monitor it in real time was really helpful.

When traveling, GPS or Google Maps is a must. However, since I'm not bad at finding my way, I rarely use GPS if it's a place I've visited multiple times.

Sometimes I can find my destination without using GPS or Google Maps. This is especially true when there are prominent landmarks or memorable buildings, which naturally guide me. Of course, GPS is still very helpful when visiting a new place or navigating a busy city.

나의 상황에 맞게 내용을 바꾸어서 말해 보세요.

Finding your way during a trip is part of the fun. Walking down unfamiliar streets, discovering unexpected attractions, or having casual conversations with locals can make the journey even richer. That's why, even when using GPS or Google Maps, I try not to miss out on the scenery around me.

PART 07 Review Quiz

1 순식간에, 단번에, 곧바로
in an _____

2 대중교통을 이용하다
use public _____

3 주변 환경을 감상하다
take _____ the surroundings

4 지하철로 갈아타다
_____ to the subway

5 안내책자를 읽다
read the _____

6 자신의 바쁜 일상에서 벗어나다
escape from one's busy _____ life

7 많은 시간을 아끼다
_____ a lot of time

8 불편해지다
become _____

배운 영어 표현들을 복습해 보세요.

9 가장 좋은 방법, 최선의 선택

the way to _____

10 중도에 포기하다

give up _____

11 가능한 많이 걷다

walk as _____ as possible

12 자신도 모르게 어떤 생각을 하게 되다

find oneself _____ about

13 현지 사람들에게 도움을 요청하다

ask _____ for help

14 더 돌아가는 길로 가다

_____ a longer route

15 풍경을 놓치다

miss _____ on the scenery

정답 01 instant 02 transportation 03 in 04 switch 05 guidebook 06 daily 07 save 08 uncomfortable 09 go 10 halfway 11 much 12 thinking 13 locals 14 take 15 out

PART 08
공공시설

TOPIC 36   시청
TOPIC 37   우체국
TOPIC 38   동사무소
TOPIC 39   공영 주차장
TOPIC 40   공립도서관

TOPIC 36 시청

스피치 가이드

키워드와 주요 표현을 활용해서 문장을 말해 보세요.

1. 시청 소개

목적: 시청에 가는 이유
- 예) I need to go to city hall to apply for a new ID card.
  새 신분증을 신청하러 시청에 가야 돼.

문화 활동: 시민들이 즐길 수 있는 문화 활동
- 예) There are exhibitions and performances held in the public hall at city hall.
  시청의 시민 홀에서는 전시회와 공연이 열려.

키워드 apply for, ID, renew, passport, resident, cultural, exhibition, performance

2. 시청 규모 소개

외관: 시청 건물의 외형적 변화
- 예) The city hall building was recently renovated with a more modern design.
  시청 건물이 최근에 더 현대적인 디자인으로 새롭게 단장되었어요.

인원: 시청에서 근무하는 공무원의 수
- 예) More than 300 people work at city hall, including administrative staff.
  행정 직원을 포함해서 300명 이상의 사람들이 시청에서 근무해요.

키워드 renovate, modern, size, grow, people, work, administrative, staff

3. 시청 내 서비스 센터 소개

서비스 센터: 시청이 운영하는 서비스 센터
- 예) There is a citizen service center inside the city hall that handles daily inquiries.
  시청 안에는 일상적인 문의를 처리하는 시민 서비스 센터가 있어요.

역할: 시민 편의를 위한 업무
- 예) The center offers support for people looking for jobs.
  그 센터는 구직 중인 사람들에게 도움을 제공해요.

키워드 citizen, handle, welfare counseling, job support, look for, help, people

대화로 연습하기

대화 속에서 문장을 늘려가는 연습을 해 보세요.

A : Have you been to a city hall? 시청에 가본 적 있어요?

B : Yes, I went there a few years ago to **renew my passport**.
네, 몇 년 전에 여권 갱신하러 갔어요.

A : I went there to register my new address. I don't visit city halls much these days. 저는 새집 주소 등록하러 갔었죠. 요즘은 시청에 갈 일이 별로 없네요.

B : Neither do I. Anyway, **the size of city halls has grown**, and **there are more people working there now**.
저도 마찬가지예요. 아무튼 시청 규모가 커졌고, 이제는 그곳에서 일하는 사람들도 많아졌죠.

A : It used to be just for administrative work, but now they also host exhibitions and concerts.
예전에는 그냥 행정 업무만 했었는데, 이제는 전시회나 콘서트도 열어요.

B : That's right. Now **residents can enjoy cultural activities** as well.
맞아요. 이제 주민들이 문화 활동도 즐길 수 있게 됐죠.

A : Also, city halls now have service centers, which makes them really convenient. 그리고 요즘 시청에 서비스 센터도 있어서 정말 편리해요.

B : Yeah, **places like welfare counseling and job support centers** make it easier **for people to get the help they need**.
복지 상담실이나 취업 지원 센터 같은 곳이 있어서 사람들이 필요한 도움을 더 쉽게 받을 수 있게 됐어요.

어휘 **cultural activities** 문화 활동 **welfare counseling** 복지 상담 **job support centers** 취업 지원 센터

You can handle various tasks at city halls. One of my memories of visiting Icheon City Hall was when I needed to ①**renew my passport**. Of course, I could have used ②**a township office** in the countryside, but handling it at Icheon City Hall saved me a bit more time.

시청에 가면 다양한 업무를 처리할 수 있습니다. 제가 이천 시청에 갔던 기억 중 하나는 여권을 갱신할 때였습니다. 물론, 시골에 있는 읍사무소를 이용할 수도 있었지만, 이천 시청에서 처리하면 시간을 조금 더 절약할 수 있었습니다.

A few years ago, I also visited Icheon City Hall to ③**register my new address** after building a new house. However, these days, I don't often ④**find myself needing to visit city halls**.

몇 년 전 새집을 짓고 새 주소를 등록해야 했을 때도 이천 시청을 찾았습니다. 하지만 요즘은 시청에 갈 일이 많지는 않습니다.

Over time, the size of city halls in different cities seems to ⑤**have expanded significantly**. Not only have their exteriors become more impressive, but the number of ⑥**civil servants** working there also seems to have increased compared to before.

시간이 지남에 따라 도시마다 시청의 규모가 크게 확장된 것 같습니다. 외관이 인상적일 뿐만 아니라 그곳에서 근무하는 공무원의 수도 역시 이전에 비해 증가한 것으로 보입니다.

City halls are no longer just places for administrative work. They also provide various facilities and ⑦**host cultural events** for local residents. For example, Icheon City Hall regularly holds exhibitions and small concerts, offering residents opportunities to ⑧**enjoy cultural experiences**.

시청은 단순히 행정업무를 처리하는 곳에 그치지 않고, 지역 주민들에게 다양한 편의 시설과 문화 행사를 제공하기도 합니다. 예를 들어, 이천 시청에서는 정기적으로 전시회나 작은 콘서트를 열어 주민들에게 문화생활을 즐길 기회를 제공합니다.

주제별로 구분하여 길게 말하는 연습을 해 보세요.

Recently, ⁹**various service centers for residents** have been established within city halls, making them more convenient to use. For example, welfare counseling offices and job support centers are available, ¹⁰**allowing local residents to access** the help they need more easily.

최근에는 시청 내에 주민들을 위한 다양한 서비스 센터가 마련되어 편리하게 이용할 수 있습니다. 예를 들어, 복지 상담실이나 취업 지원 센터가 마련되어 있어 지역 주민들이 보다 쉽게 필요한 도움을 받을 수 있습니다.

Through these services, Icheon City Hall is ¹¹**improving citizens' quality of life** and contributing to the development of the local community. I hope city halls ¹²**continue to evolve into** even more beneficial spaces for residents in the future.

이천 시청에서는 이러한 서비스를 통해 시민들의 생활수준을 높이고 지역 사회의 발전에 기여하고 있습니다. 앞으로도 시청이 주민들에게 더욱 유익한 공간으로 발전하길 기대합니다.

스피치 포인트

① renew one's passport 자신의 여권을 갱신하다 ② a township office 읍(면)사무소 ③ register one's new address 자신의 새 주소를 등록하다 ④ find oneself needing to visit city halls 시청에 가야 할 필요를 느끼다 ⑤ have expanded significantly 상당히 확장되었다 ⑥ civil servants 공무원들 ⑦ host cultural events 문화 행사들을 개최하다 ⑧ enjoy cultural experiences 문화 활동을 즐기다 ⑨ various service centers for residents 주민들을 위한 다양한 서비스 센터 ⑩ allow local residents to access 지역 주민들이 이용하도록 허락하다 ⑪ improve citizens' quality of life 시민들의 생활수준을 향상시키다 ⑫ continue to evolve into 계속해서 ~로 발전하다, 지속적으로 ~로 변화하다

You can handle various tasks at city halls. One of my memories of visiting Icheon City Hall was when I needed to renew my passport. Of course, I could have used a township office in the countryside, but handling it at Icheon City Hall saved me a bit more time.

A few years ago, I also visited Icheon City Hall to register my new address after building a new house. However, these days, I don't often find myself needing to visit city halls.

Over time, the size of city halls in different cities seems to have expanded significantly. Not only have their exteriors become more impressive, but the number of civil servants working there also seems to have increased compared to before.

City halls are no longer just places for administrative work. They also provide various facilities and host cultural events for local residents. For example, Icheon City Hall regularly holds exhibitions and small concerts, offering residents opportunities to enjoy cultural experiences.

Recently, various service centers for residents have been established within city halls, making them more convenient to use. For example, welfare counseling offices and job support centers are available, allowing local residents to access the help they need more easily.

Through these services, Icheon City Hall is improving citizens' quality of

나의 상황에 맞게 내용을 바꾸어서 말해 보세요.

life and contributing to the development of the local community. I hope city halls continue to evolve into even more beneficial spaces for residents in the future.

TOPIC 37 우체국

스피치 가이드

키워드와 주요 표현을 활용해서 문장을 말해 보세요.

1. 우체국 소개

시절: 우체국을 자주 방문했던 시절
- 예) When I was in middle school, I used to go to the post office on my way home.
  중학교 때, 저는 집에 오는 길에 우체국에 가곤했어요.

경험: 우체국 관련 과거 추억
- 예) I have good memories of sending letters to my cousin and waiting for their reply.
  사촌에게 편지를 보내고 답장을 기다리던 좋은 추억이 있어요.

키워드 middle school, home, kid, collect, stamp, letter, cousin

2. 우체국 방문 횟수 소개

과거: 과거에 얼마나 자주 우체국을 방문했는지
- 예) When I was a kid, I often went to the post office, especially around the holidays.
  어렸을 때 저는 특히 명절 즈음에 우체국에 자주 갔어요.

현재: 현재는 얼마나 자주 우체국을 방문하는지
- 예) These days, I only go there once a month to send international parcels.
  요즘은 국제 소포를 보내려고 한 달에 한 번만 그곳에 가요.

키워드 often, holiday, send, letter, once, month, at least, these days

3. 우체국의 변화 소개

쇼핑: 온라인 쇼핑과 연계
- 예) Online shopping made post offices busier with returns and parcel deliveries.
  온라인 쇼핑 때문에 반품과 소포 배송으로 우체국이 더 바빠졌어요.

불편함: 우체국 방문으로 인한 불만사항
- 예) It's hard to find time to go to the post office during weekdays.
  평일엔 우체국 갈 시간을 내기 힘들어요.

키워드 online, shopping, return, item, parcel, time, weekday, hassle

대화로 연습하기

대화 속에서 문장을 늘려가는 연습을 해 보세요.

A : **When I was a kid**, **I used to collect stamps** and went to the post office often. 어렸을 때, 저는 우표를 수집했었고 우체국에 자주 가곤 했었죠.

B : Oh, so does that mean you stopped collecting stamps?
아, 그럼 우표 수집을 그만두었다는 건가요?

A : Yes, that's right. After middle school, I lost interest. I **only went there to send letters**. 네, 맞아요. 중학교 이후로 관심이 없어졌어요. 저는 편지를 보낼 때만 그곳에 갔었어요.

B : I see. These days, I only go to the post office to send parcels.
그렇군요. 요즘 저는 소포를 보낼 때만 우체국에 가요.

A : Same here! I tend to go to the post office **at least once a month these days**. 저도 그래요! 요즘은 적어도 한 달에 한 번은 우체국에 가는 편이에요.

B : I don't do banking at the post office, but I go there to send parcels.
저는 우체국에서 은행 업무는 보지 않지만, 소포를 보내러 갑니다.

A : These days, I often go to the post office **to return items because of online shopping**. Sometimes, **it feels like a bit of a hassle**.
요즘은 온라인 쇼핑 때문에 반품하러 종종 우체국에 가죠. 가끔은 좀 귀찮게 느껴져요.

B : I hear you. But the post office has become an important hub for online shopping logistics.
이해가 돼요. 하지만 우체국은 온라인 쇼핑 물류의 중요한 중심지가 되었잖아요.

어휘 a bit of a hassle 조금 귀찮은 online shopping logistics 온라인 쇼핑 물류

When I was a child, ①**collecting stamps** was my hobby, so I would ②**visit the post office** almost once a month. However, after middle school, my interest in stamp collecting declined, and the frequency of my visits to the post office significantly reduced. I would only go there when I needed to send letters.

어렸을 때는 우표 모으는 게 취미라 매달 거의 한 번은 우체국에 가곤 했습니다. 하지만 중학교 이후로는 우표 수집에 대한 관심이 줄어들었고, 우체국을 찾는 빈도가 현저하게 줄어들었습니다. 저는 편지를 보낼 때만 그곳에 갔습니다.

When I think of the post office, I usually think of it as a place to send letters, but nowadays, I ③**hardly ever send letters**. Instead, I now only go there when I need to ④**send parcels or international mail**.

우체국이라고 하면 보통 편지를 보내는 곳이라고 생각하지만 요즘은 편지를 보낼 일이 거의 없습니다. 대신 이제 소포나 국제 우편물을 보내야 할 때만 그곳에 갑니다.

For a while, I had to ⑤**use the post office for parcel deliveries**, so I went there at least three times a week. I would also visit frequently when I had to ⑥**handle domestic or international parcels**.

한동안은 우체국 택배를 이용해야 해서 일주일에 적어도 세 번 이상 갔습니다. 또한 국내 및 국제 소포를 처리해야만 했을 때도 자주 찾아갔습니다.

Although I can also ⑦**do banking at the post office**, I don't conduct any banking transactions there. That said, the main reason I ⑧**go to the post office** is to send parcels.

우체국에서도 은행 업무를 볼 수 있지만, 저는 우체국에서 은행 거래는 하지 않습니다. 그럼에도 불구하고 제가 우체국에 가는 주된 이유는 소포를 보내기 위해서입니다.

주제별로 구분하여 길게 말하는 연습을 해 보세요.

These days, [9]**with the rise of online shopping**, I often visit the post office to [10]**return items**. In the past, people shopped in stores, but now returns are common after online orders. As a result, the post office has become an important hub for online shopping logistics. It's especially crowded after holidays, so timing your visit carefully is essential.

요즘은 온라인 쇼핑이 활성화되면서 반품을 위해 우체국에 자주 갑니다. 과거에는 사람들이 주로 매장에서 쇼핑했지만, 이제는 온라인 주문 후 반품이 흔한 일이 되었습니다. 그 결과, 우체국은 온라인 쇼핑 물류의 중요한 중심지가 되었습니다. 명절 후에는 특히 붐비므로, 방문 시간을 잘 맞추는 것이 중요합니다.

Seen this way, the post office is [11]**more than just a place** for mail services. It also [12]**serves as a financial hub** and offers administrative services in some areas. For the elderly, it's often a more familiar and accessible place, supporting communication and convenience. The post office has become an indispensable part of our daily lives.

이렇게 보면 우체국은 단순히 우편 업무만을 처리하는 곳 이상입니다. 일부 지역에서는 금융 서비스의 중심지 역할을 하며 행정 서비스도 제공합니다. 특히 어르신들에게는 더 친숙하고 접근하기 쉬운 장소로, 소통과 편의를 돕는 역할을 합니다. 우체국은 이제 우리 일상에서 없어서는 안 될 중요한 공간이 되었습니다.

스피치 포인트

① **collect stamps** 우표를 수집하다 ② **visit the post office** 우체국을 방문하다 ③ **hardly ever send letters** 거의 편지를 보내지 않는다 ④ **send parcels or international mail** 소포나 국제 우편물을 보내다 ⑤ **use the post office for parcel deliveries** 우체국 택배를 이용하다 ⑥ **handle domestic or international parcels** 국내 및 국제 소포를 처리하다 ⑦ **do banking at the post office** 우체국에서 은행 업무를 처리하다 ⑧ **go to the post office** 우체국에 가다 ⑨ **with the rise of online shopping** 온라인 쇼핑의 증가로 ⑩ **return items** 물품을 반품하다 ⑪ **more than just a place** 단순한 장소 그 이상 ⑫ **serve as a financial hub** 금융 중심지 역할을 하다

When I was a child, collecting stamps was my hobby, so I would visit the post office almost once a month. However, after middle school, my interest in stamp collecting declined, and the frequency of my visits to the post office significantly reduced. I would only go there when I needed to send letters.

When I think of the post office, I usually think of it as a place to send letters, but nowadays, I hardly ever send letters. Instead, I now only go there when I need to send parcels or international mail.

For a while, I had to use the post office for parcel deliveries, so I went there at least three times a week. I would also visit frequently when I had to handle domestic or international parcels.

Although I can also do banking at the post office, I don't conduct any banking transactions there. That said, the main reason I go to the post office is to send parcels.

These days, with the rise of online shopping, I often visit the post office to return items. In the past, people shopped in stores, but now returns are common after online orders. As a result, the post office has become an important hub for online shopping logistics. It's especially crowded after holidays, so timing your visit carefully is essential.

Seen this way, the post office is more than just a place for mail services. It

나의 상황에 맞게 내용을 바꾸어서 말해 보세요.

also serves as a financial hub and offers administrative services in some areas. For the elderly, it's often a more familiar and accessible place, supporting communication and convenience. The post office has become an indispensable part of our daily lives.

TOPIC 38 동사무소

스피치 가이드

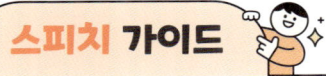

키워드와 주요 표현을 활용해서 문장을 말해 보세요.

1. 동사무소와 주민자치센터 소개

동사무소: 주민들을 위한 동사무소 역할
- 예) The district office helps with documents and resident registration.
  동사무소는 서류와 주민등록을 돕습니다.

주민자치센터: 참여하거나 담당하고 있는 활동
- 예) I help organize events at the local community center.
  저는 주민자치센터에서 행사를 조직하는 일을 도와요.

키워드 document, handle, task, organize, event, teach, English

2. 학습자로부터 받은 감동 소개

때: 인상 깊었던 순간
- 예) I was touched when a student came to every class.
  학생이 매 수업에 참석할 때 감동받았어요.

감동: 학습자의 태도에서 받은 감동
- 예) I was inspired by students who practiced English every day.
  매일 영어를 연습하는 학생들에게 영감을 받았어요.

키워드 every class, touch, from time to time, practice, enthusiasm, impress

3. 열정과 동기 소개

동기: 열정적인 학습자로부터 받은 동기
- 예) My students' passion makes me work harder.
  학생들의 열정은 저를 더 열심히 일하게 만들어요.

열정: 자신의 교육적 열정
- 예) I love teaching English because it helps my learners improve.
  저는 영어를 가르치는 것이 좋아요. 왜냐하면 학습자들이 향상하는 데 도움이 되기 때문이죠.

키워드 passion, work, thanks to, enthusiasm, improve, motivate, teach, diligently

대화로 연습하기

대화 속에서 문장을 늘려가는 연습을 해 보세요.

A : District offices **handle a variety of tasks, like issuing documents**.
동사무소는 서류 발급처럼 다양한 업무를 처리해요.

B : When I need my resident registration certificate, I usually visit the district office in my neighborhood. 저는 제 주민등록초본이 필요할 때 보통 동네에 있는 동사무소를 방문해요.

A : Oh, I see. I **teach English conversation twice a week at the local community center** for residents.
으, 그렇군요. 저는 주민들을 위해 지역 주민센터에서 주 2회 영어회화를 가르쳐요.

B : Really? I didn't know that. How is your English class going?
정말요? 몰랐더요. 영어 수업은 어때요?

A : **From time to time**, I'm **deeply impressed by people's enthusiasm to learn English**. 가끔씩 영어를 배우려는 분들의 열정에 크게 감동받아요.

B : I understand where you're coming from. 무슨 말 하려는지 이해가 돼요.

A : **Thanks to that enthusiasm**, I am also **motivated to teach more diligently** and communicate with my students.
그 열정 덕분에 저도 더 열심히 가르치고 학생들과 소통할 수 있는 동기를 얻어요.

B : That's really impressive. You're helping your students gain more confidence and communicate naturally in English.
정말 인상적이에요. 학생들이 더 자신감을 얻고 영어를 자연스럽게 구사할 수 있도록 도와주시는 거군요.

어휘 a variety of 다양한 enthusiasm 열정 be motivated to 동기부여를 받다 gain confidence 자신감을 얻다

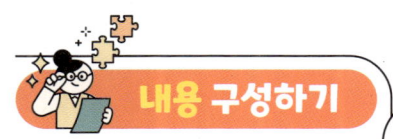

To make things more convenient for residents, local district offices in each neighborhood ①**handle a wide range of** administrative tasks. For example, residents can ②**obtain various documents** or even request university graduation certificates when needed.

주민들의 편의를 위해 각 동네마다 있는 동사무소에서는 다양한 행정 업무를 처리합니다. 예를 들어, 주민들은 각종 서류를 발급받거나 필요시 대학교 졸업증명서를 신청할 수도 있습니다.

I usually ③**visit the district office** to obtain a copy of my resident registration certificate. In addition, each district office operates a local community center that ④**provides a variety of educational programs** for residents. I also teach English conversation classes there, engaging with a diverse group of people.

저는 보통 주민등록초본을 발급받기 위해 동사무소를 방문합니다. 또한, 각 동사무소에서는 주민들에게 다양한 교육 프로그램을 제공하는 주민자치센터를 운영합니다. 저도 그곳에서 영어회화 강의를 맡아 다양한 분들과 교류하고 있습니다.

Twice a week, I commute to Icheon city to ⑤**conduct English conversation classes**. Meeting new people every quarter is always enjoyable, and I find great fulfillment in ⑥**sharing my knowledge of English with** them.

보통 일주일에 두 번 영어회화 수업을 진행하기 위해 이천시로 출근합니다. 분기마다 새로운 분들을 만날 수 있어 늘 즐겁고, 제가 가진 영어 지식을 나누며 큰 보람을 느끼고 있습니다.

During my classes, I ⑦**am** often **impressed by the enthusiasm** of those eager to learn English. Interacting with such ⑧**a diverse group of people**, from older adults to college students, not only allows me to teach but also helps me learn new things, which is always refreshing.

수업을 하다 보면 영어를 배우려는 분들의 열정에 감탄할 때가 종종 있습니다. 나이가 많으신 분들부터 대학생들까지, 다양한 분들과 소통하면서, 가르치는 것 뿐만 아니라 새로운 것을 배우게 되어 늘 신선한 자극을 받습니다.

주제별로 구분하여 길게 말하는 연습을 해 보세요.

When preparing for English conversation classes, it's important to find materials that ⁹**suit the learners' skill levels**. I ¹⁰**prepare a variety of resources** such as dialogue scripts and practical expressions for everyday use. This approach makes the learning experience more engaging and encourages active participation in class.

영어회화 수업을 준비할 때는 학습자들의 수준에 맞는 자료를 찾는 것이 중요합니다. 저는 다양한 대화 스크립트와 일상생활에서 사용할 수 있는 실용적인 표현을 준비해 수업에 활용합니다. 이러한 접근 방식은 학습 경험을 보다 흥미롭게 만들고, 수업에 적극적으로 참여하도록 유도합니다.

I also design various activities to encourage learners to ¹¹**communicate naturally in English**. For example, through role-plays and group discussions, they practice useful expressions applicable to real-life situations. This method helps them build confidence without ¹²**worrying about making mistakes**.

또한, 저는 학습자들이 영어로 자연스럽게 소통하도록 다양한 활동을 기획합니다. 예를 들어, 롤플레이와 그룹 토론을 통해 그들은 실생활에서 활용할 수 있는 유용한 표현을 연습합니다. 이러한 방법은 실수를 걱정하지 않고 자신감을 키우는 데 도움이 됩니다.

스피치 포인트

① **handle a wide range of** 다양한 범위를 다루다 ② **obtain various documents** 다양한 문서들을 발급받다 ③ **visit the district office** 동사무소를 방문하다 ④ **provide a variety of educational programs** 다양한 교육 프로그램들을 제공하다 ⑤ **conduct English conversation classes** 영어 회화 수업을 진행하다 ⑥ **share one's knowledge of English with** 자신의 영어에 대한 지식을 ~와 공유하다 ⑦ **be impressed by the enthusiasm** 열정에 감동하다, 열정에 놀라다 ⑧ **a diverse group of people** 다양한 사람들로 구성된 그룹 ⑨ **suit the learners' skill levels** 학습자들의 수준에 맞추다 ⑩ **prepare a variety of resources** 다양한 자료들을 준비하다 ⑪ **communicate naturally in English** 영어로 자연스럽게 소통하다 ⑫ **worry about making mistakes** 실수하는 걸 걱정하다

To make things more convenient for residents, local district offices in each neighborhood handle a wide range of administrative tasks. For example, residents can obtain various documents or even request university graduation certificates when needed.

I usually visit the district office to obtain a copy of my resident registration certificate. In addition, each district office operates a local community center that provides a variety of educational programs for residents. I also teach English conversation classes there, engaging with a diverse group of people.

Twice a week, I commute to Icheon city to conduct English conversation classes. Meeting new people every quarter is always enjoyable, and I find great fulfillment in sharing my knowledge of English with them.

During my classes, I am often impressed by the enthusiasm of those eager to learn English. Interacting with such a diverse group of people, from older adults to college students, not only allows me to teach but also helps me learn new things, which is always refreshing.

When preparing for English conversation classes, it's important to find materials that suit the learners' skill levels. I prepare a variety of resources such as dialogue scripts and practical expressions for everyday use. This approach makes the learning experience more engaging and

나의 상황에 맞게 내용을 바꾸어서 말해 보세요.

encourages active participation in class.

I also design various activities to encourage learners to communicate naturally in English. For example, through role-plays and group discussions, they practice useful expressions applicable to real-life situations. This method helps them build confidence without worrying about making mistakes.

스피치 메모

필요한 단어와 표현을 정리해 보세요.

TOPIC 39 공영 주차장

키워드와 주요 표현을 활용해서 문장을 말해 보세요.

1. 주차 장소 소개

장소: 평소 주차하는 장소
- 예) There's a small parking lot next to my office that I can use almost every day.
  거의 매일 사용할 수 있는 제 사무실 옆에 작은 주차장이 있어요.

공영 주차장: 공영 주차장을 사용할 때
- 예) I only use public parking spots when I really have no choice.
  정말 어쩔 수 없을 때만 공영 주차장을 이용해요.

키워드 park, small, district office, public, parking lot, choice, full

2. 주차 습관 소개

주차 요금: 주차 요금을 아끼는 방법
- 예) I tend to use free parking spots whenever possible to save on parking fees.
  가능하면 주차 요금을 아끼려 무료 주차장을 이용하는 편이에요.

상황: 공영 주차장 이용이 필요 없는 상황
- 예) Since I'm heading home, I don't need a public parking lot.
  집으로 가는 중이라 공영 주차장이 필요 없어요.

키워드 free, save, drive around, avoid, fee, back, rural, head, home

3. 주차 스트레스 소개

공간 확보: 주차 공간을 찾기 위한 습관
- 예) I try to leave earlier than usual to ensure I find a parking spot.
  주차 공간을 찾을 수 있도록 평소보다 좀 더 일찍 출발하려고 해.

주차 공간: 여유 있게 도착해서 주차 공간 확보
- 예) Arriving early gives me enough time to find a good parking spot.
  일찍 도착하면 좋은 주차 공간을 찾을 수 있는 충분한 시간이 생겨.

키워드 develop, habit, early, find, time, parking spot, ensure, arrive

대화로 연습하기

대화 속에서 문장을 늘려가는 연습을 해 보세요.

A : Parking in downtown Icheon is getting more difficult, right?
이천 시내에서 주차가 점점 더 어려워지고 있지?

B : Yeah, it's hard to find a parking spot. **I usually park near the district office**, but **if it's full, I use a public parking lot and pay**.
응. 주차자리가 찾기 힘들어. 보통 동사무소 근처에 주차하는데, 만약 자리가 없으면 공영 주차장을 이용하고 요금을 내.

A : Have you ever looked for free parking? 무료 주차장을 찾으러 돌아다니기도 해봤어?

B : Of course. **Sometimes, I drive around to avoid the parking fee**. It's less of a concern in the countryside.
물론. 가끔은 주차 요금을 아끼려고 차를 돌리기도 해. 시골에서는 그게 덜 걱정돼.

A : But you can use a public parking lot for free at night, right?
하지만 밤에는 무료로 공영 주차장을 이용할 수 있잖아. 안 그래?

B : I know, but by then, **I'm already on my way back to my rural home**, so I don't need it. 나도 알아. 하지만 그때쯤이면 이미 시골집으로 돌아가는 중이라 필요 없어.

A : I see. So, how do you try to reduce parking stress?
그렇구나. 그럼 주차 스트레스를 줄이려고 어떻게 하고 있어?

B : **I've developed a habit of leaving early**. If I get there a bit earlier, **I have more time to find a parking spot**.
나는 일찍 출발하는 습관을 들였어. 조금 더 일찍 도착하면 주차 공간을 찾는 데 여유가 생겨.

어휘 on one's way back 돌아가는 길에 rural home 시골집

I commute to Icheon city about three days a week for English classes. It takes about 35 minutes by car, but the problem is that parking in downtown Icheon is ①**becoming more and more difficult**. With the increasing number of apartment complexes and more people using cars, ②**the public parking lots are always full**.

저는 일주일에 3일 정도는 영어 수업 때문에 이천시로 출퇴근합니다. 차로 35분 정도 걸리는데, 문제는 이천 시내에서 주차하기가 점점 힘들어진다는 겁니다. 아파트 단지가 늘어나고, 차를 이용하는 사람들도 많아지다 보니 공영 주차장도 항상 차로 가득 차 있습니다.

Because my English classes usually last for two hours, I either use the parking lot near the district office or, if that's not possible, I have to ③**use a public parking lot**, though I have to ④**pay for parking**.

영어 수업은 보통 2시간씩 이어지기 때문에 동사무소 근처 주차장을 이용하거나, 상황이 안 되면 공영 주차장을 이용해야 합니다. 물론 주차 요금도 내야 합니다.

Sometimes, I hesitate to pay the parking fee and ⑤**end up driving around looking for** a free parking spot. While I don't worry much about parking in the countryside, coming to the city often ⑥**leads to parking-related stress**.

가끔은 주차 요금이 아까워서 무료로 주차할 수 있는 곳을 찾아 차를 이곳저곳 돌려야 할 때도 있어요. 시골에 살다 보니 주차 걱정은 하지 않지만, 도시로 오면 항상 주차 문제로 스트레스를 받습니다.

While I can ⑦**park for free** in public parking lots at night, by that time, I'm already ⑧**heading back to** my rural home, so I don't need to use the public parking lots in the evening.

저녁에는 공영 주차장을 무료로 이용할 수 있지만, 그때쯤 되면 퇴근해서 시골집으로 돌아가기 때문에 야간에 공영 주차장을 이용할 필요는 없습니다.

주제별로 구분하여 길게 말하는 연습을 해 보세요.

So, to ⁹**reduce parking stress**, I've developed a habit of leaving early. Arriving a bit earlier gives me more time to ⁱ⁰**find a parking spot** and allows me to prepare for my classes with ease. Of course, it's not always easy to leave early, but I believe it's worth it because I can focus on my classes without worrying about parking.

그래서 저는 주차 스트레스를 줄이기 위해 일찍 출발하는 습관을 들였습니다. 조금 더 일찍 도착하면 주차 공간을 찾는 데 여유가 있고, 수업도 더 여유롭게 준비할 수 있어 도움이 됩니다. 물론, 일찍 출발하는 것이 항상 쉬운 일은 아니지만, 주차 걱정 없이 수업에 집중할 수 있어 그만한 가치가 있다고 생각합니다.

I've heard that Icheon city is working to ⁱⁱ**address the parking problem** by ⁱ²**expanding public parking lots** and adding more roadside parking spaces. Some areas have even introduced a smart parking system that allows drivers to check available spots in real time, so I'm hopeful the parking situation will improve soon.

이천시에서도 공영 주차장을 확장하고 도로변 주차 공간을 더 추가하는 등의 방법으로 주차 문제를 해결하기 위해 노력하고 있다고 들었습니다. 일부 지역에서는 운전자가 실시간으로 빈 주차 공간을 확인할 수 있는 스마트 주차 시스템까지 도입했다고 하니, 앞으로 주차 상황이 나아지길 기대하고 있습니다.

스피치 포인트

① **become more and more difficult** 더욱 더 어려워지게 되다　② **the public parking lots are always full** 공영 주차장들이 항상 만차이다　③ **use a public parking lot** 공영 주차장을 이용하다　④ **pay for parking** 주차 요금을 내다　⑤ **end up driving around looking for** 결국 차를 몰고 다니며 찾게 되다　⑥ **lead to parking-related stress** 주차와 관련된 스트레스를 초래하다　⑦ **park for free** 무료로 주차하다　⑧ **head back to** 되돌아가다　⑨ **reduce parking stress** 주차 스트레스를 줄이다　⑩ **find a parking spot** 주차 공간을 찾다　⑪ **address the parking problem** 주차 문제를 해결하다　⑫ **expand public parking lots** 공영 주차장을 확장하다

I commute to Icheon city about three days a week for English classes. It takes about 35 minutes by car, but the problem is that parking in downtown Icheon is becoming more and more difficult. With the increasing number of apartment complexes and more people using cars, the public parking lots are always full.

Because my English classes usually last for two hours, I either use the parking lot near the district office or, if that's not possible, I have to use a public parking lot, though I have to pay for parking.

Sometimes, I hesitate to pay the parking fee and end up driving around looking for a free parking spot. While I don't worry much about parking in the countryside, coming to the city often leads to parking-related stress.

While I can park for free in public parking lots at night, by that time, I'm already heading back to my rural home, so I don't need to use the public parking lots in the evening.

So, to reduce parking stress, I've developed a habit of leaving early. Arriving a bit earlier gives me more time to find a parking spot and allows me to prepare for my classes with ease. Of course, it's not always easy to leave early, but I believe it's worth it because I can focus on my classes without worrying about parking.

나의 상황에 맞게 내용을 바꾸어서 말해 보세요.

I've heard that Icheon city is working to address the parking problem by expanding public parking lots and adding more roadside parking spaces. Some areas have even introduced a smart parking system that allows drivers to check available spots in real time, so I'm hopeful the parking situation will improve soon.

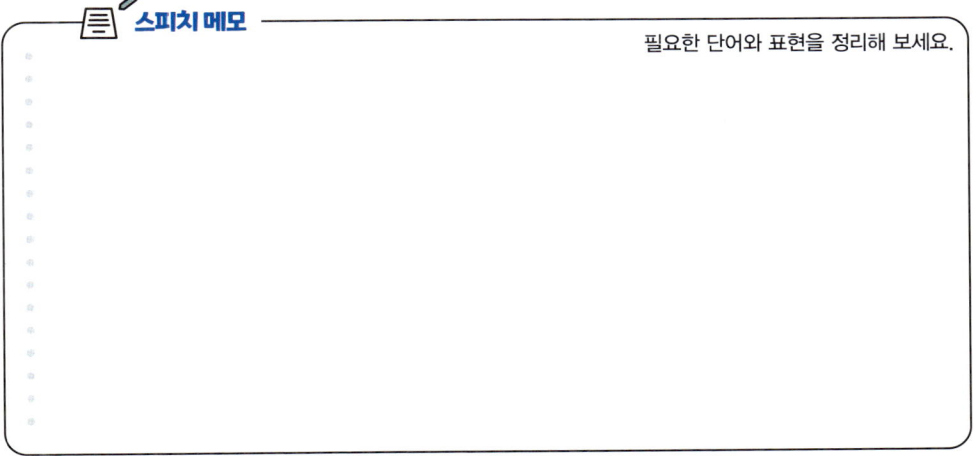

스피치 메모

필요한 단어와 표현을 정리해 보세요.

공립도서관

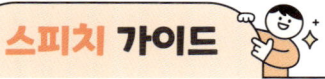

키워드와 주요 표현을 활용해서 문장을 말해 보세요.

1. 공립도서관 소개

방문: 도서관에 가는 목적

예) Sometimes I go to the library to read or use the computer.
가끔은 책을 읽거나 컴퓨터를 사용하려고 도서관에 가.

습관: 도서관에서의 공부 습관

예) I try to go to the library every weekend.
난 주말마다 도서관에 가려고 해.

키워드 read, use, computer, study, great, habit, every weekend

2. 공립도서관에서의 활동 소개

활동: 도서관에서 즐길 수 있는 활동

예) I sometimes join book clubs or writing workshops.
가끔 책모임이나 글쓰기 워크숍에 참여해요.

유혹: 도서관을 더 방문하게 만드는 매력

예) It's hard to resist when the place is so comfortable.
너무 편안해서 자꾸 가고 싶어져요.

키워드 book club, writing, coffee, reading, comfortable, be tempted, visit

3. 공립도서관 프로그램 소개

프로그램: 도서관에서 제공하는 프로그램

예) The library offers language classes, book discussions, and cultural lectures.
도서관은 어학 강좌, 독서 토론, 그리고 문화 강연을 제공해요.

관심: 참여 경험이나 관심 표현

예) I think these programs are a great way to learn and meet people.
이런 프로그램들은 배우고 사람들과 교류하기에 좋은 방법 같아요.

키워드 language, discussion, cultural, English conversation, meet, opportunity

대화로 연습하기 대화 속에서 문장을 늘려가는 연습을 해 보세요.

A : More people seem to **be going to local libraries to study** these days. It's **such a great habit**.

요즘 지역 도서관에 가서 공부하는 사람들이 많아졌어요. 정말 좋은 습관 같아요.

B : Yes, the library has such a calming atmosphere. I heard they've added small cafés, like book cafés.

맞아요. 도서관에 가면 마음이 차분해져요. 최근에 북카페처럼 작은 카페가 생겼다면서요?

A : That's right. It's nice to **enjoy coffee while reading**.

네, 맞아요. 거기서 커피 마시면서 책을 읽을 수 있어서 좋아요.

B : I always check out new books when I visit the library.

저도 도서관에 가면 항상 신간 도서를 빌려요.

A : Me too. The facilities are great, so **I'm tempted to visit more often**.

저도요. 도서관이 제공하는 시설들이 좋아서 꽤 자주 가고 싶어져요.

B : Same here. I think the library is really convenient.

저도 마찬가지예요. 도서관은 정말 편리한 것 같아요.

A : I've noticed **there are more programs at the library, like English conversation groups**. **They seem like great opportunities**.

도서관에서 영어 회화 모임 같은 프로그램들이 많이 생긴 것 같아요. 좋은 기회인 것 같습니다.

B : Yes, the library is not just for reading, but also a great place to connect with others.

맞아요. 도서관은 단지 책을 읽는 곳이 아니라 사람들과 교류할 수 있는 좋은 장소예요.

어휘 calming atmosphere 차분한 분위기 | be tempted to ~하라고 유혹받다

내용 구성하기

Some of the people taking my English classes mentioned that they ① **continue their studies** by visiting local libraries. It's truly a great thing to do, and I admire their dedication to ②**self-improvement**.

제 영어 수업을 듣고 있는 몇몇 분들은 지역 도서관에 가서 공부를 계속한다고 말씀하셨습니다. 이는 정말 훌륭한 일이며, 저는 그들의 자기 계발에 대한 헌신을 존경합니다.

There is ③**a city library operated by** Icheon city, but there are also smaller libraries run by local communities. There is a Cheongmi Library in the countryside where I live, and of course, there is a Gamgok Library, which is just ④**a 5-minute drive** from my home.

이천시에서 운영하는 시립 도서관도 있지만, 지역에서 운영하는 작은 도서관들도 있습니다. 제가 살고 있는 시골에도 청미 도서관이 있어요. 물론 집에서 차로 5분 거리에는 감곡 도서관이 있죠.

When I visit the library, I ⑤**feel a sense of calm** and nostalgia, as if I've returned to my school days. Recently, the library began operating a small café, ⑥**like a book café**. There, I can relax, enjoy a cup of coffee, and read books or newspapers.

도서관에 가면 마음이 차분해지고, 학창 시절로 돌아간 듯한 향수를 느낍니다. 최근에 도서관에서 북카페처럼 작은 카페를 운영하기 시작했어요. 그곳에서 편히 쉬며 커피를 마시고 책이나 신문을 읽을 수 있습니다.

I really appreciate that libraries ⑦**provide various facilities** for local residents. With many new books to read or check out, I often ⑧**visit the local libraries**.

지역 주민들을 위해 도서관에서 다양한 편의 시설을 제공하는 점이 너무 좋습니다. 읽고 빌려갈 수 있는 신간 도서들도 많아서, 저는 자주 지역 도서관을 방문합니다.

주제별로 구분하여 길게 말하는 연습을 해 보세요.

Libraries ⁹**offer more than just reading**. They also host various activities. Some libraries provide programs such as English conversation groups or book discussion meetings. Participating in these programs allows you to connect with new people and ⁱ⁰**expand your learning opportunities**.

도서관은 단순히 책을 읽는 곳이 아닙니다. 다양한 활동도 제공합니다. 일부 도서관에서는 영어 회화 모임이나 독서 토론회와 같은 프로그램을 운영합니다. 이러한 프로그램에 참여하면 새로운 사람들과 교류하고 배움의 기회를 넓힐 수 있습니다.

I've led an English conversation group at the library. People ⁱⁱ**from various age groups and backgrounds** actively participated, engaging in conversations with enthusiasm. Watching participants grow in confidence and improve their English skills ⁱ²**was incredibly rewarding**. Experiences like this remind me that libraries are valuable spaces for learning and connection.

저는 도서관에서 영어 회화 모임을 진행한 적이 있습니다. 다양한 연령대와 배경을 가진 사람들이 적극적으로 참여하여 열정적으로 대화에 임했습니다. 참가자들이 자신감을 얻고 영어 실력이 향상되는 모습을 지켜보는 것은 정말 보람 있었습니다. 이런 경험은 도서관이 배움과 교류의 소중한 공간임을 다시 한 번 일깨워줍니다.

스피치 포인트

① **continue one's studies** 자신의 공부를 계속하다 ② **self-improvement** 자기 개발 ③ **a city library operated by** ~에 의해 운영되는 시립 도서관 ④ **a 5-minute drive** 차로 5분 거리 ⑤ **feel a sense of calm** 차분함을 느끼다 ⑥ **like a book café** 북카페처럼 ⑦ **provide various facilities** 다양한 시설들을 제공하다 ⑧ **visit the local libraries** 지역 도서관들을 방문하다 ⑨ **offer more than just reading** 단순히 독서만 제공하는 것이 아니다 ⑩ **expand one's learning opportunities** 자신의 배움의 기회를 넓히다 ⑪ **from various age groups and backgrounds** 다양한 연령대와 배경을 가진 ⑫ **be incredibly rewarding** 매우 보람 있다

Some of the people taking my English classes mentioned that they continue their studies by visiting local libraries. It's truly a great thing to do, and I admire their dedication to self-improvement.

There is a city library operated by Icheon city, but there are also smaller libraries run by local communities. There is a Cheongmi Library in the countryside where I live, and of course, there is a Gamgok Library, which is just a 5-minute drive from my home.

When I visit the library, I feel a sense of calm and nostalgia, as if I've returned to my school days. Recently, the library began operating a small café, like a book café. There, I can relax, enjoy a cup of coffee, and read books or newspapers.

I really appreciate that libraries provide various facilities for local residents. With many new books to read or check out, I often visit the local libraries.

Libraries offer more than just reading. They also host various activities. Some libraries provide programs such as English conversation groups or book discussion meetings. Participating in these programs allows you to connect with new people and expand your learning opportunities.

I've led an English conversation group at the library. People from various age groups and backgrounds actively participated, engaging

나의 상황에 맞게 내용을 바꾸어서 말해 보세요.

in conversations with enthusiasm. Watching participants grow in confidence and improve their English skills was incredibly rewarding. Experiences like this remind me that libraries are valuable spaces for learning and connection.

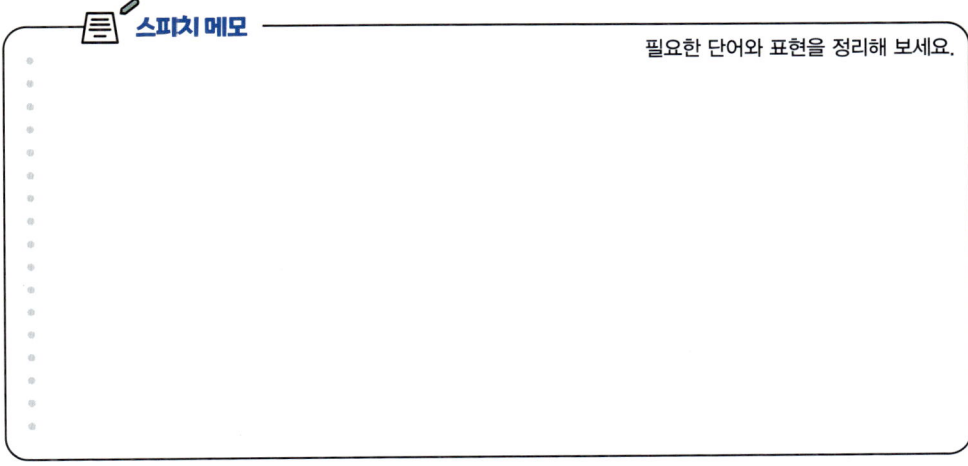

필요한 단어와 표현을 정리해 보세요.

PART 08 Review Quiz

1 자신의 새 주소를 등록하다
　　　_____ one's new address

2 문화 행사들을 개최하다
　　　host _____ events

3 시민들의 생활수준을 향상시키다
　　　improve citizens' _____ of life

4 거의 편지를 보내지 않는다
　　　hardly _____ send letters

5 국내 및 국제 소포를 처리하다
　　　_____ domestic or international parcels

6 우체국에서 은행 업무를 처리하다
　　　do _____ at the post office

7 다양한 범위를 다루다
　　　handle a wide _____ of

8 영어 회화 수업을 진행하다
　　　_____ English conversation classes

배운 영어 표현들을 복습해 보세요.

9 학습자들의 수준에 맞다

_____ the learners' skill levels

10 공영 주차장을 이용하다

use a public parking _____

11 무료로 주차하다

park for _____

12 주차 문제를 해결하다

_____ the parking problem

13 자신의 공부를 계속하다

_____ one's studies

14 차분함을 느끼다

feel a sense of _____

15 매우 보람 있다

be _____ rewarding

정답 01 register 02 cultural 03 quality 04 ever 05 handle 06 banking 07 range 08 conduct
       09 suit 10 lot 11 free 12 address 13 continue 14 calm 15 incredibly

PART 09
건강과 질병

TOPIC 41 운동
TOPIC 42 건강
TOPIC 43 안과
TOPIC 44 치과
TOPIC 45 다이어트

TOPIC 41 운동

스피치 가이드

키워드와 주요 표현을 활용해서 문장을 말해 보세요.

1. 운동 습관, 패턴 소개

습관: 평소에 헬스장을 가는 횟수
- 예) I try to work out at the gym every other day.
  저는 이틀에 한 번씩 헬스장에서 운동하려고 노력해요.

패턴: 헬스장에서 하는 운동 종류
- 예) I usually lift weights and then run on the treadmill for half an hour.
  저는 보통 근력 운동을 하고 나서 러닝머신에서 30분 정도 달려요.

키워드 three, a week, every other day, lift weights, treadmill, strength training

2. 운동 상태, 효과 소개

상태: 현재 운동 상태
- 예) These days, I can enjoy my workout at the gym without any stress.
  요즘에는 헬스장에서 운동을 스트레스 없이 즐길 수 있어.

효과: 운동을 통해서 얻는 효과
- 예) Regular exercise has improved my sleep and reduced stress.
  규칙적인 운동은 내 수면의 질을 높여주었고 그리고 스트레스를 줄여줬어.

키워드 workout, stress, enjoy, comfortably, improve, reduce, healthier, happier

3. 운동 장소, 기분 소개

장소: 보통 바쁜 날에 운동하는 곳
- 예) On busy days, I go for a quick walk near my office.
  바쁜 날에는 제 사무실 근처에서 짧게 산책해요.

기분: 운동할 때 느끼는 기분
- 예) Even a short workout makes me feel more energized.
  짧은 운동이라도 저를 더 에너지가 넘치게 만들어줘요.

키워드 office, lake, brisk, walk, energized, lighter, refreshed

 **대화로 연습하기** 대화 속에서 문장을 늘려가는 연습을 해 보세요.

A : Hey, Sam! What do you usually do to stay healthy?
이봐, 쌤! 건강을 유지하려고 보통 뭐 해?

B : **I go to the gym about three times a week. I do strength training and run on the treadmill** for an hour.
난 일주일에 세 번 정도 헬스장에 가. 근력 운동을 하고, 러닝머신에서 한 시간 동안 뛰어.

A : That sounds great! Do you enjoy it? 멋지다! 그거 재미있어?

B : At first, it was a bit challenging, but **now I enjoy working out comfortably**.
처음엔 좀 힘들었는데, 이제는 편하게 운동하는 게 즐거워.

A : What if you're too busy to go to the gym? 너무 바빠서 헬스장에 못 가면 어떻게 해?

B : **On busy days, I just take a brisk walk around the lake** near my neighborhood. It's a great way to **feel lighter and refreshed**.
바쁜 날에는 그냥 동네에 있는 호수 주변을 빠르게 걸어. 좀 더 가볍고 상쾌한 기분을 느낄 수 있는 좋은 방법이야.

A : Sounds like you've built a solid routine. What keeps you motivated?
꽤 탄탄한 루틴을 세운 것 같아. 무엇이 널 계속 움직이게 해?

B : Well, **working out makes me feel healthier and happier**. That's what keeps me going.
글쎄, 운동을 하면 더 건강하고 행복하게 느껴져. 그게 내가 운동을 계속하는 이유야.

어휘 refreshed (기분이) 상쾌한 solid 탄탄한 keep ~ motivated 계속 의욕을 갖게 하다

As I get older, I feel like I'm ①**gaining weight**, so I started ②**working out at the gym** a few days ago. At first, it was a bit challenging to get used to the exercises, but now I enjoy working out comfortably.

나이가 들어가면서 점점 살이 찌는 느낌이 들어 며칠 전부터 헬스장에서 운동을 시작했습니다. 처음에는 운동에 적응하는 데 조금 힘들었지만, 이제는 편하게 운동을 즐기고 있습니다.

There's a gym near my house, so I try to work out about ③**three times a week**. I do strength training and ④**run on the treadmill** for an hour. After working out, I head home, take a shower, and then enjoy my favorite coffee while listening to music.

집 근처에 헬스장이 있어 가급적 일주일에 세 번 정도 운동하려고 합니다. 근력 운동도 하고 러닝머신 위에서 1시간 동안 달리기도 합니다. 운동 후에는 집에 돌아와 샤워를 하고 그리고 나서 음악 들으며 제가 좋아하는 커피를 마십니다.

However, sometimes when I don't have time to work out ⑤**because of a busy schedule**, I simply ⑥**take a brisk walk** around the lake near my neighborhood. After walking for over 30 minutes, I start to feel much lighter.

하지만 때때로 바쁜 일정을 이유로 운동할 시간이 없으면 그냥 동네 근처에 있는 호수 주위를 빠른 걸음으로 걷습니다. 30분 이상 걷고 나면 마음이 한결 가벼워지는 느낌이 듭니다.

For me, exercising is ⑦**a must-do routine**. If I don't work out, I feel uncomfortable ⑧**throughout the day**, so I make sure to find time for it. But, as with everything, it's not always easy.

저에게 운동은 반드시 해야 하는 일과입니다. 운동을 하지 않으면 하루 종일 불편한 느낌이 들기 때문에 반드시 시간을 내서 운동하려고 합니다. 하지만 모든 일이 그렇듯 그게 항상 쉬운 일은 아닙니다.

주제별로 구분하여 길게 말하는 연습을 해 보세요.

When I exercise, I feel like not only my body but also my mind becomes healthier. Especially after feeling stressed, working out helps clear my mind and ⁹**significantly improves my mood**. Thanks to this, my cluttered thoughts become more organized, and I ¹⁰**develop a more positive mindset**.

운동을 하면 몸뿐만 아니라 마음도 건강해지는 것 같습니다. 특히 스트레스를 많이 받았을 때 운동을 하면 머리가 맑아지고 기분이 한층 좋아집니다. 덕분에 복잡했던 생각들이 정리되고 더 긍정적인 마음가짐을 갖게 됩니다.

Experiencing these positive changes through exercise has motivated me to ¹¹**keep it up consistently**. I want to continue exercising to live a healthier and more energetic life. Thanks to the energy I ¹²**gain from working out**, I feel I can approach my daily life with greater enthusiasm.

운동을 통해 이런 긍정적인 변화를 경험하면서 꾸준히 운동을 해야겠다는 동기를 갖게 되었습니다. 더 건강하고 활기찬 삶을 살기 위해 앞으로도 운동을 계속하고 싶습니다. 운동을 통해 얻는 에너지 덕분에 일상생활에서도 더 큰 열정을 가지고 생활할 수 있을 것 같습니다.

스피치 포인트

① **gain weight** 살찌다　② **work out at the gym** 헬스장에서 운동하다　③ **three times a week** 일주일에 세 번　④ **run on the treadmill** 러닝머신에서 달리다　⑤ **because of a busy schedule** 바쁜 일정 때문에　⑥ **take a brisk walk** 빠르게 걷다, 활기차게 걷다　⑦ **a must-do routine** 반드시 해야 하는 일과　⑧ **throughout the day** 하루 종일　⑨ **significantly improve one's mood** 자신의 기분을 크게 개선하다　⑩ **develop a more positive mindset** 더 긍정적인 사고방식을 기르다　⑪ **keep it up consistently** 지속적으로 계속하다　⑫ **gain from working out** 운동으로부터 얻다

As I get older, I feel like I'm gaining weight, so I started working out at the gym a few days ago. At first, it was a bit challenging to get used to the exercises, but now I enjoy working out comfortably.

There's a gym near my house, so I try to work out about three times a week. I do strength training and run on the treadmill for an hour. After working out, I head home, take a shower, and then enjoy my favorite coffee while listening to music.

However, sometimes when I don't have time to work out because of a busy schedule, I simply take a brisk walk around the lake near my neighborhood. After walking for over 30 minutes, I start to feel much lighter.

For me, exercising is a must-do routine. If I don't work out, I feel uncomfortable throughout the day, so I make sure to find time for it. But, as with everything, it's not always easy.

When I exercise, I feel like not only my body but also my mind becomes healthier. Especially after feeling stressed, working out helps clear my mind and significantly improves my mood. Thanks to this, my cluttered thoughts become more organized, and I develop a more positive mindset. Experiencing these positive changes through exercise has motivated me to keep it up consistently. I want to continue exercising to live a healthier

나의 상황에 맞게 내용을 바꾸어서 말해 보세요.

and more energetic life. Thanks to the energy I gain from working out, I feel I can approach my daily life with greater enthusiasm.

필요한 단어와 표현을 정리해 보세요.

TOPIC 42 건강

스피치 가이드

키워드와 주요 표현을 활용해서 문장을 말해 보세요.

1. 건강 유지 소개

방법: 건강을 지키기 위한 개인적인 방법
- 예) I try to stay active by walking every day and eating a balanced diet.
  나는 매일 걷고 균형 잡힌 식사를 해서 활동적이려고 노력해.

목적: 건강을 유지하는 목적과 목표
- 예) My goal is to stay healthy and avoid diseases by following a good routine.
  내 목표는 좋은 일정을 따라 질병을 피하면서 건강을 유지하는 거야.

키워드 avoid, alcohol, cigarette, walk, eat, less, healthy, follow

2. 건강을 위한 노력 소개

노력: 건강을 유지하기 위한 노력
- 예) I'm making an effort to exercise regularly and get enough sleep every night.
  저는 규칙적으로 운동하고 매일 충분히 자려고 노력하고 있어요.

계획: 생활 습관 개선을 위한 계획
- 예) I plan to cut down on junk food to improve my health.
  건강을 개선하기 위해 정크푸드를 줄일 계획이에요.

키워드 exercise, regularly, eat, less, belly, fat, cut down on, change, habit

3. 건강을 위한 습관 소개

습관: 꾸준한 습관을 통한 건강 향상
- 예) I have made a habit of stretching every morning, and it really helps my flexibility.
  매일 아침 스트레칭을 하는 습관을 들였는데, 그게 제 유연성에 정말 도움이 돼요.

변화: 일상적인 습관의 변화와 긍정적인 결과
- 예) Since I started drinking more water, I feel more energetic and less tired.
  물 마시는 양을 늘린 이후로 저는 더 에너지가 넘치고 덜 피곤해요

키워드 stretch, flexibility, consistently, practice, water, feel, energetic, healthier

대화로 연습하기
대화 속에서 문장을 늘려가는 연습을 해 보세요.

A : These days, I'm trying to **avoid alcohol and cigarettes and eat less to stay healthy**. 요즘 건강을 위해 술, 담배를 피하고 음식을 적게 먹으려고 해요.

B : Same here. As I get older, I feel like my body isn't what it used to be. 저도요. 나이가 들수록 몸이 예전 같지 않더라고요.

A : Exactly. **By eating less, I've lost some belly fat**, and it feels great. 맞아요. 먹는 양을 줄이니 뱃살도 빠지고 기분이 좋아요.

B : They say, "Losing your health is like losing everything." I completely agree. 건강을 잃으면 모든 걸 잃는다는 말이 있잖아요. 정말 공감해요.

A : That's why I'm trying to **exercise and change my lifestyle habits**. 그래서 운동도 하고 생활 습관을 바꾸려고 노력 중이에요.

B : Absolutely. It's so important to take care of your health while you still have it. 맞아요. 건강할 때 잘 지키는 게 정말 중요하죠.

A : So, **I've been consistently practicing small habits**, and **I'm starting to feel healthier**. 그래서 꾸준히 작은 습관들을 실천하고 있어요. 점점 더 건강해지는 느낌이 들어요.

B : That's true. I can feel that small efforts are adding up and creating big changes. 정말 그렇죠. 작은 노력들이 쌓여서 큰 변화를 만든다는 걸 느낄 수 있어요.

어휘 consistently 꾸준히 add up 점차적으로 쌓이다

Everyone acknowledges that health is ①**the most important thing**. However, maintaining good health is not as easy as it sounds. These days, I am trying to eat smaller portions to ②**stay healthy**. I avoid alcohol and cigarettes and try not to eat late-night snacks as much as possible.

건강이 제일 중요하다는 사실은 누구나 인정합니다. 하지만 건강을 유지하는 것은 말처럼 쉽지 않습니다. 요즘 저는 건강을 위해 식사량을 줄이려고 노력하고 있습니다. 술과 담배는 멀리하고, 야식도 되도록 피하려고 합니다.

As I get older, I often feel that my body isn't what it used to be. I ③**get tired more easily** and seem to need more sleep. However, since I started eating less, I've noticed ④**a significant decrease in belly fat**, which makes me feel great.

나이가 들면서 몸이 예전 같지 않다는 것을 자주 느낍니다. 쉽게 피곤해지고 잠도 많아진 것 같습니다. 하지만 식사량을 줄이기 시작한 후부터 뱃살이 많이 줄어든 것을 느꼈고, 덕분에 기분이 좋아졌습니다.

I know very well that I need to exercise and ⑤**change my lifestyle habits** to stay healthy. People often say, "Losing your health is like losing everything." I ⑥**completely agree with** this sentiment.

건강을 위해 운동을 해야 하고 생활 습관도 바꿔야 한다는 것을 잘 알고 있습니다. "건강을 잃으면 모든 것을 잃는 것과 같다"는 말을 흔히들 하죠. 저도 이 말에 깊이 공감합니다.

It's crucial to ⑦**maintain your health** while you still have it. Once you ⑧**lose your health**, even the simplest things feel bothersome, and you truly come to realize just how valuable it is.

건강할 때 건강을 지키는 것이 정말 중요합니다. 건강을 잃으면 작은 일조차 귀찮게 느껴지고, 건강의 소중함을 뼈저리게 깨닫게 되니까요.

주제별로 구분하여 길게 말하는 연습을 해 보세요.

To maintain good health, it's important to ⁹**stick to** even small, **healthy habits** consistently. By exercising regularly and eating a balanced diet, I can start to ¹⁰**notice positive changes** in my body, which greatly benefit my overall well-being.

건강을 유지하려면 작은 건강 습관이라도 꾸준히 실천하는 것이 중요합니다. 규칙적으로 운동하고 균형 잡힌 식사를 하면 제 몸에서 긍정적인 변화를 느낄 수 있으며, 이는 전반적인 건강에 크게 도움이 됩니다.

As these efforts accumulate, I come to ¹¹**realize the true value** of maintaining good health. With continued effort, I've gradually started to feel my body improving and my energy increasing. Fatigue decreases, and I ¹²**begin to feel refreshed**, which enhances my daily life.

이러한 노력이 쌓이면서 저는 건강을 유지하는 것의 진정한 가치를 깨닫게 됩니다. 지속적인 노력 덕분에 제 몸이 점차 좋아지고 에너지가 증가하는 것을 느끼기 시작했습니다. 피로는 줄어들고, 상쾌함을 느끼기 시작하며, 이는 제 일상생활을 더욱 활기차게 만들어 줍니다.

스피치 포인트

① the most important thingt 가장 중요한 것은 ② stay healthy 건강을 유지하다 ③ get tired more easily 더 쉽게 피곤해지다 ④ a significant decrease in belly fat 뱃살의 현저한 감소 ⑤ change one's lifestyle habits 자신의 생활 습관을 바꾸다 ⑥ completely agree with 완전히 공감하다, 완전히 동의하다 ⑦ maintain one's health 자신의 건강을 유지하다 ⑧ lose one's health 자신의 건강을 잃다 ⑨ stick to healthy habits 건강한 습관을 유지하다 ⑩ notice positive changes 긍정적인 변화를 알아차리다 ⑪ realize the true value 진정한 가치를 깨닫다 ⑫ begin to feel refreshed 개운해지기 시작하다

Everyone acknowledges that health is the most important thing. However, maintaining good health is not as easy as it sounds. These days, I am trying to eat smaller portions to stay healthy. I avoid alcohol and cigarettes and try not to eat late-night snacks as much as possible.

As I get older, I often feel that my body isn't what it used to be. I get tired more easily and seem to need more sleep. However, since I started eating less, I've noticed a significant decrease in belly fat, which makes me feel great.

I know very well that I need to exercise and change my lifestyle habits to stay healthy. People often say, "Losing your health is like losing everything." I completely agree with this sentiment.

It's crucial to maintain your health while you still have it. Once you lose your health, even the simplest things feel bothersome, and you truly come to realize just how valuable it is.

To maintain good health, it's important to stick to even small, healthy habits consistently. By exercising regularly and eating a balanced diet, I can start to notice positive changes in my body, which greatly benefit my overall well-being.

As these efforts accumulate, I come to realize the true value of maintaining good health. With continued effort, I've gradually started

나의 상황에 맞게 내용을 바꾸어서 말해 보세요.

to feel my body improving and my energy increasing. Fatigue decreases, and I begin to feel refreshed, which enhances my daily life.

스피치 메모

필요한 단어와 표현을 정리해 보세요.

TOPIC 43 안과

스피치 가이드

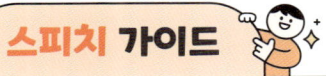

키워드와 주요 표현을 활용해서 문장을 말해 보세요.

1. 안경 착용 소개

착용: 안경을 착용하게 된 시기
- 예) I started wearing glasses in high school because my vision got worse.
  고등학교 때 시력이 나빠져서 안경을 쓰기 시작했어.

의미: 자신에게 안경이란 어떤 의미
- 예) Now, glasses are part of my daily routine and my style.
  이제 안경은 내 일상과 스타일의 일부야.

키워드 wear, glasses, high school, middle school, part, daily routine, style

2. 눈 관리 습관 소개

불편함: 눈과 관련된 불편함 말하기
- 예) My eyes get really tired after using the computer for a long time.
  컴퓨터를 오래 쓰면 눈이 정말 피곤해져요.

관리: 눈을 관리하는 자신만의 비법
- 예) I try to blink more often and use artificial tears.
  저는 자주 깜빡이려고 하고 인공눈물을 사용해요.

키워드 tired, computer, blurry, red, rest, far away, blink, artificial tears

3. 눈 건강 소개

중요성: 왜 눈 건강이 중요한지 설명
- 예) Good eyesight is essential for studying, working, and everyday life.
  좋은 시력은 공부, 일, 일상생활에 꼭 필요해요.

방법: 눈 건강을 지키는 방법
- 예) It's important to check my eyesight regularly to maintain good eye health.
  좋은 눈 건강을 유지하기 위해 정기적으로 시력을 체크하는 것이 중요해요.

키워드 essential, important, studying, maintain, eye health, check-up, regularly

대화로 연습하기

대화 속에서 문장을 늘려가는 연습을 해 보세요.

A : **I've been wearing glasses since middle school**, and **they've become a part of me**.
중학교 때부터 안경을 써왔고, 이제는 내 일부처럼 느껴져.

B : I know what you mean. My eyes get easily tired from looking at my smartphone screen all day.
무슨 말인지 알아. 하루 종일 스마트폰 화면을 봐서 눈이 쉽게 피곤해져.

A : Sometimes **my vision gets blurry, and my eyes get red**.
가끔 시야가 흐릿해지고, 눈이 빨갛게 돼.

B : I'm trying to reduce my smartphone use, but it's not easy.
스마트폰 사용을 줄이려고 하는데, 쉽지 않아.

A : For me, I **rest my eyes or look at something far away** for a while.
내 경우에는 눈을 쉬게 하거나 멀리 있는 것을 잠시 동안 봐.

B : That's a good idea. 좋은 생각이네.

A : **To maintain good eye health, healthy lifestyle habits and regular check-ups are important**.
좋은 눈 건강을 유지하려면, 건강한 생활 습관과 정기적인 검진이 중요해.

B : You're right. I think I need to pay more attention to my eye health. 맞아. 눈 건강에 더 신경 써야겠어.

어휘 pay attention to ~에 집중하다, ~에 신경을 쓰다

내용 구성하기

I've been ①**wearing glasses** since middle school, and now they've become a part of my body. These days, I do a lot of writing on the computer, so my eyes get tired easily and sometimes ②**get bloodshot**. Occasionally, my vision also becomes blurry.

저는 중학교 때부터 안경을 썼고, 이제 안경은 제 몸의 일부분이 되어버렸습니다. 요즘은 컴퓨터로 글을 많이 쓰다 보니 눈이 쉽게 피로해지고, 가끔 충혈이 됩니다. 때때로 시야가 흐려지기도 합니다.

As I get older, I can feel that my eyesight isn't what it used to be. There is only one eye clinic in my neighborhood, so I go there for simple eye tests or to ③**address common eye issues**. However, for more thorough examinations, I ④**visit an eye hospital** in Chungju or a university hospital.

나이가 들수록 제 눈이 예전 같지 않다는 걸 느낍니다. 우리 동네에는 안과가 하나밖에 없어서, 간단한 시력 검사나 흔한 안과 문제는 그곳에서 해결합니다. 하지만 더 정밀한 검사를 받으려면 충주에 있는 안과 병원이나 대학 병원을 방문합니다.

As the saying goes, "Good eyesight is as valuable as the body itself." I believe that ⑤**having good eyesight** is truly a blessing. Lately, I've been trying to ⑥**cut down on my smartphone use**.

"좋은 눈은 몸만큼 귀하다"는 말이 있듯이, 좋은 시력을 갖는 것은 정말 축복이라고 생각합니다. 최근에는 스마트폰 사용을 줄이려고 노력하고 있었습니다.

When ⑦**my eyes feel tired**, I just close them and rest for a while, or I look at a distant mountain to relieve the strain. I also think it's important to regularly ⑧**visit the eye clinic for checkups**.

눈이 피곤할 때는 그저 잠시 눈을 감고 쉬거나, 먼 산을 바라보며 눈의 피로를 풀려고 합니다. 또한, 정기적으로 안과에 가서 검사를 받는 것이 중요하다고 생각합니다.

주제별로 구분하여 길게 말하는 연습을 해 보세요.

To [9]**maintain healthy eyes**, I believe lifestyle habits are also important. I try to eat a balanced diet and consume foods rich in eye-friendly vitamins. I also adjust the indoor lighting to [10]**ease eye strain**.

건강한 눈을 유지하기 위해서는 생활 습관도 중요하다고 생각합니다. 저는 균형 잡힌 식사를 하고, 눈에 좋은 비타민이 풍부한 음식을 섭취하려고 노력합니다. 또한, 실내조명을 조절하여 눈의 피로를 줄이려고 합니다.

Above all, the most important thing is to cherish and consistently [11]**care for eye health**. Since it's difficult to [12]**regain vision** once it gets worse, I believe prevention and maintenance are the best approaches.

무엇보다 중요한 것은 눈의 건강을 소중히 여기고 꾸준히 관리하는 것입니다. 눈은 한 번 나빠지면 회복하기 어려우므로, 미리 예방하고 관리하는 것이 최선이라고 생각합니다.

스피치 포인트

① **wear glasses** 안경을 쓰다 ② **get bloodshot** 충혈되다 ③ **address common eye issues** 일반적인 눈 문제를 해결하다 ④ **visit an eye hospital** 안과 병원에 방문하다 ⑤ **have good eyesight** 좋은 시력을 가지다 ⑥ **cut down on one's smartphone use** 자신의 스마트폰 사용을 줄이다 ⑦ **one's eyes feel tired** 자신의 눈이 피로하다 ⑧ **visit the eye clinic for checkups** 검진을 위해 안과를 방문하다 ⑨ **maintain healthy eyes** 건강한 눈을 유지하다 ⑩ **ease eye strain** 눈의 피로를 줄이다 ⑪ **care for eye health** 눈 건강을 관리하다 ⑫ **regain vision** 시력을 회복하다

I've been wearing glasses since middle school, and now they've become a part of my body. These days, I do a lot of writing on the computer, so my eyes get tired easily and sometimes get bloodshot. Occasionally, my vision also becomes blurry.

As I get older, I can feel that my eyesight isn't what it used to be. There is only one eye clinic in my neighborhood, so I go there for simple eye tests or to address common eye issues. However, for more thorough examinations, I visit an eye hospital in Chungju or a university hospital.

As the saying goes, "Good eyesight is as valuable as the body itself." I believe that having good eyesight is truly a blessing. Lately, I've been trying to cut down on my smartphone use.

When my eyes feel tired, I just close them and rest for a while, or I look at a distant mountain to relieve the strain. I also think it's important to regularly visit the eye clinic for checkups.

To maintain healthy eyes, I believe lifestyle habits are also important. I try to eat a balanced diet and consume foods rich in eye-friendly vitamins. I also adjust the indoor lighting to ease eye strain.

나의 상황에 맞게 내용을 바꾸어서 말해 보세요.

Above all, the most important thing is to cherish and consistently care for eye health. Since it's difficult to regain vision once it gets worse, I believe prevention and maintenance are the best approaches.

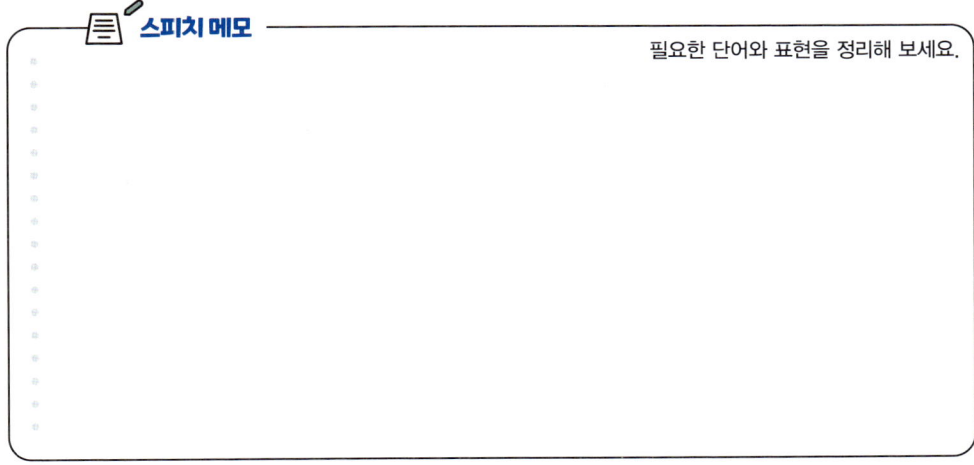

TOPIC 44 치과

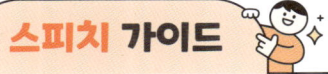

키워드와 주요 표현을 활용해서 문장을 말해 보세요.

1. 치과 방문 경험 소개

방문: 치과를 얼마나 자주 방문하는지
- 예) I go to the dentist twice a year for regular check-ups.
  나는 정기 검진을 위해 1년에 두 번 치과에 가.

목적: 치과에 가는 이유나 목적
- 예) I usually go to the dentist for cleanings and to check for cavities.
  보통 스케일링이나 충치 검사를 위해 치과에 가.

키워드 twice, a year, dentist, take good care of, cleaning, cavity

2. 치아 상태 소개

후회: 예전 치아 관리에 대한 아쉬움
- 예) I regret not flossing regularly when I was in my twenties.
  20대였을 때 치실을 꾸준히 사용하지 않은 걸 후회해요.

시절: 치아 관리를 소홀히 했던 시기
- 예) Back in college, I ate too many snacks and skipped brushing sometimes.
  대학교 때는 간식을 너무 많이 먹고 양치도 가끔 빼먹었어요.

키워드 regret, floss, twenties, younger, in college, take better care of

3. 치아 관리 방법 소개

양치질: 하루에 몇 번 양치질을 하는지
- 예) I try to brush my teeth three times a day, after every meal.
  저는 하루 세 번, 매 식사 후에 양치질하려고 해요.

상황: 양치질을 못할 경우에는 어떻게 대처하는지
- 예) If I can't brush after lunch, I use mouthwash or chew gum.
  점심 먹고 양치 못할 땐 가글을 하거나 껌을 씹어요.

키워드 brush, teeth, three, day, mouthwash, gum, use, lunch

 **대화로 연습하기** 대화 속에서 문장을 늘려가는 연습을 해 보세요.

A : **I visit the dentist twice a year** to keep my teeth healthy.
내 치아를 건강하게 유지하려고 일 년에 두 번 치과를 방문해.

B : I get scaling every six months too. 나도 6개월마다 스케일링을 받아.

A : **I regret not taking better care of my teeth when I was younger.** 어렸을 때 치아를 더 잘 관리하지 못한 게 후회가 돼.

B : I feel the same way. 나도 같은 기분이야.

A : **I brush three times a day** and **use gum or mouthwash if I can't after lunch**.
나는 하루에 세 번 양치질하고 점심 후 혹시 양치할 수 없으면 껌이나 구강 청결제를 사용해.

B : For me, I try to use interdental brushes or floss to clean between my teeth.
내 경우에는 치간 칫솔이나 치실을 사용하여 치아 사이를 깨끗하게 하려고 해.

A : So, we need to visit the dentist regularly and **take good care of our teeth**.
그래서 우리는 정기적으로 치과에 가고 치아를 잘 관리해야 해.

B : That's right, because dental health greatly affects overall health too. 맞아. 치아 건강이 전체적인 건강에도 큰 영향을 미치니까.

어휘 take good care of ~을 잘 돌보다, ~을 잘 관리하다 affect overall health 전체적인 건강에 영향을 주다

내용 구성하기

There are an unusually large number of dental clinics in the rural area where I live. ①**After some thought**, I realized it's probably because there are more elderly people here than younger ones. Since they've been using their teeth for a long time, their ②**dental health** may not be as good as it once was.

제가 사는 시골에는 유난히 치과가 많습니다. 곰곰이 생각해 보니, 젊은 사람들보다는 어르신들이 더 많이 살고 계시고, 오랫동안 치아를 사용하다 보니 치아 상태가 예전만큼 좋지 않은 경우가 많아서 그런 것 같습니다.

I make sure to ③**visit the dentist** twice a year. Knowing the importance of dental health, I try to ④**take good care of my teeth**. I often regret not managing them better when I was younger, and it's a thought that has crossed my mind more than once.

저는 일 년에 두 번은 꼭 치과를 방문합니다. 치아의 소중함을 알기에 열심히 관리하려고 노력하고 있습니다. 젊었을 때 치아들을 더 잘 관리하지 못한 것을 자주 후회하며, 이런 생각이 여러 번 떠오르곤 했습니다.

When I visit the dentist, I have tartar that has built up over time removed, treat any gum issues, and ⑤**address cavities** if they're found. I make it a priority to ⑥**get scaling done every six months**.

치과에 가면, 오랫동안 쌓였던 치석을 제거하고, 잇몸 문제가 있으면 치료하며, 충치가 발견되면 바로 치료를 합니다. 저는 6개월에 한 번씩 스케일링을 받는 것을 우선시합니다.

I ⑦**brush my teeth** three times a day. If I'm in a situation where I can't brush after lunch, I chew gum or use mouthwash to freshen my mouth. When brushing, I ⑧**use interdental brushes or dental floss** to remove food particles stuck between my teeth. Since I know how precious my teeth are, I continue to take diligent care of them every day.

저는 하루에 세 번 양치질을 합니다. 점심 식사 후 양치질을 할 수 없는 상황에 처하면 껌을 씹거나 구강 청결제를 사용하여 입안을 상쾌하게 합니다. 양치질을 할 때는 치간 칫솔이나 치실을 사용하여 치아 사이에 낀 음식물을 제거합니다. 치아의 소중함을 알기에 매일 꾸준히 치아 관리를 열심히 하고 있습니다.

주제별로 구분하여 길게 말하는 연습을 해 보세요.

⁹**Going to the dentist** often can be annoying sometimes, but I know it helps ¹⁰**prevent big problems later on**, so I keep going. Thanks to the treatments, I haven't had any major issues, and no more discomfort. Dental care has just become part of my routine, so I can live without worrying about it.

치과에 자주 가는 것이 때때로 귀찮을 수 있지만, 나중에 큰 문제가 생기지 않도록 도와준다는 것을 알기 때문에 계속 가고 있습니다. 치료 덕분에 이제 큰 문제도 없고, 불편함도 사라졌습니다. 치아 관리는 이제 제 일상적인 루틴의 일부가 되었으며, 걱정 없이 지낼 수 있습니다.

Dental health isn't just for looks. It's actually really ¹¹**important for overall health**. I've been realizing more and more that I need to visit the dentist often and take care of my teeth. ¹²**When my teeth are healthy**, digestion works better, and I can take care of my overall health too.

치아 건강은 단지 외모를 위한 것이 아닙니다. 사실, 전체적인 건강에 정말 중요합니다. 저는 치과를 자주 방문하고 치아를 잘 관리해야 한다는 것을 점점 더 깨닫고 있었습니다. 치아가 건강하면 소화가 더 잘 되고, 전체적인 건강도 챙길 수 있습니다.

스피치 포인트

① after some thought 곰곰이 생각한 후, 잠시 생각한 후 ② dental health 치아 건강 ③ visit the dentist 치과를 방문하다 ④ take good care of one's teeth 자신의 치아를 잘 관리하다 ⑤ address cavities 충치를 치료하다 ⑥ get scaling done every six months 6개월마다 스케일링을 받다 ⑦ brush one's teeth 양치질하다 ⑧ use interdental brushes or dental floss 치간 칫솔이나 치실을 사용하다 ⑨ go to the dentist 치과에 가다 ⑩ prevent big problems later on 나중에 큰 문제를 예방하다 ⑪ important for overall health 전체적인 건강에 중요한 ⑫ when one's teeth are healthy 자신의 치아가 건강할 때

There are an unusually large number of dental clinics in the rural area where I live. After some thought, I realized it's probably because there are more elderly people here than younger ones. Since they've been using their teeth for a long time, their dental health may not be as good as it once was.

I make sure to visit the dentist twice a year. Knowing the importance of dental health, I try to take good care of my teeth. I often regret not managing them better when I was younger, and it's a thought that has crossed my mind more than once.

When I visit the dentist, I have tartar that has built up over time removed, treat any gum issues, and address cavities if they're found. I make it a priority to get scaling done every six months.

I brush my teeth three times a day. If I'm in a situation where I can't brush after lunch, I chew gum or use mouthwash to freshen my mouth. When brushing, I use interdental brushes or dental floss to remove food particles stuck between my teeth. Since I know how precious my teeth are, I continue to take diligent care of them every day.

Going to the dentist often can be annoying sometimes, but I know it helps prevent big problems later on, so I keep going. Thanks to the treatments, I haven't had any major issues, and no more discomfort. Dental care has just become part of my routine, so I can live without worrying about it. Dental health isn't just for looks. It's actually really important for overall health. I've been realizing more and more that I need to visit the dentist often and take care of my teeth. When my teeth are healthy, digestion works better, and I can take care of my overall health too.

TOPIC 45 다이어트

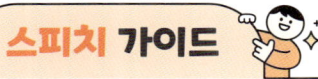

키워드와 주요 표현을 활용해서 문장을 말해 보세요.

1. 다이어트 소개

연령: 다이어트에 관심이 많은 연령대
- 예) People in their 20s care about dieting for both appearance and health.
  20대는 외모와 건강을 위해 다이어트에 관심이 많아요.

사람: 다이어트에 특히 민감한 사람들
- 예) Celebrities and models are especially sensitive to weight and body shape.
  연예인이나 모델은 체중과 체형에 특히 민감해요.

키워드 in one's 20s, all ages, care, models, sensitive, young, women

2. 다이어트 부작용 소개

요요현상: 다이어트 후 다시 살이 찌는 현상
- 예) Many people experience the yo-yo effect after losing weight quickly.
  많은 사람들이 급하게 살을 뺀 후 요요현상을 겪어요.

부작용: 신체에 생기는 다양한 문제
- 예) Extreme dieting can lead to hair loss and fatigue.
  극단적인 다이어트는 탈모와 피로를 유발할 수 있어요.

키워드 experience, rapid, yo-yo effect, cause, hair loss, strain, body, fatigue

3. 효과적인 다이어트 소개

방법: 건강하게 천천히 감량하는 습관
- 예) A balanced diet and regular exercise are the best way to lose weight.
  균형 잡힌 식단과 규칙적인 운동이 살을 빼는 최고의 방법이야.

효과: 지속 가능한 감량을 위한 핵심 요소
- 예) Building good habits is more important than short-term results.
  단기적인 결과보다 좋은 습관을 만드는 게 더 중요해.

키워드 balanced, healthy, exercise, depend on, habit, patience, consistency

대화 속에서 문장을 늘려가는 연습을 해 보세요.

A : **People of all ages care about dieting**. 모든 연령대가 다이어트에 관심이 있어요.

B : True. Gaining weight is easy, but losing it is hard. Both dieting and exercise help.
맞아요. 체중을 늘리는 것은 쉽지만, 빼는 것은 어렵죠. 다이어트와 운동 모두 도움이 됩니다.

A : **Many young women are into dieting**, but **rapid weight loss often causes yo-yo effects**.
많은 젊은 여성들이 다이어트에 관심이 있지만, 급격한 체중 감소는 종종 요요 현상을 일으킬 수 있어요.

B : I completely agree with that. 그 점에는 전적으로 동의해요.

A : I think **extreme dieting strains the body**, so **a slow and healthy approach might be better**.
지나치게 다이어트를 하면 몸에 부담을 주는 것 같아요. 그래서 천천히 건강하게 하는 게 더 좋을 수 있죠.

B : That's exactly what I'm trying to say. 제가 하려는 말이 그 말이에요.

A : The effects of dieting really **depend on patience and consistency**. I believe small changes can eventually make a big difference.
다이어트의 효과는 정말로 인내와 꾸준함에 달려 있어요. 저는 작은 변화들이 결국 큰 차이를 만들 수 있다고 믿어요.

B : I totally agree. Maintaining consistent and healthy habits is key.
완전 동의해요. 일관되고 건강한 습관을 유지하는 것이 핵심입니다.

어휘 strain 몸을 상하게 하다 make a big difference 큰 영향을 미치다, 중요한 변화를 일으키다

People of all ages ①**have been interested in dieting**, both in the past and now. It will probably remain a lifelong concern. I, too, have often wondered how I could lose weight when I ②**gained too much weight** for my height.

예전부터 지금까지 남녀노소 모두 다이어트에 관심을 가져왔습니다. 아마도 평생의 관심사가 될 것입니다. 저도 한때는 제 키에 비해 살이 너무 많이 쪄서 어떻게 체중을 감량할 수 있을지 고민한 적이 많았습니다.

Gaining weight is easy, but on the other hand, losing weight is not. You can lose weight through exercise, but dieting can also help you with weight loss. When dieting, you need to ③**reduce your food intake**. If you reduce your food intake and exercise at the same time, ④**the effects of dieting** can be amplified.

체중을 늘리는 것은 쉽지만, 반면에 체중을 감량하는 것은 쉽지 않습니다. 운동을 통해 체중을 감량할 수 있지만, 다이어트 역시 체중 감량에 도움이 될 수 있습니다. 다이어트를 할 때는 음식 섭취를 줄여야 합니다. 음식 섭취를 줄이고 운동을 동시에 하면 다이어트 효과가 배가될 수 있습니다.

These days, many young women are highly interested in dieting. If you ⑤**lose weight rapidly** over a short period, you will almost certainly ⑥**experience the yo-yo effect**.

요즘 많은 젊은 여성들이 다이어트에 매우 관심이 많습니다. 만약 짧은 기간 동안 급격히 체중을 감량하면, 거의 확실히 요요 현상을 겪게 될 것입니다.

In my opinion, dieting too harshly can ⑦**put a strain on your body**. Therefore, it's better to ⑧**follow a gradual and healthy diet** or engage in your favorite exercises while dieting.

제 생각에는 너무 과도하게 다이어트를 하면 몸에 부담을 줄 수 있습니다. 따라서 천천히 건강한 식단을 따르거나 다이어트 중에 좋아하는 운동을 하는 것이 더 좋습니다.

주제별로 구분하여 길게 말하는 연습을 해 보세요.

To [9]**see the effects of dieting**, you need to be patient. It's not something that will happen overnight. Consistency is key, and making small, sustainable changes to your lifestyle will [10]**bring better long-term results**.

다이어트의 효과를 보려면 인내심이 필요합니다. 그것은 하룻밤 사이에 일어나는 일이 아닙니다. 일관성이 핵심이며, 생활습관에 작은 변화를 지속적으로 주는 것이 더 나은 장기적인 결과를 가져올 것입니다.

The effects of dieting [11]**depend on your eating habits**. A well-balanced diet can improve not only your physical health but also your mental well-being. Eating the right foods and [12]**avoiding extreme diets** is essential for overall health.

다이어트의 효과는 식습관에 달려 있습니다. 균형 잡힌 식단은 신체 건강뿐만 아니라 정신 건강도 개선할 수 있습니다. 올바른 음식을 섭취하고 극단적인 다이어트를 피하는 것이 전반적인 건강에 필수적입니다.

스피치 포인트

① **have been interested in dieting** 다이어트에 관심이 있어 왔다 ② **gain too much weight** 너무 많이 체중이 증가하다 ③ **reduce one's food intake** 자신의 음식 섭취를 줄이다 ④ **the effects of dieting** 다이어트의 효과 ⑤ **lose weight rapidly** 급격히 체중을 줄이다 ⑥ **experience the yo-yo effect** 요요 현상을 경험하다 ⑦ **put a strain on one's body** 자신의 몸에 부담을 주다 ⑧ **follow a gradual and healthy diet** 천천히 건강한 식단을 따르다 ⑨ **see the effects of dieting** 다이어트의 효과를 보다 ⑩ **bring better long-term results** 더 나은 장기적인 결과를 가져오다 ⑪ **depend on one's eating habits** 자신의 식습관에 달려있다 ⑫ **avoid extreme diets** 극단적인 다이어트를 피하다

People of all ages have been interested in dieting, both in the past and now. It will probably remain a lifelong concern. I, too, have often wondered how I could lose weight when I gained too much weight for my height.

Gaining weight is easy, but on the other hand, losing weight is not. You can lose weight through exercise, but dieting can also help you with weight loss. When dieting, you need to reduce your food intake. If you reduce your food intake and exercise at the same time, the effects of dieting can be amplified.

These days, many young women are highly interested in dieting. If you lose weight rapidly over a short period, you will almost certainly experience the yo-yo effect.

In my opinion, dieting too harshly can put a strain on your body. Therefore, it's better to follow a gradual and healthy diet or engage in your favorite exercises while dieting.

To see the effects of dieting, you need to be patient. It's not something that will happen overnight. Consistency is key, and making small, sustainable changes to your lifestyle will bring better long-term results.

나의 상황에 맞게 내용을 바꾸어서 말해 보세요.

The effects of dieting depend on your eating habits. A well-balanced diet can improve not only your physical health but also your mental well-being. Eating the right foods and avoiding extreme diets is essential for overall health.

스피치 메모

필요한 단어와 표현을 정리해 보세요.

PART 09 Review Quiz

1 헬스장에서 운동하다
work _____ at the gym

2 빠르게 걷다, 활기차게 걷다
take a _____ walk

3 자신의 기분을 크게 개선하다
significantly _____ one's mood

4 자신의 생활 습관을 바꾸다
change one's lifestyle _____

5 자신의 건강을 잃다
_____ one's health

6 긍정적인 변화를 알아차리다
notice _____ changes

7 일반적인 눈 문제를 해결하다
address _____ eye issues

8 눈의 피로를 줄이다
ease eye _____

배운 영어 표현들을 복습해 보세요.

9 시력을 회복하다
　　＿＿＿＿＿＿ vision

10 자신의 치아를 잘 관리하다
　　take good ＿＿＿＿＿＿ of one's teeth

11 양치질하다
　　＿＿＿＿＿＿ one's teeth

12 전체적인 건강에 중요한
　　important for ＿＿＿＿＿＿ health

13 자신의 음식 섭취를 줄이다
　　reduce one's food ＿＿＿＿＿＿

14 요요 현상을 경험하다
　　experience the yo-yo ＿＿＿＿＿＿

15 다이어트의 효과를 보다
　　＿＿＿＿＿＿ the effects of dieting

정답　01 out　02 brisk　03 improve　04 habits　05 lose　06 positive　07 common　08 strain　09 regain
　　　10 care　11 brush　12 overall　13 intake　14 effect　15 see

PART 10
K-콘텐츠

TOPIC 46　　K-Pop
TOPIC 47　　K-Food
TOPIC 48　　K-Movie
TOPIC 49　　K-Drama
TOPIC 50　　K-Culture

TOPIC 46 K-Pop

스피치 가이드

키워드와 주요 표현을 활용해서 문장을 말해 보세요.

1. 케이팝 반응과 영감 소개

반응: 케이팝에 대한 해외 팬들의 반응
- 예) Some fans even learn Korean just because of K-Pop!
  어떤 팬들은 케이팝 때문에 한국어까지 배워요!

영감: 케이팝의 컨셉, 안무 등의 영감
- 예) Many K-Pop choreographies are inspired by Korean traditions or games.
  많은 케이팝 안무는 한국의 전통이나 놀이에서 영감을 받아요.

키워드 learn, Korean, fan, react, international, inspire, drinking, tradition

2. 케이팝의 매력과 힘 소개

매력: 케이팝의 좋은 점이나 매력
- 예) The performances are so addictive and high-quality.
  그 공연들은 정말 중독성 있고 퀄리티가 높아.

원동력: 케이팝이 자신에게 주는 힘
- 예) K-Pop gives me strength and keeps me going every day.
  케이팝은 나에게 힘이 되고 매일 버틸 수 있게 해줘.

키워드 addictive, high-quality, cheer up, strength, keep going

3. 케이팝의 의미와 영향력 소개

정의: 장르, 스타일, 구성요소 등 기본적인 설명
- 예) K-Pop is a genre of Korean popular music that includes singing and dancing.
  케이팝은 노래와 춤을 포함한 한국 대중음악 장르예요.

영향력: 케이팝이 주는 영향력
- 예) K-Pop has a huge global influence, especially through social media.
  케이팝은 특히 SNS를 통해 세계적인 영향을 끼치고 있어요.

키워드 popular, music, more than, singing, huge, influence, bring together

대화로 연습하기
대화 속에서 문장을 늘려가는 연습을 해 보세요.

A : K-Pop is so popular worldwide now. You can even listen to it live on YouTube! 케이팝은 요즘 전 세계적으로 정말 인기가 많아. 유튜브로 실시간으로 들을 수도 있잖아!

B : I know! I love **watching international fans react to K-Pop**. It makes me proud as a Korean. 맞아! 해외 팬들이 케이팝에 반응하는 영상 보는 거 너무 좋아. 한국인으로서 자랑스러워.

A : Recently, I've been into 'APT' by BLACKPINK's Rosé and Bruno Mars. 요즘 나는 블랙핑크의 로제랑 브루노 마스가 부른 'APT'에 빠져 있었어.

B : Me too! It's cool that it **was inspired by a Korean drinking game**. 나도 마찬가지야! 한국 술 게임에서 영감을 받았다니 신기하더라.

A : K-Pop's global fame started with Psy's 'Gangnam Style,' don't you think? 세계적인 케이팝의 명성이 싸이의 '강남스타일'로 시작된 거 맞지?

B : Definitely. **K-Pop always cheers me up** and **gives me strength when I need it**. 당연하지. 케이팝은 언제나 기운을 북돋아주고 내가 필요할 때 힘을 줘.

A : K-Pop is amazing. It connects people around the world and inspires us. 케이팝은 정말 대단해. 전 세계 사람들을 연결하고 영감을 주는 음악이야.

B : Yes, **K-Pop is more than just music**. I think **it brings people together**. 맞아. 케이팝은 단순한 음악 그 이상이지. 사람들을 하나로 모은다고 생각해.

어휘 cheer up 기운을 내다 bring together 하나로 만들다, 모으다

내용 구성하기

The popularity of K-Pop around the world is truly amazing. One of its great advantages is that you can ①**listen to K-Pop music** live on YouTube. These days, I often watch ②**overseas fans' reactions to K-Pop music** on YouTube, and every time I do, I feel proud as a Korean of our popular music.

전 세계에서 케이팝의 인기는 정말 대단합니다. 케이팝의 큰 장점 중 하나는 유튜브를 통해 케이팝 음악을 실시간으로 들을 수 있다는 점입니다. 요즘은 유튜브를 통해 케이팝 음악에 대한 해외 팬들의 반응을 자주 보는데, 그럴 때마다, 저는 한국인으로서 우리의 대중음악에 자부심을 느낍니다.

Recently, I've been listening to 'APT,' a song performed by BLACKPINK's Rosé and Bruno Mars, which ③**caused a global sensation**. The song is said to have been inspired by a Korean drinking game. The title, 'APT,' means 'apartment' in Korean, but it might ④**sound a bit unfamiliar to** non-Korean listeners.

최근에 저는 블랙핑크의 로제와 브루노 마스가 함께 불러 전 세계적으로 큰 반향을 일으켰던 'APT'를 듣고 있는 중이었습니다. 한국의 술 게임에서 영감을 받아 만들어진 노래라고 합니다. 제목의 'APT'는 한국어로 '아파트'를 뜻하지만, 한국인이 아닌 청취자들에게는 다소 생소하게 들릴 수도 있습니다.

I think ⑤**the worldwide popularity of K-Pop** began with Psy's 'Gangnam Style.' The song captured aspects of Korean life and was sung in Korean, yet it ⑥**gained tremendous global popularity**. Even now, I find it incredible when I think about it.

케이팝이 세계적인 인기를 얻게 된 것은 싸이의 '강남스타일'이 시초가 아니었나 생각해 봅니다. 그 노래는 한국인의 생활 모습을 담고 있었고 한국어로 불렀지만 전 세계적으로 엄청난 인기를 얻었습니다. 지금도, 그것에 대해 생각할 때면 여전히 믿기지가 않습니다.

I love music. Since high school, music has been an integral part of my life. I enjoy both pop music and K-Pop. Music is ⑦**a precious part of my life** that makes happy moments more joyful and ⑧**provides comfort and strength** during tough times.

저는 음악을 좋아합니다. 고등학교 때부터 음악은 제 삶의 필수적인 부분이었습니다. 팝송도 좋아하고 케이팝 도 좋아합니다. 음악은 행복한 순간을 더 즐겁게 만들어주고 힘든 시기에 위로와 힘을 주는 소중한 삶의 일부입니다.

주제별로 구분하여 길게 말하는 연습을 해 보세요.

Another reason I love K-Pop is ⁹**the dedication and hard work of the artists**. K-Pop idols ¹⁰**undergo years of intense training** to improve their singing, dancing, and stage presence. Their passion and commitment are truly impressive, and I believe this is one of the key reasons K-Pop has gained such massive popularity worldwide.

제가 케이팝을 좋아하는 또 다른 이유는 아티스트들의 헌신과 노력입니다. 케이팝 아이돌은 노래, 춤, 그리고 무대 매너를 향상시키기 위해 몇 년간의 혹독한 훈련을 거칩니다. 그들의 열정과 헌신은 정말 인상적이며, 이것이 케이팝이 전 세계적으로 엄청난 인기를 얻은 핵심 이유 중 하나라고 생각합니다.

In conclusion, K-Pop is ¹¹**more than just music**. It's a cultural phenomenon that connects people worldwide. Through powerful performances, creative concepts, and meaningful lyrics, K-Pop continues to inspire and ¹²**unite fans across the globe**.

결론적으로, 케이팝은 단순한 음악을 넘어 전 세계 사람들을 연결하는 문화적 현상입니다. 강렬한 퍼포먼스, 창의적인 콘셉트, 그리고 의미 있는 가사를 통해 케이팝은 전 세계 팬들에게 계속해서 영감을 주고 하나로 모읍니다.

스피치 포인트

① **listen to K-Pop music** 케이팝 음악을 듣다 ② **overseas fans' reactions to K-Pop music** 케이팝 음악에 대한 해외 팬들의 반응 ③ **cause a global sensation** 전 세계적으로 큰 반향을 일으키다 ④ **sound a bit unfamiliar to** 조금 낯설게 들리다 ⑤ **the worldwide popularity of K-Pop** 케이팝의 전 세계적인 인기 ⑥ **gain tremendous global popularity** 전 세계적으로 엄청난 인기를 얻다 ⑦ **a precious part of one's life** 자신의 삶에서 소중한 부분 ⑧ **provide comfort and strength** 위로와 힘을 주다 ⑨ **the dedication and hard work of the artists** 아티스트들의 헌신과 노력 ⑩ **undergo years of intense training** 수년간의 혹독한 훈련을 받다 ⑪ **more than just music** 단순한 음악 그 이상 ⑫ **unite fans across the globe** 전 세계 팬들을 하나로 모으다

The popularity of K-Pop around the world is truly amazing. One of its great advantages is that you can listen to K-Pop music live on YouTube. These days, I often watch overseas fans' reactions to K-Pop music on YouTube, and every time I do, I feel proud as a Korean of our popular music.

Recently, I've been listening to 'APT,' a song performed by BLACKPINK's Rosé and Bruno Mars, which caused a global sensation. The song is said to have been inspired by a Korean drinking game. The title, 'APT,' means 'apartment' in Korean, but it might sound a bit unfamiliar to non-Korean listeners.

I think the worldwide popularity of K-Pop began with Psy's 'Gangnam Style.' The song captured aspects of Korean life and was sung in Korean, yet it gained tremendous global popularity. Even now, I find it incredible when I think about it.

I love music. Since high school, music has been an integral part of my life. I enjoy both pop music and K-Pop. Music is a precious part of my life that makes happy moments more joyful and provides comfort and strength during tough times.

Another reason I love K-Pop is the dedication and hard work of the artists. K-Pop idols undergo years of intense training to improve their

나의 상황에 맞게 내용을 바꾸어서 말해 보세요.

singing, dancing, and stage presence. Their passion and commitment are truly impressive, and I believe this is one of the key reasons K-Pop has gained such massive popularity worldwide.

In conclusion, K-Pop is more than just music. It's a cultural phenomenon that connects people worldwide. Through powerful performances, creative concepts, and meaningful lyrics, K-Pop continues to inspire and unite fans across the globe.

TOPIC 47 K-Food

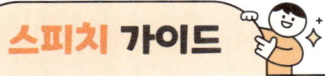

키워드와 주요 표현을 활용해서 문장을 말해 보세요.

1. 케이푸드 소개

사진: 사진을 보낸 사람, 장소
- 예) I got some pictures from my brother showing the Korean food craze in Japan.
  일본에서 케이푸드 열풍을 보여주는 사진들을 동생이 보내줬어.

반응: 케이푸드의 인기나 풍경 묘사
- 예) So many people were waiting in line to get kimbap and tteokbokki.
  김밥과 떡볶이를 사기 위해 많은 사람들이 줄을 서 있었어.

키워드 brother, Japan, photo, wait, line, long, kimbap, tteokbokki, shop

2. 케이푸드의 힘 소개

목격담: 해외에서 케이푸드를 보거나 먹은 경험
- 예) I ran into a Korean snack bar while I was traveling abroad.
  해외여행 중에 한국식 분식집을 우연히 봤어요.

자부심: 케이푸드가 세계에 미치는 영향에 대한 생각
- 예) Seeing K-Food spread globally really makes me happy.
  케이푸드가 세계로 퍼져나가는 걸 보니 정말 기뻐요.

키워드 Korean, snack, bar, Hong Kong, abroad, happy, feel, power, K-Food

3. 케이푸드의 인기 소개

인기: 케이푸드의 세계적인 인기
- 예) Korean dishes are gaining popularity all around the world.
  한국 요리들이 전 세계적으로 인기를 얻고 있어요.

건강: 케이푸드가 건강식으로 받아들여지는 점
- 예) Korean cuisine is known for its fresh ingredients and healthy balance.
  한국 요리는 신선한 재료와 건강한 균형으로 잘 알려져 있어요.

키워드 gain, popularity, popular, fresh, ingredient, healthy, balance, option

대화로 연습하기

대화 속에서 문장을 늘려가는 연습을 해 보세요.

A : **I saw photos from my brother in Japan.** It **showed long lines at kimbap and tteokbokki shops** in Ikebukuro.
일본에 있는 내 동생이 보낸 사진을 봤어. 이케부쿠로에 있는 김밥과 떡볶이 가게 앞에 긴 줄이 있는 사진이었어.

B : Wow, K-Food is getting so popular, especially among young people! 와, 케이푸드가 특히 젊은 세대들 사이에서 정말 인기 많아졌구나!

A : Yes, I was surprised when **I found a Korean snack bar in Hong Kong.** 맞아. 홍콩에서 한국식 분식점을 발견했을 때도 놀랐어.

B : The Korean Wave really made Korean food famous everywhere. 한류 덕분에 한국 음식이 전 세계적으로 유명해졌어.

A : **I feel the power of K-Food.** 케이푸드의 힘이 느껴져.

B : Same here! It's amazing how much people love it.
나도! 사람들이 그렇게 좋아하다니 정말 놀라워

A : I'm really glad that **Korean food has become popular as a healthy option** too. 한국 음식이 건강에 좋은 선택지로도 인기가 많아졌다니 정말 기뻐.

B : I feel the same way! I hope even more people get to taste and enjoy it in the future. 나도 마찬가지야! 앞으로 더 많은 사람들이 맛보고 즐기면 좋겠어.

어휘 **healthy option** 건강한 좋은 선택지

Along with K-Pop, K-Food has been gaining popularity worldwide lately. In particular, K-Food is becoming more popular among younger generations. Some people ①**love Korean instant noodles**, while many young people ②**enjoy Korean snacks** like kimbap and tteokbokki.

케이팝과 함께 케이푸드는 요즘 전 세계적으로 인기를 얻고 있었습니다. 특히 케이푸드는 젊은 세대들 사이에서 더 인기가 높아지고 있죠. 어떤 사람들은 한국 라면을 좋아하는 반면에 많은 젊은이들은 김밥이나 떡볶이 같은 한국 간식을 즐깁니다.

A few days ago, I saw some photos sent by my younger brother, who lives in Japan. The photos were from Ikebukuro, showing people ③**waiting in line** in front of a kimbap shop and a long line of young Japanese people ④**waiting for** tteokbokki at another shop.

며칠 전에 일본에 사는 남동생이 보낸 사진 몇 장을 보았습니다. 김밥 가게 앞에서 줄을 서서 기다리는 사람들과 다른 가게에서 떡볶이를 기다리는 일본 젊은이들의 긴 줄을 보여주는 이케부쿠로의 사진이었습니다.

Almost 7 years ago, when I visited Hong Kong again, I was walking around the hotel area to ⑤**find a place for breakfast** and accidentally ⑥**discovered a snack bar** run by Koreans. When I went inside, I was a bit surprised to see many Hong Kong people enjoying Korean snacks.

거의 7년 전에, 홍콩을 다시 방문했을 때, 아침 먹을 곳을 찾기 위해 호텔 근처를 돌아다니다가 우연히 한국인이 운영하는 분식점을 발견했습니다. 안으로 들어가 보니, 많은 홍콩 사람들이 한국 간식을 즐기고 있는 모습을 보고 조금 놀랐습니다.

It's true that, ⑦**thanks to the Korean Wave**, interest in Korean food is growing just like Korean pop music. Once again, I can ⑧**feel the power of K-Food**, and it makes me happy.

한류 덕택으로 한국 대중음악처럼 한국 음식에 대한 관심도 점점 높아지고 있는 게 사실입니다. 다시 한 번 케이푸드의 힘을 느낄 수 있어 기분이 좋습니다.

주제별로 구분하여 길게 말하는 연습을 해 보세요.

The popularity of Korean food isn't new. ⁹**Over the past few years**, more and more Korean restaurants have opened in many countries, and Korean food is known for being healthy, so many people choose it ¹⁰**for dieting or health reasons**.

한국 음식의 인기는 이제 시작된 것이 아닙니다. 몇 년 전부터 점점 더 많은 나라에서 한국 음식점이 생기고 있고, 한국 음식은 건강에도 좋다고 알려져 많은 사람들이 다이어트나 건강을 위해 선택하고 있습니다.

I'm proud that Korean food is loved around the world. Many Korean dishes ¹¹**have been adapted to different tastes**, so more people can enjoy them. I hope ¹²**the popularity of Korean food** continues to grow.

한국 음식이 세계에서 사랑받는 것이 자랑스럽습니다. 다양한 한국 음식들이 각국의 입맛에 맞게 변형되어 더 많은 사람들이 즐기고 있습니다. 앞으로도 한국 음식의 인기가 더 커지기를 바랍니다.

스피치 포인트

① love Korean instant noodles 한국 라면을 정말 좋아하다 ② enjoy Korean snacks 한국 간식을 즐기다 ③ wait in line 줄서서 기다리다 ④ wait for ~을 기다리다 ⑤ find a place for breakfast 아침 식사할 장소를 찾다 ⑥ discover a snack bar 분식점을 발견하다 ⑦ thanks to the Korean Wave 한류 덕택으로 ⑧ feel the power of K-Food 케이푸드의 힘을 느끼다 ⑨ over the past few years 지난 몇 년 동안 ⑩ for dieting or health reasons 다이어트나 건강상의 이유로 ⑪ have been adapted to different tastes 다양한 입맛에 맞게 변형되었다 ⑫ the popularity of Korean food 한국 음식의 인기

Along with K-Pop, K-Food has been gaining popularity worldwide lately. In particular, K-Food is becoming more popular among younger generations. Some people love Korean instant noodles, while many young people enjoy Korean snacks like kimbap and tteokbokki.

A few days ago, I saw some photos sent by my younger brother, who lives in Japan. The photos were from Ikebukuro, showing people waiting in line in front of a kimbap shop and a long line of young Japanese people waiting for tteokbokki at another shop.

Almost 7 years ago, when I visited Hong Kong again, I was walking around the hotel area to find a place for breakfast and accidentally discovered a snack bar run by Koreans. When I went inside, I was a bit surprised to see many Hong Kong people enjoying Korean snacks.

It's true that, thanks to the Korean Wave, interest in Korean food is growing just like Korean pop music. Once again, I can feel the power of K-Food, and it makes me happy.

The popularity of Korean food isn't new. Over the past few years, more and more Korean restaurants have opened in many countries, and Korean food is known for being healthy, so many people choose it for dieting or health reasons.

나의 상황에 맞게 내용을 바꾸어서 말해 보세요.

I'm proud that Korean food is loved around the world. Many Korean dishes have been adapted to different tastes, so more people can enjoy them. I hope the popularity of Korean food continues to grow.

TOPIC 48 K-Movie

스피치 가이드

키워드와 주요 표현을 활용해서 문장을 말해 보세요.

1. 한국영화와 홍콩영화 비교 소개

한국: 현재 한국영화의 인기
- 예) Recently, Korean films have even won major international awards.
  최근에는 한국 영화가 주요 국제 영화제에서도 상을 받았어요.

홍콩: 과거 홍콩영화의 전성기
- 예) Hong Kong movies were very popular in the 1980s and 1990s
  홍콩 영화는 1980년대와 1990년대에 매우 인기가 있었어요.

키워드 win, international, award, popular, these days, a thing, the past

2. 한국 영화의 글로벌 영향력 소개

영향력: 한국 배우들의 글로벌 진출
- 예) Actors like Ma Dong-seok and Lee Jung-jae are gaining international fame.
  마동석과 이정재 같은 배우들이 국제적인 명성을 얻고 있어요.

인정: 한국 영화의 국제적 인정
- 예) Critics praise Korean films for their storytelling and emotional depth.
  평론가들은 한국 영화의 스토리 전개와 감정의 깊이를 칭찬해요.

키워드 gain, fame, appear, Hollywood, praise, storytelling, recognize, worldwide

3. 한국 영화의 발전과 미래 소개

성장: 한국 영화의 발전
- 예) The quality of Korean movies has improved dramatically.
  한국 영화의 퀄리티가 눈에 띄게 향상됐어요.

기대: 한국 영화의 미래
- 예) The future of Korean movies looks very bright.
  한국 영화의 미래는 매우 밝아 보여요.

키워드 quality, improve, dramatically, amazing, grow, bright, wait, next

대화로 연습하기

대화 속에서 문장을 늘려가는 연습을 해 보세요.

A : **K-movies are really popular these days. Hong Kong movies are kind of a thing of the past now**.
요즘 케이무비가 대세예요. 홍콩 영화는 이제 좀 한물갔어요.

B : That's true! Director Bong Joon-ho won big at the Oscars.
맞아요! 봉준호 감독이 오스카에서 큰 상을 받았잖아요.

A : Now, **Korean actors are appearing in Hollywood movies more often**. 이제 한국 배우들이 할리우드 영화에 많이 나옵니다.

B : Exactly, even Hollywood stars want to work with Korean directors. 맞아요. 할리우드 배우들조차도 한국 감독과 함께 작업하고 싶어 해요.

A : **K-movies are truly recognized worldwide**.
케이무비는 전 세계적으로 진정으로 인정받고 있어요.

B : I totally agree with you on that. 그 점에는 완전 동의합니다.

A : It's **amazing to see how Korean movies have grown**, and I **can't wait to see where they go next**.
한국 영화가 이렇게 성장한 걸 보는 건 정말 놀라워요. 앞으로 어디로 가게 될지 너무 기대돼요.

B : Same here! The future of K-movies is definitely bright, and the world is watching!
저도 마찬가지예요! 케이무비의 미래는 분명 밝고, 전 세계가 지켜보고 있어요!

어휘 **a thing of the past** 과거의 일 **can't wait to** 몹시 ~하고 싶다

During the COVID-19 pandemic, when Korea was going through a difficult time, the Academy Awards were taking place in the United States. I was ①**watching the live broadcast** on TV when Bong Joon-ho, a director from Korea, won four awards, including Best Picture. I still ②**vividly remember** how thrilled I was at that moment and how I couldn't help but cheer out loud.

코로나19 팬데믹으로 한국이 힘든 시기를 겪고 있던 그때, 미국에서는 아카데미 시상식이 열리고 있었습니다. 저는 TV로 생중계를 보고 있었는데, 한국 출신의 봉준호 감독이 작품상을 포함해 4개의 상을 받는 장면이 나왔습니다. 그 순간 얼마나 기뻤는지 아직도 생생하게 기억나며, 저도 모르게 큰 소리로 환호했던 기억이 납니다.

I'm ③**a huge movie buff**, so I enjoy watching both Hollywood and Korean films without much preference. Back when I was in my twenties, Hong Kong movies ④**were all the rage** in Korea. But now, after all these years, it's amazing to see Korean films gaining popularity all over the world.

저는 영화광이라 할리우드 영화든 한국 영화든 특별히 가리지 않고 즐겨 봅니다. 제가 20대였을 때만 해도 그 당시 한국에서는 홍콩 영화가 대세였습니다. 그런데 지금, 이렇게 시간이 많이 흐른 후에 한국 영화가 전 세계적으로 인기를 얻고 있다는 사실이 놀랍습니다.

The fact that ⑤**well-written scripts** and the outstanding performances of Korean actors have come together to create great movies has become ⑥**an undeniable reality**.

잘 짜여진 대본과 탁월한 한국 배우들의 연기가 결합되어 훌륭한 영화들이 만들어지고 있다는 사실은 이제 누구도 부인할 수 없는 현실이 되었습니다.

It's now quite natural to see Korean actors in Hollywood films, and the fact that famous Hollywood stars want to ⑦**work with Korean directors** might be ⑧**a result of the growing popularity** of K-movies.

이제는 한국 배우들을 할리우드 영화 속에서 보는 것도 아주 자연스러워졌고, 유명한 할리우드 배우들이 한국 감독과 함께 영화를 만들고 싶어 하는 것도, 어쩌면 케이무비의 커져가는 인기에 따른 결과일지도 모르겠습니다.

주제별로 구분하여 길게 말하는 연습을 해 보세요.

I think the success of Korean movies didn't just happen by chance. It's the result of years of hard work and constant innovation. ⁹**Trying out new genres** and telling fresh stories really connected with audiences, and I believe that's what ⁱ⁰**fueled the K-Movie boom** we see today.

저는 한국 영화의 성공이 단지 우연히 일어난 일이 아니라고 생각합니다. 그것은 수년간의 노력과 끊임없는 혁신의 결과입니다. 새로운 장르를 시도하고 신선한 이야기를 전하는 것이 관객들과 잘 맞아떨어졌고, 저는 그것이 오늘날 우리가 보고 있는 케이무비 열풍을 일으킨 원동력이라고 믿습니다.

I really hope Korean movies ⁱ¹**keep winning hearts** and blending beautifully with different cultures as they continue to grow. Thinking about ⁱ²**the endless potential of K-movies** makes me super excited for what's to come.

저는 한국 영화가 계속 성장하면서 사람들의 마음을 얻고, 다양한 문화와 아름답게 어우러지기를 진심으로 바랍니다. 케이무비의 끝없는 잠재력을 생각하면, 앞으로 일어날 일들이 너무 기대됩니다.

스피치 포인트

① **watch the live broadcast** 생방송을 시청하다 ② **vividly remember** 생생하게 기억하다 ③ **a huge movie buff** 영화광 ④ **be all the rage** 대유행하다 ⑤ **well-written scripts** 잘 쓰인 대본 ⑥ **an undeniable reality** 부인할 수 없는 현실(사실) ⑦ **work with Korean directors** 한국 감독들과 함께 일하다 ⑧ **a result of the growing popularity** 커져가는 인기에 따른 결과 ⑨ **try out new genres** 새로운 장르를 시도하다 ⑩ **fuel the K-Movie boom** 케이무비 열풍을 일으키다 ⑪ **keep winning hearts** 계속해서 사람들의 마음을 얻다 ⑫ **the endless potential of K-movies** 케이무비의 끝없는 잠재력

During the COVID-19 pandemic, when Korea was going through a difficult time, the Academy Awards were taking place in the United States. I was watching the live broadcast on TV when Bong Joon-ho, a director from Korea, won four awards, including Best Picture. I still vividly remember how thrilled I was at that moment and how I couldn't help but cheer out loud.

I'm a huge movie buff, so I enjoy watching both Hollywood and Korean films without much preference. Back when I was in my twenties, Hong Kong movies were all the rage in Korea. But now, after all these years, it's amazing to see Korean films gaining popularity all over the world.

The fact that well-written scripts and the outstanding performances of Korean actors have come together to create great movies has become an undeniable reality.

It's now quite natural to see Korean actors in Hollywood films, and the fact that famous Hollywood stars want to work with Korean directors might be a result of the growing popularity of K-movies.

I think the success of Korean movies didn't just happen by chance. It's the result of years of hard work and constant innovation. Trying out new genres and telling fresh stories really connected with audiences, and I believe that's what fueled the K-Movie boom we see today.

나의 상황에 맞게 내용을 바꾸어서 말해 보세요.

I really hope Korean movies keep winning hearts and blending beautifully with different cultures as they continue to grow. Thinking about the endless potential of K-movies makes me super excited for what's to come.

필요한 단어와 표현을 정리해 보세요.

K-Drama

키워드와 주요 표현을 활용해서 문장을 말해 보세요.

1. 한국 드라마 소개

인기: 한국 드라마의 인기

예) K-dramas have become extremely popular recently.
한국 드라마가 최근에 매우 인기를 끌게 되었어.

시청: 얼마나 많은 사람들이 시청하고 있는지

예) I've noticed that millions of people around the world are watching K-dramas.
전 세계 수백만 명의 사람들이 한국 드라마를 보고 있다는 걸 알게 되었어.

키워드 extremely, popular, everyone, millions of, people, watch

2. 넷플릭스 소개

느낌: 넷플릭스에 대한 생각

예) I enjoy watching Netflix shows because they're so diverse and entertaining.
매우 다양하고 재미있기 때문에 넷플릭스 프로그램 시청하는 걸 즐겨요.

드라마: 넷플릭스를 통해 접하는 한국 드라마에 대한 생각

예) K-dramas are my favorite because they are always so emotional and captivating.
한국 드라마는 항상 감동적이고 몰입감이 있어서 제 최애에요.

키워드 diverse, entertaining, great, show, fun, exciting, emotional, captivating

3. 한국 드라마의 미래 소개

미래: 한국 드라마의 미래

예) I wonder if K-dramas will keep growing in popularity.
한국 드라마가 계속해서 인기를 끌게 될 지 궁금해요.

영향력: 전 세계에 어떤 영향을 주고 있는지

예) It's amazing how K-dramas are having such a big impact worldwide.
한국 드라마가 전 세계에 이렇게 큰 영향을 미치고 있다는 것이 놀라워요.

키워드 wonder, grow, popularity, hit, the next, definitely, take over, impact

대화로 연습하기

대화 속에서 문장을 늘려가는 연습을 해 보세요.

A : **K-dramas are so popular** these days. **Everyone's watching them**. 요즘 한국 드라마들이 진짜 인기 많아. 모든 사람들이 보고 있잖아.

B : Yeah, after 'Squid Game,' people started loving Korean content. 맞아. '오징어 게임' 이후로 사람들이 한국 콘텐츠를 엄청 좋아하기 시작했어.

A : **Netflix has great shows** like 'The Glory' and 'Extraordinary Attorney Woo.' I think **they're really fun and exciting to watch**. 넷플릭스에는 '더 글로리'랑 '이상한 변호사 우영우' 같은 훌륭한 작품들이 있어. 정말 재밌고 흥미진진한 것 같아.

B : And Disney Plus isn't bad either with 'Moving.' 디즈니 플러스도 '무빙' 같은 작품 괜찮던데.

A : **I wonder what the next hit will be**. 다음 히트 작품이 뭐가 될지 궁금해.

B : Whatever it is, I'm already excited. 뭐든 난 벌써 기대가 돼.

A : Korean dramas **are definitely taking over the world** right now. 한국 드라마가 지금 전 세계를 휩쓸고 있어.

B : Totally. They're not just popular in Korea anymore, but everywhere. 맞아. 이제는 한국에서만 인기 있는 게 아니라, 전 세계 어디서나 인기가 많아.

어휘 take over the world 세계를 장악하다, 전 세계적으로 유행하다

내용 구성하기

①**K-dramas are all the rage** these days, right? Thanks to platforms like Netflix and Disney Plus, Korean dramas are loved all over the world. Ever since 'Squid Game,' people have been saying, 'Korean content ②**is always worth watching.**' When I meet foreign friends, they naturally know words like 'Annyeong' or 'Gamsahamnida' now.

요즘 한국 드라마가 완전 대세죠? 넷플릭스랑 디즈니 플러스 덕분에 한국 드라마가 전 세계에서 사랑받고 있어요. 특히 '오징어 게임' 이후로는 '한국 콘텐츠는 믿고 본다'는 말이 생겼을 정도예요. 외국 친구들 만나면 이제 '안녕'이나 '감사합니다' 같은 한국어를 당연히 알더라고요.

Netflix keeps ③**releasing new Korean dramas** lately. 'The Glory' and 'Extraordinary Attorney Woo' were huge hits, weren't they? Honestly, you can easily lose track of time just ④**binge-watching** on Netflix.

넷플릭스는 요즘도 새로운 한국 드라마를 계속 선보이고 있죠. '더 글로리', '이상한 변호사 우영우' 같은 작품도 엄청 화제였잖아요? 솔직히 말해서, 넷플릭스에서 정주행을 하다 보면 시간 가는 줄 모를 수 있어요.

Disney Plus isn't staying quiet either. Korean original series like 'Big Bet' and 'Moving' have made it a platform to ⑤**keep an eye on.** I love how there's such ⑥**a variety of Korean dramas** coming out now, giving us so many options to enjoy!

디즈니 플러스도 가만히 있을 리가 없죠. '카지노'나 '무빙' 같은 한국 오리지널 시리즈가 나와서 점점 더 기대되는 플랫폼이 되었어요. 지금 이렇게 다양한 한국 드라마들이 나오고 있어, 우리가 즐길 수 있는 선택지가 많아져서 정말 좋아요!

Aren't you curious about what's coming next? I hope Korean dramas ⑦**continue to gain global popularity** and introduce more people to our culture. I'm already excited to see which show will ⑧**create the next big sensation**!

앞으로도 어떤 작품들이 나올지 너무 궁금하지 않나요? 한국 드라마가 계속해서 세계적인 인기를 얻고 더 많은 사람들에게 우리 문화를 소개했으면 좋겠어요. 다음 광풍을 일으킬 작품은 뭐가 될지 벌써 기대됩니다!

주제별로 구분하여 길게 말하는 연습을 해 보세요.

As [9]**the popularity of Korean dramas grows**, many Korean actors are [10]**gaining attention abroad**. It's now common for Korean actors to appear in Hollywood films. I think this is proof of how much influence K-dramas have gained.

한국 드라마들의 인기가 높아지면서 해외에서도 많은 한국 배우들이 주목받고 있죠. 이제는 한국 배우들이 할리우드 영화에도 출연하는 일이 흔해졌습니다. 그만큼 한국 드라마의 영향력이 커졌다는 증거라고 생각해요.

As Korean dramas become more popular worldwide, interest in our culture is growing as well. Dramas that beautifully combine [11]**traditional and modern elements** of Korea are [12]**receiving a lot of love**. I hope Korean dramas continue to be loved in every corner of the world!

한국 드라마가 전 세계적으로 인기를 끌고 있는 만큼, 우리 문화에 대한 관심도 커지고 있습니다. 한국의 전통과 현대적인 요소가 잘 결합된 드라마들이 많은 사랑을 받고 있어요. 앞으로도 한국 드라마가 세계 곳곳에서 사랑받기를 바랍니다.

스피치 포인트

① **K-dramas are all the rage** 한국 드라마들이 대유행이다 ② **be always worth watching** 항상 시청할 가치가 있다 ③ **release new Korean dramas** 새로운 한국 드라마들을 공개하다 ④ **binge-watch** 몰아서 보다, 정주행하다 ⑤ **keep on eye on** ~에 주목하다, ~을 지켜보다 ⑥ **a variety of Korean dramas** 다양한 한국 드라마들 ⑦ **continue to gain global popularity** 계속해서 세계적으로 인기를 얻다 ⑧ **create the next big sensation** 다음 큰 반향을 일으키다 ⑨ **the popularity of Korean dramas grows** 한국 드라마들의 인기가 커지다 ⑩ **gain attention abroad** 해외에서 주목을 받다 ⑪ **traditional and modern elements** 전통과 현대적인 요소 ⑫ **receive a lot of love** 많은 사랑을 받다

K-dramas are all the rage these days, right? Thanks to platforms like Netflix and Disney Plus, Korean dramas are loved all over the world. Ever since 'Squid Game,' people have been saying, 'Korean content is always worth watching.' When I meet foreign friends, they naturally know words like 'Annyeong' or 'Gamsahamnida' now.

Netflix keeps releasing new Korean dramas lately. 'The Glory' and 'Extraordinary Attorney Woo' were huge hits, weren't they? Honestly, you can easily lose track of time just binge-watching on Netflix.

Disney Plus isn't staying quiet either. Korean original series like 'Big Bet' and 'Moving' have made it a platform to keep an eye on. I love how there's such a variety of Korean dramas coming out now, giving us so many options to enjoy!

Aren't you curious about what's coming next? I hope Korean dramas continue to gain global popularity and introduce more people to our culture. I'm already excited to see which show will create the next big sensation!

As the popularity of Korean dramas grows, many Korean actors are gaining attention abroad. It's now common for Korean actors to appear in Hollywood films. I think this is proof of how much influence K-dramas have gained. As Korean dramas become more popular worldwide,

나의 상황에 맞게 내용을 바꾸어서 말해 보세요.

interest in our culture is growing as well. Dramas that beautifully combine traditional and modern elements of Korea are receiving a lot of love. I hope Korean dramas continue to be loved in every corner of the world!

스피치 메모

필요한 단어와 표현을 정리해 보세요.

K-Culture

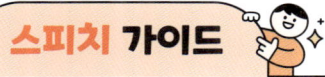

키워드와 주요 표현을 활용해서 문장을 말해 보세요.

1. 한국 문화 소개

인지도: 한국 문화에 대한 외국인의 관심

예) Korean culture has gained global recognition thanks to K-Pop and K-Drama.
케이팝과 한국 드라마 덕분에 한국 문화가 전 세계적으로 인지도를 얻었어요.

여행객: 한국을 방문하는 외국 여행객의 수

예) Millions of tourists visit Korea every year to enjoy K-Culture.
매년 수백만 명의 관광객이 케이컬처를 즐기기 위해 한국을 방문해요.

키워드 recognition, thanks to, amazing, interested, millions of, number, increase

2. 한국 문화에 대한 자부심 소개

생각: 한국 문화에 대한 개인적인 생각, 느낌

예) I think Korean culture is very dynamic and influential.
한국 문화가 매우 역동적이고 영향력 있는 것 같아.

자부심: 한국인으로서 느끼는 자부심

예) I'm proud that people around the world love Korean culture.
전 세계 사람들이 한국 문화를 정말 좋아하는 걸 보면 자랑스러워.

키워드 dynamic, influential, think about, proud, Korean

3. 한국 패션 소개

패션: 요즘 한국 패션의 동향

예) Korean street fashion is getting a lot of attention for its unique style.
한국의 거리 패션은 독특한 스타일로 많은 주목을 받고 있어요.

대중성: 어떤 스타일이 인기를 얻고 있는지

예) Styles worn by K-Pop idols are especially popular among young people abroad.
케이팝 아이돌들이 입는 스타일은 특히 해외 젊은 층 사이에서 인기가 많아요.

키워드 attention, unique, trendy, popular, young, idol, style

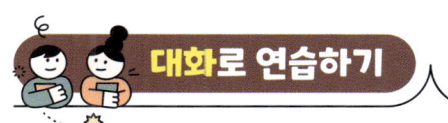 **대화로 연습하기** 대화 속에서 문장을 늘려가는 연습을 해 보세요.

A : These days, **isn't it amazing how many foreigners are interested in Korean culture**? 요즘 한국 문화에 관심 있는 외국인들이 많다는 게 놀랍지 않아요?

B : Yes, it's incredible, especially how popular Korean cosmetics are worldwide. 네 특히 한국 화장품이 전 세계적으로 인기라니 정말 대단해요.

A : Also, **the number of foreign tourists visiting Korea has been increasing** every year. 게다가 매년 한국을 방문하는 외국인 관광객도 늘고 있다고 하더라고요.

B : That's right. More people are eager to experience Korean culture in person. 맞아요. 더 많은 사람들이 한국 문화를 직접 경험하고 싶어 합니다.

A : **When I think about it**, I really **feel proud to be Korean.** 그것에 대해 생각해보면, 저는 정말 한국인이라는 것이 자랑스러워요.

B : Likewise! I also want to share our traditions with the world more. 저도 마찬가지에요! 우리 전통을 더 많이 세계와 공유하고 싶어요.

A : **Korean fashion is really trendy** these days too. I heard **idol styles are especially popular**. 한국 패션도 요즘 정말 핫하잖아요. 특히 아이돌 스타일이 인기라면서요.

B : Exactly! It seems like a lot of people are trying to emulate their looks. 맞아요! 많은 사람들이 그 스타일을 따라 하려고 노력하는 것 같아요.

어휘 incredible 믿기 힘든 be eager to ~하기를 열망하다 trendy 최신 유행을 따르는

Thanks to the Korean Wave, ①**interest in Korean culture** is steadily growing. In particular, Korean cosmetics ②**are incredibly popular** among young women all around the world.

한류 덕분에 한국 문화에 대한 관심이 점점 커지고 있습니다. 특히 전 세계의 젊은 여성들 사이에서는 한국 화장품에 대한 인기가 하늘을 찌를 정도죠.

As a result, ③**the number of foreign tourists** visiting Korea has been increasing every year, and the trend of people wanting to ④**experience Korean culture in person** is also on the rise.

그 결과, 한국을 방문하는 외국인 관광객 수가 매년 증가하고 있으며, 한국 문화를 직접 체험하고자 하는 사람들의 추세도 역시 증가하고 있습니다.

⑤**Those interested in traditional Korean culture** visit palaces like Gyeongbokgung, while those curious about traditional Korean food head to markets like Dongdaemun or Namdaemun to ⑥**taste local dishes**.

한국 전통 문화에 관심 있는 사람들은 경복궁처럼 고궁을 찾게 되고, 한국 전통 음식에 흥미가 있는 사람들은 동대문이나 남대문과 같은 시장으로 가서 현지 음식을 맛봅니다.

The fact that there are so many foreigners ⑦**showing interest in Korean culture** around us makes me simply proud to be Korean, and it also motivates me to ⑧**share** more of **our rich traditions with** the world.

한국 문화에 관심을 보이는 외국인들이 우리 주위에 많다는 사실에 그냥 한국인으로서 자랑스러울 따름이며, 또한 우리나라의 풍부한 전통을 세계와 더 많이 공유하고 싶은 마음이 듭니다.

주제별로 구분하여 길게 말하는 연습을 해 보세요.

Korean fashion has also been gaining massive popularity recently. In particular, the styles worn by Korean idols ⁹**have become a global trend**, with many people trying to ¹⁰**emulate their looks**.

한국 패션도 최근 큰 인기를 얻고 있었습니다. 특히 한국 아이돌들이 입는 스타일은 전 세계적으로 화제가 되었고, 많은 사람들이 이를 따라 하려고 하죠.

From Korean dramas and music to food, cosmetics, and fashion, Korean culture continues to ¹¹**captivate people worldwide** in so many ways. I hope even more people get to experience and ¹²**fall in love with Korean culture** in the future.

한국 드라마, 음악, 음식, 화장품, 패션까지, 한국 문화는 정말 다양한 면에서 전 세계 사람들의 관심을 끌고 있습니다. 앞으로도 더 많은 사람들이 한국 문화를 경험하고 사랑하게 되길 바랍니다.

스피치 포인트

① **interest in Korean culture** 한국 문화에 대한 관심 ② **be incredibly popular** 엄청나게 인기가 있다 ③ **the number of foreign tourists** 외국 여행객들의 수 ④ **experience Korean culture in person** 몸소 한국 문화를 경험하다 ⑤ **those interested in traditional Korean culture** 전통 한국 문화에 관심 있는 분들 ⑥ **taste local dishes** 현지 음식들을 맛보다 ⑦ **show interest in Korean culture** 한국 문화에 관심을 보이다 ⑧ **share one's rich traditions with** 자신의 풍부한 전통을 ~와 공유하다 ⑨ **have become a global trend** 세계적으로 유행하게 되었다 ⑩ **emulate one's look** 자신의 외모나 스타일을 따라 하다 ⑪ **captivate people worldwide** 전 세계 사람들의 마음을 사로잡다 ⑫ **fall in love with Korean culture** 한국 문화에 푹 빠지다

Thanks to the Korean Wave, interest in Korean culture is steadily growing. In particular, Korean cosmetics are incredibly popular among young women all around the world.

As a result, the number of foreign tourists visiting Korea has been increasing every year, and the trend of people wanting to experience Korean culture in person is also on the rise.

Those interested in traditional Korean culture visit palaces like Gyeongbokgung, while those curious about traditional Korean food head to markets like Dongdaemun or Namdaemun to taste local dishes.

The fact that there are so many foreigners showing interest in Korean culture around us makes me simply proud to be Korean, and it also motivates me to share more of our rich traditions with the world.

Korean fashion has also been gaining massive popularity recently. In particular, the styles worn by Korean idols have become a global trend, with many people trying to emulate their looks.

나의 상황에 맞게 내용을 바꾸어서 말해 보세요.

From Korean dramas and music to food, cosmetics, and fashion, Korean culture continues to captivate people worldwide in so many ways. I hope even more people get to experience and fall in love with Korean culture in the future.

PART 10
Review Quiz

1 전 세계적으로 엄청난 인기를 얻다
gain _____ global popularity

2 위로와 힘을 주다
provide _____ and strength

3 전 세계 팬들을 하나로 모으다
_____ fans across the globe

4 한국 라면을 정말 좋아하다
love Korean instant _____

5 케이푸드의 힘을 느끼다
feel the _____ of K-Food

6 다이어트나 건강상의 이유로
for dieting or _____ reasons

7 생생하게 기억하다
_____ remember

8 대유행하다
be all the _____

배운 영어 표현들을 복습해 보세요.

9 케이무비 열풍을 일으키다
_____ the K-Movie boom

10 항상 시청할 가치가 있다
be always _____ watching

11 다음 큰 반향을 일으키다
_____ the next big sensation

12 해외에서 주목을 받다
gain _____ abroad

13 몸소 한국 문화를 경험하다
_____ Korean culture in person

14 현지 음식들을 맛보다
taste _____ dishes

15 자신의 외모나 스타일을 따라 하다
_____ one's look

정답 01 tremendous 02 comfort 03 unite 04 noodles 05 power 06 health 07 vividly 08 rage
      09 fuel 10 worth 11 create 12 attention 13 experience 14 local 15 emulate